DOING
COMMUNITY
ECONOMIC
DEVELOPMENT

Edited by
John Loxley,
Jim Silver and
Kathleen Sexsmith

Fernwood Publishing
Halifax & Winnipeg

and Canadian Centre
for Policy Alternatives–MB

This book is dedicated
to the memory of
Lloyd le Van (Van) Hall,
for his commitment over
the years to improving the
lives of Aboriginal People.

Editing: Eileen Young
Cover Art: Jackie Traverse
Printed and bound in Canada by Hignell Book Printing

Published in Canada by Fernwood Publishing
Site 2A, Box 5, 32 Oceanvista Lane
Black Point, Nova Scotia, B0J 1B0
and 324 Clare Avenue, Winnipeg, Manitoba, R3L 1S3
www.fernwoodpublishing.ca

and Canadian Centre for Policy Alternatives–Manitoba
309-323 Portage Ave, Winnipeg, MB, R3B 2C1
www.policyalternatives.ca

Fernwood Publishing Company Limited gratefully
acknowledges the financial support of the Government
of Canada through the Book Publishing Industry
Development Program (BPDIP), the Canada Council for
the Arts and the Nova Scotia Department of Tourism and
Culture for our publishing program.

Library and Archives Canada Cataloguing in Publication

Doing community economic development / John Loxley,
Kathleen Sexsmith and Jim Silver, editors.

Co-Published by: CCPA.
Includes bibliographical references and index.
ISBN 978-1-55266-221-2

1. Community development. 2. Economic development
projects. I. Loxley, John, 1942- II. Sexsmith, Kathleen III.
Silver, Jim IV. Canadian Centre for Policy Alternatives

HC79.E44D63 2007   338.9   C2007-903348-2

CONTENTS

ABOUT THE AUTHORS

Sarah Amyot is a graduate of the University of Winnipeg's Women's Studies Program. She was a research assistant for the Manitoba Research Alliance on Community Economic Development. Sarah currently works at the University of Winnipeg Students' Association and has been/is active in a number of women's organizations and projects in Winnipeg and in Nicaragua.

Myles Brown graduated from the University of Winnipeg with a Bachelor of Arts in History.

Robert Buck is a long time resident and former mayor of Grand Rapids.

Lawrence Deane is an associate professor at the Inner City Social Work Program of the University of Manitoba. Lawrie is on the boards of several Winnipeg inner-city community economic development initiatives including the North End Housing Project and Ogijiita Pimatiswin Kinamatwin, an organization that provides employment, training, and education to inner-city Aboriginal residents. He is the author of *Under One Roof: Community Economic Development in Winnipeg's North End*.

Kreesta Doucette grew up in Northern Manitoba. She has completed a master's degree in Rural Planning and Development. Kreesta is currently the coordinator of the Manitoba Food Charter, where she has worked with volunteers to conduct over seventy province-wide government, community and organizational consultations on food in Manitoba.

Kate Dykman is a University of Winnipeg graduate in philosophy and international development studies. She works and volunteers in the environmental sector.

Lynne Fernandez recently completed her Master of Economics degree, with a focus on CED and government policy in Manitoba. She is now a sessional instructor in the University of Manitoba's Labour Studies Department and a research associate with the Canadian Centre for Policy Alternatives– Manitoba.

Parvin Ghorayshi is a professor of sociology at the University of Winnipeg. Her research interests involve global and local issues with a focus on women and Diaspora communities. Her most recent publications are: "Unholy Alliances: The Discourse of Globalization and Our Global Future," in *Power and Resistance, 4th Edition*; and (with Heather Graydon and Benita Kliewer)

"Towards Social Theory in CED: Idealizing of Community in the Era of Globalization," in *Transforming or Reforming Capitalism*.

Julie Guard teaches in and coordinates the Labour Studies Program at the University of Manitoba. Her research on gender, ethnicity and working-class identity has been published in *Labour/le travail* and the *Journal of Women's History* and her work on call centre organizing has appeared in *Labor: Studies in Working-Class History of the Americas*. She is a board member of the Canadian Centre for Policy Alternatives–Manitoba and the Joseph Zuken Memorial Association and is active in the women's, labour and peace movements.

Blair Hamilton is a consultant in community economic development and cooperative development. Based in Arnaud, Manitoba, he works with both urban and rural community organizations in pursuing values-based development strategies.

Joan Hay is the program coordinator at House of Opportunities, a community-based, inner-city employment development agency. She is pursuing a social work degree through the University of Manitoba's Inner City Social Work program. A long-time inner-city resident, community activist and radio show co-host, she also sits on numerous local boards and committees.

Darlene Klyne is a Cree and Dakota mother and grandmother. She is the project coordinator for the Aboriginal Visioning Strategy for the Renewal of the North End. She is passionate about Aboriginal value-based and directed community development as a decolonization tool for her community. Darlene works with the Aboriginal community and other partners in supporting an Aboriginal focus to community renewal in Winnipeg's North End.

Glen Koroluk has been an environmental researcher and advocate since the late 1980s. He works as the water caucus coordinator for the Manitoba Eco-Network and is a community organizer for the Beyond Factory Farming Coalition, which he helped co-found in 2002. Glen currently sits on the board of Food Secure Canada and is a representative on the Canadian Environmental Network's Agricultural Caucus steering committee. Previously, Glen was the coordinator for Hog Watch Manitoba and served as the executive director of Resource Conservation Manitoba.

Peter Kulchyski is a professor of native studies at the University of Manitoba. His most recent book is *Like the Sound of a Drum: Aboriginal Cultural Politics in Denendeh and Nunavut*.

Laura Lamb teaches in the Department of Economics at Thompson Rivers University. She was also a researcher for the Manitoba Research Alliance on Community Economic Development in the New Economy. Her fields of study include community economic development, applied microeconomic theory and industrial organization. She has recently co-authored a chapter in *Community Economic Development: Building for Social Change.*

Geoff Lloyd has a Bachelor of Arts from the University of Manitoba, graduating with an Advanced Major in Labour Studies. He worked for over a year as an officer at the Employment Standards Branch of the Manitoba Department of Labour and is now teaching English overseas.

Garry Loewen has extensive experience in poverty reduction and community economic development. He was the founding Executive Director of the North End Community Renewal Corporation, SEED Winnipeg (a micro-enterprise development organization), and the Canadian Community Economic Development Network. He was also the founding president of Opportunities For Employment, an organization that assists welfare recipients to make the transition from welfare to work. He currently works as a self-employed community economic development consultant.

Ivy Lopez is a counsellor at the Build-A-Business Program and the Youth Business Development Program at SEED (Supporting Employment and Economic Development) Winnipeg.

John Loxley is a professor of economics and co-ordinator of research, Global Political Economy Program, University of Manitoba. He specializes in international finance, international development and community econommic development. He is the author of *Alternative Budgets*; *Debt and Disorder*; and, most recently, he edited *Transforming or Reforming Capitalism.*

Andrew McIsaac is a student in the Advanced Major Program in labour studies at the University of Manitoba, where he has recently been accepted into the School of Law.

Gerald McKay is a long time resident and former municipal councillor of Grand Rapids.

Molly McCracken is a community organizer who lives and works in Winnipeg's inner city. She is executive director of the West Broadway Development Corporation. She has also done research in child care and housing issues.

Ramona Neckoway is Inwewiwin from Nisichiwaysihk Cree Nation and a doctoral candidate in Native Studies at the University of Manitoba.

Francine Parent is a staff member at the Andrews Street Family Centre in Winnipeg's North End, where she works with Andrews Street Girls Club. She is a graduate of Children of the Earth High School, Winnipeg's Aboriginal high school.

Aaron Pettman was a graduate student in economics at the University of Manitoba.

Cheryl Selig is a junior planner with the Greater Moncton Planning District Commission.

Kathleen Sexsmith recently graduated with her B.A. (Honours) in economics from the University of Manitoba. After graduating, she spent six months working in Peru as an agricultural development intern with Mennonite Economic Development Associates (MEDA). She is currently a Master of Philosophy in Development Studies student at the University of Oxford, where she specializes in Latin American development issues.

Byron Sheldrick is the chair of the Department of Political Science at the University of Guelph. His research interests are in social movements, law and politics, and the restructuring of the welfare state. He taught law at Keele University in the United Kingdom before joining the Politics Department at the University of Winnipeg in 1998 and the University of Guelph in 2006. He is the author of *Perils and Possibilities: Social Activism and the Law* and is the co-editor (with Joan Grace) of *Canadian Politics: Democracy and Dissent*.

Jim Silver is a professor of politics, chair of the Politics Department and co-director of the Urban and Inner-City Studies program at the University of Winnipeg. He is a founding member and currently a board member of the Canadian Centre for Policy Alternatives–Manitoba. His latest book is *In Their Own Voices: Building Urban Aboriginal Communities*.

Ian Skelton works in the Department of City Planning at the University of Manitoba. His research interests centre around social housing and social policy, and he edits *Canadian Planning and Policy — Aménagement et politique au Canada*.

Olufemi Sowemimo is a student in the Advanced Major Program in labour studies at the University of Manitoba. He plans to graduate in 2008.

Sara Stephens graduated from the University of Manitoba with a masters in anthropology. Her thesis was a study of Community Economic Development in Winnipeg. She is currently working as a researcher.

Sherry Sullivan has worked in adult learning for eighteen years and has taught, administered, developed and learned life and learning skills and Recognition of Prior Learning (RPL) processes and systems. She has worked for community and private-sector organizations, government and technical-vocational, university and college education institutions in Aboriginal, rural, northern and military settings. For the past thirteen years she has worked specifically in RPL and is currently the RPL Director at the University of Manitoba.

Fred Tait is a farmer in western Manitoba, a board member of the National Farmers Union, and a former board member of the Canadian Centre for Policy Alternatives-Manitoba.

Kevin Warkentin was an honours student in the Politics Department at the University of Winnipeg, and a legislative intern with the Manitoba Legislature.

Raymond Wiest is professor emeritus of the Department of Anthropology, University of Manitoba. His research focus has been on Mexican transnational labour and on gendered labour commodification in the garment industry in Bangladesh and in Winnipeg. He has published widely on these and related themes, including a recent co-edited book, *Globalization and Community: Canadian Perspectives* (2004).

Cory Willmott is an assistant professor, Department of Anthropology, Southern Illinois University at Edwardsville. Her research interests focus on the politics of clothing and land, including the roles of clothing and textiles in the relations between Algonquian peoples and colonizers, as well as issues of representation in visual and museum anthropology. Her recent publications include "From Stroud to Strouds" (in *Textile History*) and "The Lens of Science" (in *Visual Anthropology*).

ACKNOWLEDGEMENTS

This book was prepared with the generous financial support of the Social Sciences and Humanities Research Council (grant # 538-2002-1003) and the Manitoba Research Alliance on Community Economic Development in the New Economy, the research consortium headed by the Canadian Centre for Policy Alternatives Manitoba, which secured and administered the grant.

A special word of thanks to Garry Loewen not only for holding together the Research Alliance, administratively and financially, but also for reading and providing helpful comments on several of the draft chapters. Thanks also to the rest of the Research Committee for their hard work and humour and to the members of the Research Alliance for their continued support and input over the past four years. The help, support and assistance of the universities of Manitoba, Winnipeg and Brandon are also gratefully acknowledged. Thanks also for the invaluable assistance of Shauna MacKinnon, director, and Todd Scarth, former director of the CCPA-Manitoba, who provided leadership and guidance both to the project as a whole and to the production of this book.

The fine editing job of Doug Smith is noted with great appreciation, as are the efforts of Wayne Antony of Fernwood Publishing in bringing the book to fruition. Thanks also to those involved in the production of the book: Tara Prakash and Andrew Donachuk, who worked on the manuscript; and to the production staff at Fernwood — Eileen Young, Beverley Rach, Debbie Mathers and Brenda Conroy.

The excellent art work of Jackie Traverse has special significance to the editors for its relevance to the concerns of this book with Aboriginal aspirations and Aboriginal views on appropriate approaches to CED.

The authors acknowledge their huge debt of gratitude to the members of the many community-based economic development organizations in Manitoba who took time from their various day-to-day challenges to participate in this research project and who helped in so many ways to shape the views of the authors on CED. Several government departments at both federal and provincial levels gave generously of their time and resources to assist this project.

Once more, JL would like to acknowledge the importance of his teammates in CSSC, for their help and support. He would also like to thank Aurelie, Raina and Matthew for being there throughout this project, which though on the whole, enjoyable and fulfilling was, nonetheless, both long and inevitably, at times, stressful. JS thanks all the members of the Research Alliance team, and especially our community partners, who worked to put together this book and the other papers and books arising from this collective project. We have learned a lot together, with more to come. A special heart-felt thanks, as always, to Loa Henry for her love and support.

Chapter One

COMMUNITY ECONOMIC DEVELOPMENT
An Introduction

Jim Silver and John Loxley

This is a book about community economic development. The chapters are among the outcomes of a large, three-year research project undertaken by the Manitoba Research Alliance on Community Economic Development in the New Economy, and funded by the Social Science and Humanities Research Council as part of their New Economy Initiative.[1] The chapters address current issues in Manitoba, but we believe that they have a much broader relevance and applicability. We examine inner-city, rural and northern aspects of community economic development (CED); Aboriginal and non-Aboriginal forms of CED; the role of women in CED; issues related to employment development and CED; agriculture and CED; and the economics of CED.

In this introductory chapter we first describe the logic and consequences of the capitalist organization of most of the world's economic activity. We argue that this way of organizing economic affairs not only produces great wealth, but also, and necessarily, produces deep and widespread poverty and human despair. We then examine community economic development as an alternative way of organizing economic affairs. We discuss the different logic of CED, consider some principles of CED, and examine some of the difficulties in implementing CED. Difficulties notwithstanding, we argue that CED holds great promise for those many communities and people who are disadvantaged by the current organization of economic activity, and we argue further that CED may even have potential as an alternative to the current dominant way of organizing economic activity.

In the book's concluding chapter we describe how the Manitoba Research Alliance — a unique collaboration of university-based researchers, community-based organizations and a community-based, public policy research institute — organized its work, and we reflect upon the research on community economic development that still needs to be done.

THE PREVAILING ECONOMIC SYSTEM

Most of the world's economic activity is organized in a capitalist fashion: goods and services are produced and distributed, and resources are allocated, based upon the profit motive. What gets produced, and where and how, is a function of what is profitable. Who gets what is a function of peoples' (wildly differing) levels of income and wealth. This way of arranging economic activity is capable of producing enormous wealth, cheek by jowl with deep and widespread poverty and related ills. Economic activity need not necessarily be organized this way, but it is. Some of the consequences are very adverse.

The prevailing capitalist system has certain intrinsic features, chief among which is the constant, competitive drive of individual business firms to earn profits. This relentless drive for ever more profits has certain inevitable results. One is a constant revolutionizing of the means of production, leading to rapid technological change, as firms relentlessly innovate in order to gain advantage over their competitors. A second is the concentration of production in ever larger units so that geographically, some areas become highly populated and developed while others become marginalized in terms of people, jobs and incomes. Yet another feature is the constant drive to expand, which results both in ever-larger firms and in geographic expansion, as transnational corporations scour the globe in search of lower wages, larger markets, and cheaper raw materials, in order to maximize their profits.

While economic activity has become much more global in the past thirty-five years, globalization is not a new phenomenon, but rather an accentuation of the drive to expand that is intrinsic to capitalism. In the past few decades trade between nations, and investment and flows of money across national borders, have increased dramatically. Companies no longer confine their production to their home nations. They can, and do, set up production facilities anywhere in the world, choosing to locate wherever they are most likely to be able to maximize profits. This often means relocating production to areas where government regulations are weakest and wages are lowest (Teeple 2000: 91). Typically, corporations benefit more from this than do people.

This trend has been accelerated by international trade agreements, such as the Canada-U.S. Free Trade Agreement and the North American Free Trade Agreement (NAFTA), which significantly reduce the capacity of elected governments to regulate the profit-seeking activities of transnational corporations. They "free" these corporations from many of the "obstacles" — or what most of us would see, from a human, non-corporate point of view, as benefits — created by governments, such as environmental regulations and labour standards. Free trade increases the freedom of transnational corporations to search the globe for the most profitable production sites, making it more likely that they will set up shop wherever they can maximize their profits. This is especially the case for heavily unionized, relatively high-wage, mass-production industries. According to Teeple (2000: 67): "The effects of this emerging global labour market began to become visible from the early 1970s on with a general downward pressure on wages in the industrial world."

In the face of the intensified competition created by globalization, companies have sought not only to reduce wage levels, but also to create what the corporate sector calls more "flexible" work forces. Corporations have sought to move away from the relatively fixed and permanent high-wage regime characteristic of the mass-production industries of the 1950s and 1960s — sometimes referred to as "Fordism," after the mass-production, relatively high-wage system introduced early in the century by Henry Ford — to a more flexible labour force, increasingly characterized by the use of part-time, lower-waged, less secure and non-unionized work. The resultant increase in part-time work and decrease in wages at the lower end of the income scale have been significant factors in creating persistently high levels of poverty.

The increased degree of globalization and the problems the phenomenon creates for many working people and for those who would like to be but are not now employed — especially those with relatively little formal education and relatively few skills — have been facilitated by the particularly rapid technological change associated with the microelectronics revolution, and more particularly by the widespread use of computers. This has contributed to what some have referred to as a "new economy," which is characterized by the need for higher levels of education and the even more rapid flows of money and capital around the globe. We would argue that, for the most part, the "new economy" is not so much a new one: rather, it is an accentuation of the existing capitalist economy, operating on the basis of the same punishing logic it has always employed.

By the mid-1970s computers were beginning to be widely employed in industry, with dramatic results. Not only has their use facilitated the increased globalization of economic activity, including an acceleration of the ease and rapidity by which investments can be moved around the globe, but their use in industry — in both factories and offices — has often resulted in massive job losses. Those job losses have exerted downward pressure on wage levels at the lower end of the wage scale and have contributed to the growth of generally low-paid and contingent (i.e., non-full-time, non-secure) forms of employment. Most of the jobs open to relatively unskilled school-leavers in the 1950s and 1960s — jobs that could support a family — have now disappeared. These jobs have relocated elsewhere or have been eliminated by technology, only to be replaced by low-wage and often part-time work in the service sector.

A result of these powerful forces that have been unleashed by the fiercely competitive character of capitalism has been rapidly growing inequality and poverty. Nor have inequality and poverty been confined to the "developing" countries, or the "third world." The dynamic, market-driven character of capitalism marginalizes and excludes large numbers of people in advanced capitalist countries in the North as well. Inner cities have decayed as a result of capital and population flight; rural areas have been depopulated and are home to growing levels of economic distress as small farms are swallowed by larger, often corporate enterprises, and small towns atrophy; and Canada's north has become home to some particularly egregious examples of poverty and its associated indignities, the result in large part of the expansion of capitalism in search of resources.

One response to inequality and poverty has been the promotion of "development." Development is seen by most to be a "good" thing: those who have benefited from the current economic arrangements can help those who have yet to "develop" — in other words, to become more like their benefactors, to become more modern, more capitalist.

This notion of development has been subjected to much criticism. It has been argued that development premised upon the western notion of modernization and unbounded capitalist expansion has predominantly benefited those who already have economic power (Hart-Landsberg and Burkett 2001; Sparr 1994). Development strategies have ignored or underestimated the key factors crucial for human well-being. Far from benefiting most of the poor, some have argued that development has created barriers to human well-being and freedom (Sen 1999). A growing body of literature questions the concept of "development." Some have argued that development has become a new colonialism, involving the imposition upon the poor of control from the outside, to the benefit less of the poor than of those from the outside.

Disadvantaged groups in northern countries, like their counterparts elsewhere, have been the target of development strategies. What came to be labelled as the key characteristics of underdevelopment in Southern countries, such as poverty, and lack of access to education, health care and paid employment, for example, also exist among various groups of people in the North (Veltmeyer and O'Malley 2001; Labrecque 1991). Aboriginal people, for example, have been living in what came to be known as "underdeveloped conditions" and have been the target of development policies (Loxley 1981; 2000).

Awareness of the limitations, disparities and non-sustainability that are intrinsic to the capitalist model of development has led to the consideration of alternative development frameworks. That is, theorizing has begun to consider development initiatives whose purpose is less to produce profit than to create human well-being, freedom and democratic involvement (Woodiwiss

2002; Sen 1999; Korten 1999; Brandt 1995; Schumacher 1973).

In debating how to achieve this different form of development — one whose aim is to produce benefits for, and to build the capacities of, all people rather than just some — many have focused on community economic development (CED) and the revitalization of local economies (Schumacher 1973; Henderson 1996; Brandt 1995; Korten 1999). There are considerable differences among CED strategies, but in general CED involves the continuous process of capacity-building: building upon existing local resources, including people, to generate broadly based economic and social well-being (Dreier 1996; Fals-Borda 1992; Fisher and Shragge 2002; Perry n.d.: 1–21; Lewis 1994; Fontan et al.1999).

AN ALTERNATIVE: COMMUNITY ECONOMIC DEVELOPMENT

The logic of community economic development (CED) differs from that of capitalism. Where capitalism is predicated upon the search for profits, and people are required to fit their lives to corporate demands, CED starts from the assumption that people have to be directly involved in determining what "development" means to them. If "development" is imposed from the outside — as is the case with the operations of transnational corporations, for instance, or even with interventions of well-intentioned development "experts" and "advisors" — the results are too often unsuccessful from a human well-being and capacity-building point of view. In CED, people have to be directly involved in determining what kind of development they want, and in implementing that development. This is because a central purpose of CED is capacity building.

Community economic development can be thought to be the polar opposite of capitalist forms of development in, among others, this one important way: where capitalist development typically brings the "development" to a community from the outside, CED promotes development from the "inside." CED starts from the assumption that the people in a community are to be the authors, architects and builders of their development. Too often in the past the recipients of "development" have been excluded from shaping what development is. Development is imposed upon them. Such forms of development are not likely to be successful. Development is much more likely to be successful if it is rooted in the reality of, and is the product of, the conscious decisions of the community — as is the case with CED. When CED is adopted, people themselves choose how they want to develop; if they lack certain skills and abilities, then those are to be nurtured so that they themselves can be the builders of their future. The people of a community may well need assistance and supports in building their community's future, but they themselves are the designers and the builders.

6

This approach to community economic development has been codified in a set of CED principles that were developed by an Aboriginal workers' co-op, called Neechi Foods, that is located in the North End of Winnipeg's inner city. These principles are now widely used. They are described as follows:

CED Principles
1. Use of locally produced goods and services;
2. Production of goods and services for local use;
3. Local re-investment of profits;
4. Long-term employment of local residents;
5. Local skill development;
6. Local decision-making;
7. Promotion of public health;
8. Improvement of the physical environment;
9. Promotion of neighbourhood stability;
10. Promotion of human dignity; and
11. Mutual aid support among organizations adhering to these principles. (Neechi 1993)

These principles are rooted in what we would call a "convergence" approach to development, by which we mean that, rather than looking beyond the community for development, CED seeks to produce to meet local needs, to hire locally, to purchase locally, to invest locally, and thus to create internal rather than external economic "linkages." This approach emphasizes the importance of small-scale production, promoting backward, forward and final-demand linkages between different sectors of local economies, minimizing leakages of income and replacing imports where possible.[2] It also enhances social capital, human well-being, community safety and stability, and local decision-making, without which the economic basis cannot be realized (Loxley 1986a). Maximizing the use of local resources — human and otherwise — to meet local needs is essential to this process. Thus, in the case of Neechi Foods, for example, supermarkets had for the most part abandoned Winnipeg's inner city as part of the post-World War Two process of suburbanization. Food retailers' profits could be maximized by building ever-larger supermarkets in suburban areas where people with higher incomes were located. Inner cities, where people with lower incomes were concentrated, were abandoned. Neechi Foods consciously formed in order to meet local inner city needs for good quality food, and to create good jobs for local people in the process. Doing so is consistent with the principles of producing to meet local inner-city needs, hiring locally and purchasing locally. Economic linkages in this model converge within the local economy.

✘ This convergence model is sometimes explained by means of a "rusty bucket" metaphor. If one pours water into a rusty bucket, the water pours out through the holes in the bucket and is lost. Similarly, in a non-convergent — or divergent — economy, if money comes into a local economy much of it pours right out again as the result of the need to purchase food at a suburban supermarket (imports), or it pours out to absentee landlords if housing is not owned locally (surplus outflow). When the money pours out through the holes in the rusty bucket, it is not available to benefit the local community and it is thus lost to the local community. When this happens, the economic linkages do not converge; they diverge. Community economic development operates to maximize the convergence of economic linkages, in order to maximize the benefits to the local economy. Doing so may not maximize profits, but it will improve the economic and social well-being of those otherwise omitted from the benefits of profit-oriented economies.

We believe that there are two ways of imagining how community economic development might be used. First, by operating on the basis of the principles described above, thereby consciously adopting a convergence strategy, community economic development can be the means by which "gaps" that are left by the capitalist economy can be filled. The profit-driven logic of capitalism has, as one of its inevitable consequences, the result that many people and communities are left out of the benefits that it creates. CED can be seen as a means by which to meet the needs of those left out of the capitalist economy. It can "fill the gaps" left by capitalism. In this use of CED, it co-exists with capitalism. CED in this case seeks to operate within the interstices of the more dominant, capitalist economy and its associated culture.

A second way of imagining how community economic development might be used is to see it as being potentially "transformative." By that we mean that the benefits of CED might come to be seen as being so great that it (CED) expands beyond the interstices of the capitalist economy, thus transforming the existing economic system from one that is profit-driven and relentlessly expansionary, to one that is needs-driven and focused on building peoples' capacities, as well as their economic and social well-being. Most of the chapters in this book consider CED in the former sense — as an economic and social strategy aimed at benefiting those left out of the dominant economy. Some consider CED in both senses: they see it as providing not only a "gap-filling" strategy but also potentially, a "transformative" strategy. In Chapter 16 Loxley and Lamb examine some of the matters that would have to be considered if community economic development were to become transformative. The challenges of building a transformative CED would be formidable. The benefits, in our view, would be considerable.

SOME CHALLENGES IN IMPLEMENTING
COMMUNITY ECONOMIC DEVELOPMENT

Promoting community economic development is never easy, even when CED is limited to the "gap-filling" variety. In this section we briefly discuss some of these difficulties and their implications. Our point is that, as valuable as we consider community economic development to be in meeting the needs and developing the capacities of all people, it does not represent an easy solution. Community economic development involves hard, skilled work, and is fraught with difficulty in its implementation.

Consider the notion of community. Community is a contested concept. It might refer to those living in a shared geographic area, or those who share particular values or characteristics or interests. But, in either case, communities are rarely, if ever, homogenous entities. Communities are always characterized by conflict, usually arising from inequalities of power and/or wealth along lines of gender, class or ethnicity, for example. The ideal view of community as being coherent, democratic and inclusive, overlooks various forms of repression — of women, of people of colour, of those who are "different" in any way   and neglects the tendency for bureaucratic and elitist forms of organization to emerge. There is no magic "solution" to these difficulties. But an awareness of these realities, together with a philosophical commitment to egalitarianism, of *all* people being valued equally — can be a foundation upon which to build community economic development.

Consider also the notion of democracy. Community economic development is committed, by its very character and principles, to the promotion of democratic decision-making. Yet here too, many of the same problems arise: the dangers of the bureaucratization and professionalization of CED organizations; the risks of the emergence of elites, and of patriarchal power strategies; the likelihood that, in the absence of special measures being taken, those who are different or less strong will be marginalized and excluded. All of these are sociological realities, and powerful tendencies. In the absence of an awareness of such dangers, in the absence of the adoption of measures aimed at specifically preventing their emergence, these tendencies will manifest themselves, making the promotion of community economic development still more difficult. It is necessary to consciously and deliberately ensure that women, for example, are fully included, and that Aboriginal people, recent immigrants and refugees, to take another example, are fully included. It is necessary to ensure that organizational processes that promote democratic decision-making are so institutionalized that they become the "common sense" of a community. Again, this is not easy, and many are the potential pitfalls. Yet an awareness of these dangers, and a commitment to contesting them, is a necessary part of the foundation upon which community economic development can be built.

Consider, too, the complex issue of management skills, and more generally the need for education and training to enable the development of the skills and capacities that local people may need to build their own futures. Community economic development can be complex. According to its principles, it is committed to local control and the development of local capacities: this requires a conscious awareness of the need to take the time, and to develop the means, to ensure that control is in local hands. Specially designed education and training initiatives may be required. The search for profits that characterizes capitalism is so relentlessly competitive that time cannot be taken to develop local capacities. Corporations rely upon mainstream systems to produce for them their skilled managers and technicians: this process simply reinforces existing inequalities. Community economic development is committed to overcoming those inequalities: this means always taking the time to develop the means to ensure that local capacities and local control are developed. Like everything about community economic development, this is not easy. But if it is not done, it is not CED.

Consider next the role of government. Much, if not all, of what we are discussing is predicated upon a supportive role being played by governments. If community economic development is to succeed, governments must make public investments in support of CED initiatives. The whole point of CED is that it is not driven by the profit-maximizing principles of capitalism. It is driven by other, more people-oriented and community-oriented principles. Thus CED organizations may not be able to "compete" in the private market for investment. Governments must provide public investment. Yet governments have been extremely reluctant to do so, and even in those cases when governments appear to be committed to CED, their commitment has been lukewarm (Loxley 1990; 1981; Chapter 17 this volume). This has placed tight restrictions upon what community economic development has been able to achieve.

For governments to become more meaningful participants in the process of community economic development, those active in CED must become more politicized. Yet this too constitutes a significant challenge. The poor and socially excluded tend not to participate much, if at all, in the political process. Political power, like so many other resources, is inequitably distributed. But because the poor and excluded participate little in the political process, governments feel little pressure to respond to their needs, and thus to the needs of community economic development. Without government support, the capacity of CED to effect significant change is limited: in an economy that is capitalist-dominated, the result is inevitably that poverty grows. The political empowerment of the poor and socially excluded thus becomes an essential ingredient in the success of community economic development: the difficulties associated with the political empowerment of those who are currently dis-empowered, and who are therefore poor and excluded, becomes one of the most significant challenges facing CED. This is especially the case if we consider community economic development not just as "gap-filling," but as transformative. If CED is to be transformative, it will require new forms of political mobilization that include, but also go beyond, those who are currently excluded from the benefits of the dominant system. This, like so much else about community economic development, will not be easy, as it will, of necessity, entail transforming the nature of the state (see Sheldrick and Warkentin, Chapter 17 in this volume).

IF CED IS SO HARD, WHY BOTHER?

The benefits of community economic development are worth the substantial effort needed to make it a success. It ought to be clear by now that this is partly a philosophical, or ideological, issue. Community economic development is committed to the creation of a more egalitarian, participatory and democratic society. It seeks to ensure that those who are poor and excluded in the current economic system become the authors of a better future that they themselves participate in imagining and building. This objective clearly rests on a set of ideological preferences with which not all will agree. Yet in our view, these are objectives worth pursuing. The eradication of poverty — or at least a dramatic reduction in its incidence and its severity — is in itself a laudatory goal, the benefits of which ought to be obvious in a world in which millions are hungry. But community economic development goes further. It would include, if successfully implemented, a significant move in the direction of meaningful gender equality, and the equality of those who are, in any of a wide variety of ways, characterized by difference or "otherness." It would involve a greater degree of democratization and meaningful involvement in life than is now the case for most. It would empower people, by making them, much more than is now the case, the authors of their own destiny.

These are goals that are, for the most part, beyond the purview of the chapters in this book. This book arises out of a large research project — the Manitoba Research Alliance on Community Economic Development in the New Economy — that attempted to deepen our understanding of, and contribute to the development of, solutions to more immediate and more localized problems. Community economic development, we maintain, has much to offer in this gap-filling way, and the chapters in this book offer some examples. At the same time, what is possible at a local level may hold the seeds for the broader and deeper gains that would follow if and when the logic of capitalism is replaced by the different logic and principles of community economic development.

THEMES

Several crucial themes will be seen to emerge in the chapters in this book.

First, the fundamental importance of genuine community involvement emerges over and over again: at the neighbourhood level in local revitalization initiatives; in the process of employment development; in Aboriginal forms of community development; in the many community development initiatives led by women; and even in the participatory action research methodology used for many of the chapters in the book. Participation entails capacity building, a theme long since developed in political philosophy (McPherson 1965; Pateman 1970): with its emphasis on community involvement, CED contests the well-known tendencies to bureaucratization, professionalization and elite rule, and promotes the fundamental value of economic, social and political equality.

Second, the development and use of the Neechi CED principles emerge repeatedly as a central guiding force in the promotion of community economic development. The notion of purchasing, hiring and investing locally, of linking the needs of the community with local resources, of building on local strengths, and of creating linkages within, and stemming leakages from, the community, are all overarching principles that, while rooted in economic theory, are easily grasped, and are capable of guiding the work undertaken in the many manifestations of community economic development.

Third, the need for and use of non-market solutions arises repeatedly in the chapters in this book. The market and the related search for ever-more profits are capable of unleashing enormous productive power. But the other side of that same coin is the massive inequalities and poverty and the marginalization and social exclusion that *inevitably* accompany this way of organizing economic affairs. It is non-market solutions that, over and over, are identified by the authors of these chapters as the means by which to rectify and overcome these problems.

Fourth, the community economic development initiatives described in this book reveal the enormous creativity that can be unleashed by CED. While it is true that the market can induce creativity, the evidence presented in these chapters suggests not only that people working collectively to build their communities and solve community problems can be similarly creative but also, in most cases, that their creativity can lead to more meaningful ends.

Fifth, these chapters reveal repeatedly the central importance of the role of the state in promoting and supporting CED. Successful community economic development requires the active and effective support of the state. But it is clear that to be effective promoters of community economic development, governments need to act not in a top-down, bureaucratic fashion, but rather as "facilitators" of participatory forms of development (see Silver 2000).

Finally, the chapters in this book reveal that success in promoting CED not only involves a philosophical issue — a way of thinking about economic and social affairs — it also raises various technical considerations. Promoting CED makes us look at the kind of society that we want to build, and how we want to build it. The more people who come to adopt this way of thinking about building community, the more successful will CED initiatives be.

The many obstacles to the successful promotion of community economic development emerge repeatedly in these tough-minded and well-researched chapters. But the potential for the use of CED to contribute to the building of a better world is equally obvious.

NOTES

1. Other outcomes include the following: (1) a book on the theory of community economic development: John Loxley et al., *Transforming or Reforming Capitalism: Towards a Theory of Community Economic Development* (Halifax and Winnipeg: Fernwood Publishing and CCPA-MB, 2007); (2) a book on urban Aboriginal people and community development. Jim Silver, *In Their Own Voices: Urban Aboriginal Community Development* (Halifax: Fernwood Publishing, 2006); (3) a book of John Loxley's essays on community economic development: John Loxley, *Community, Aboriginal and Northern Economic Development* (Arbeiter Ring Publishing, forthcoming); (4) a series of monographs published by the Canadian Centre for Policy Alternatives–Manitoba and available on their Web site <www.policyalternatives. ca>; and (5) a video on urban Aboriginal community development, based on the final chapter of *In Their Own Voices* and done by award-winning Aboriginal film-maker Coleen Rajotte.

2. A backward linkage occurs when a local enterprise's output depends on inputs purchased from other enterprises in the community. As purchases from inside the community increase, backward linkages become stronger. Thus, a community restaurant buying food and employing labour from within the community is creating backward linkages. A forward linkage is created when a company's output is sold as an input to other projects in the community. Thus, a community restaurant that sells its baked goods to local stores who, in turn, resell them to customers, is creating a forward linkage. A final demand linkage occurs when investment in a local project produces goods for consumption, investment, or government purchase, as opposed to purchase by the export sector. The greater the proportion of domestic production sold inside the community or region, rather than as exports, the larger the final demand linkage effect will be (see Lamb 2007).

Chapter Two

THE STATE OF COMMUNITY ECONOMIC DEVELOPMENT IN WINNIPEG

John Loxley

The main purpose of this chapter is to reflect a little on the nature of the momentum in the CD/CED movement in Winnipeg and on what lies behind it.[1] I will also suggest some of the measures that might be needed to maintain and strengthen that momentum.

It seems to me that Winnipeg is rapidly becoming a major focal point in Canada for community economic development and I think there are eight reasons for this. These are:

1. CED in Winnipeg is guided by a clear set of principles, the Neechi Principles, to which almost all groups and activists adhere (see Chapter 1 in this volume by Silver and Loxley). These are clear, unambiguous and demanding. They have received national attention and were developed in Winnipeg by an Aboriginal workers' cooperative.

2. Activists in Winnipeg have demonstrated a willingness to engage nationally, with people across the country, in promoting the philosophy and practice of CED. Because of their eagerness to learn from what others have done across Canada and internationally, we have benefited from the experience of activists who have come to Winnipeg to share their experiences. The annual conferences of the Canadian CED Network (CC-EDNET), the CED Technical Assistance Program (CEDTAP) and workers' cooperatives, which were held in Winnipeg in 2002, provided us with an excellent opportunity to connect constructively with both theorists and practitioners from elsewhere. Our own practitioners are also actively involved in these national organizations. For some years now, a regional representative of CCEDNET has been appointed to Winnipeg and is based in the office of the Canadian Centre for Policy Alternatives–Manitoba.

3. We have a very strong institutional base for CED in Winnipeg, with several institutions now having a long track record. The Community

Education Development Agency (CEDA), which celebrated its twenty-fifth anniversary in 2003, has provided animation of both CD and CED. Financial support has been provided by the Assiniboine Credit Union (ACU), which has won national awards not only for its CED work but also for its progressive human resource policies, SEED Winnipeg, LITE (Local Investment Toward Employment), the Alternative Financial Services Coalition, The Jubilee Fund, Community Ownership Solutions and the Urban Entrepreneurs with Disabilities Program (these are described in more detail in Loxley 2003b). We also have a growing number of delivery agencies on the ground which are maturing and making an impact, notably the development corporations in West Broadway, Spence and the North End (see Chorney 2003). CED-based housing institutions, such as Inner City Renovations (which replaced Just Housing and the North End Community Renovation Enterprise), the North End Housing Project and housing associations in West Broadway and Spence and Ogijiita Pimatiswin Kinamatwin (the Aboriginal Youth Housing Renovation Project, for ex-inmates) have proliferated (see Cates 2003). Housing is, in my opinion, particularly important to CED: it clearly fulfils a crucial basic human need; it provides opportunities for the acquisition of skills by local residents; it offers opportunities for well-paying jobs; it potentially helps create linkages with other service and production ventures (e.g., training and building supplies); and it can play an important role in helping promote neighbourhood stability, which is crucial for long-term CED. Winnipeg also has a multitude of employment and training agencies, as well as social service agencies, and it also has an embryonic social enterprise sector (see papers by Loewen 2003a and 2003b). It also has a social purchasing portal established by SEED, which directs businesses via the web to suppliers of goods and services that create employment opportunities for individuals or groups "that face multiple barriers to employment" <http://www.sppwinnipeg.org/> (accessed July 2007). This creates jobs in inner-city and social-purpose businesses while enabling purchasers to be socially responsible.

4. Since 1999, government support of CED has improved markedly. The election of an NDP provincial government in that year led to a substantial increase in support for CED, in a number of different ways. First of all, the creation of a Community and Economic Development Committee of Cabinet (CEDC) elevated CED policy to an unprecedented level in the province. Second, and through CEDC, a CED policy lens has been introduced through which the contribution of all government activities will be evaluated. This lens is unique in Canada and is based on the Neechi principles, which now have the support of the provincial government (see Chapter 17 in this volume for an elaboration as well as a critical

assessment). Thirdly, provincial financial support for CED has been increased markedly through the Neighbourhoods Alive! Program, which provides core funding for many of the institutions mentioned earlier. The NDP government has also brought in legislation making financial contributions to CED eligible for tax credits, and it is the first government in Canada to introduce tax increment financing, which enables municipalities to reinvest property tax revenues into CED initiatives. It has taken steps to support CED projects, both Aboriginal and otherwise, through its procurement policies (these and other initiatives supported by the province are described more fully in the Manitoba Budget, 2006). While many within and outside the provincial government would like to see it do more, this is an impressive record. The federal government also made an important contribution to CED in Winnipeg through Western Economic Diversification (WED), which was instrumental in helping SEED Winnipeg get off the ground. The Winnipeg Partnership Agreement, between all three levels of government, has given CED a significant boost in the city and will invest $75 million over five years in CED and urban renewal (Winnipeg Partnership Agreement 2005).

5. Winnipeg CED has benefited significantly in recent years from the active involvement of a number of charitable foundations. The Thomas Sill Foundation and the United Way have provided important strategic assistance to a number of local CED organizations, with the latter assuming an increasingly important coordinating role in the CED movement generally. Most recently, the Winnipeg Foundation has joined them, funding a large CED initiative in the hitherto relatively neglected Centennial neighbourhood. That these foundations would depart so significantly from a narrow charity model of assistance represents a remarkable transformation in approach over the last decade or so and is a great credit to their boards and leadership.

6. There is a very supportive academic environment for CED in Winnipeg. All three universities have an interest in CED and have done extensive research in the field. The approach to research is both interdisciplinary and participatory. Research findings and non-academic participants in CED are brought into the classroom to strengthen teaching and to bring the subject alive for students. Many academics are actively involved in CED ventures. In 2002, the three universities cooperated with the Canadian Centre for Policy Alternatives–Manitoba, a number of community organizations and the provincial and federal governments, to form the Manitoba Research Alliance: the alliance obtained an $895,000 SSHRC/INE grant to conduct research into CED and the new economy, one outcome of which is this volume. This was a unique project, led by a non-academic community-based research organization and sup-

ported by such CED agencies as the North End Community Renewal Corporation, the West Broadway Development Corporation and SEED. This alliance was based on cooperation between academics and non-academics interested in CED and has helped push back the frontiers of knowledge, examining what works, what does not and what are the best practice opportunities for promoting CED. It gave unprecedented opportunities for a number of young people to become involved in CED through research: in this process, it has been important in helping create the next generation of CED activists and intellectuals.

7. Winnipeg is fortunate to have a fairly large number of remarkable people involved in promoting CED. Many of them have slogged away in the trenches for years when there was little to show for their efforts. Some have stayed involved with early CED initiatives, such as Neechi or SEED, over many years, through thick and thin. Many have cut their teeth in CEDA. For over a decade now many have hung in with the Assiniboine Credit Union (ACU), watching it grow from strength to strength. Many more have sat as volunteers on CED boards, receiving little thanks or acknowledgement for their efforts. Without such people — and my sense is that Winnipeg is unusually well endowed with them — CED would not be as well-developed as it is.

8. There is, therefore, a strong cultural foundation for CED in the city, underpinned by a widely held belief in the need for, and the importance of, collective action to improve social well-being. It is based on irreverence towards the establishment and a willingness to challenge it in order to address issues of poverty, deprivation and exclusion. It is also based on mutual respect for fellow CED activists, even though they may often draw their inspiration from quite different ideological perspectives. It is quite pragmatic, building on what works, working with the establishment where it helps and doing what it takes to get things done, but all activities generally fall within the framework of the Neechi principles.

It is this combination of factors that makes Winnipeg such a dynamic place for CED today. Many of them are difficult to replicate elsewhere because they originated, uniquely, in the history, politics and sociology of the city. Nonetheless, we can expect interest in our CED experience to grow as successes in the city are consolidated. This is not to denigrate or belittle the CED experience elsewhere in Canada or to suggest that the Winnipeg experience does not borrow from and build on those experiences: in fact, I am suggesting quite the opposite. The Winnipeg CED community has benefited enormously from lessons learned in Quebec, British Columbia, Saskatchewan, Nova Scotia, Prince Edward Island and elsewhere, bringing in visitors from these provinces to help shape our policies and approaches.

Without this input, which is greatly appreciated, CED in Winnipeg would be much less developed than it is.

This description of accomplishments is also not meant to suggest that there are no problems facing CED in Winnipeg. On the contrary, if the momentum of the CED movement here is to be maintained, then some important challenges have to be met: among them, are the following.

THE TRAINING AND
REPLACEMENT OF PEOPLE

The challenge here is one of succession and growth: we need to produce a sufficient number of people trained in CED to provide both for the replacement of current practitioners and for the inevitable growth in CED activities in the city. This challenge was recognized some time ago and provision was made for coordinating existing and developing new CED training programs. This was a cooperative effort involving many CED groups in Winnipeg: it led to the establishment of a CD/CED Training Intermediary, a partnership between the community and provincial government, with associated courses at Red River Community College. This partnership, however, has been beset with problems and has not worked well. There have also been problems of accreditation with Red River. Skills shortages, especially in finance and bookkeeping, appear to be a significant problem in existing institutions, and staff need to have the opportunity to upgrade. Succession needs more careful planning as well as provision of financial resources for a smooth transition. Leadership relies too heavily on a few skilled individuals.

STABILIZING AND DIVERSIFYING
THE FUNDING OF OPERATIONS

It is generally acknowledged that the success of CED in recent years in raising grant funding from the government for operations also contains the seeds of a potential vulnerability should government or government policy change (Loxley 2003b). It is one thing to recognize this danger, quite another to address it. Three possibilities are a) reducing dependence on any single grant source by diversifying funders as much as possible; b) seeking to build an endowment or trust approach which, in effect, means obtaining funding up-front for use in future years; and c) building up personal or corporate donations through the new tax credit program. Each of these presents its own challenges, but pursuing them is worthwhile given what is at stake.

FUNDING CAPITAL EXPENDITURES

It is also generally acknowledged that there is currently a crucial gap in CED financing in Winnipeg, specifically the financing that affects capital spending. There is a need to build an equity fund or to secure grant financing for long-term capital expenditures if the development of social enterprises, in particular, is to be achieved. There are tentative beginnings in Community Ownership Solutions (COS), a non-profit development corporation that promotes market based solutions to CED (COS n.d.) and, to a smaller degree, in SEED: the issue has been studied systematically. COS received a big set-back with the collapse of the Crocus Investment Fund, which sponsored it.

THE PROMOTION OF
SOCIAL ENTERPRISES

There is a widely held view in Winnipeg that, if CED is to make a big impact, we must move aggressively into building commercially viable social enterprises. As suggested by the cautious progress of social enterprises in the city to date, this is not an easy challenge; it is, nonetheless, a necessary one if CED efforts are to be scaled up significantly. There have been a number of unique opportunities that could have been, or could still be, pivotal for social enterprises in the city, but up to this point in time they appear to have been missed. The largest civic infrastructure project by far, the Winnipeg flood-way extension, is now in progress. A new Hydro building is being constructed downtown, presenting potential social enterprise opportunities for both construction and maintenance. A new spate of Hydro dam building, in which some provision has been made for partnerships with local First Nations communities, is about to start in the north of the city. There may be logical extensions to social enterprises in Winnipeg. A new wave of infrastructure spending, funded in part by senior levels of government, is under way in the city. Proposals for building a road up the east side of Lake Winnipeg could result in enormous potential spin-off benefits for companies in Winnipeg. Momentum is also building for expansion of programs to provide accessible housing, especially for recent immigrants: these programs might be set up on a cooperative basis. Each of these developments presented, and may still present, potential economic opportunities for social enterprises.

There is also a growing interest in alternative delivery mechanisms in the social service area which might be ideal for social enterprises. Finally, the Winnipeg Partnership Agreement cries out for fresh ideas on community economic development: it could help finance pursuit of social enterprises in areas outlined here.

Each of these opportunities offers the possibility of pursuing social enterprise on a scale large enough to promise viability, the possibility of decent wages and salaries, the potential of significant linkages among a number of social enterprises and a degree of stability which can only be envied by existing social enterprises that struggle for survival in the highly competitive and fickle commercial service sector.

It is apparent, however, that the CED community lacks the organizational capacity to make inroads using social enterprises into most of these areas, despite a sympathetic and supportive government policy environment. What is needed is an organization that has roots in the community and that can respond to economic opportunities by mobilizing people and putting together a business plan: such an organization would need to have the capability to establish and run, or find others to run, competent social economy enterprises. This need was acknowledged in the CED symposium held in Winnipeg in April 2006. It remains to be seen what employment opportunities still exist by the time such a vehicle is up and running.

The most successful forms of social enterprise in Winnipeg appear to be cooperatives: these include a co-op gas company, which is both large and, with the rising price of gasoline, rapidly growing; credit unions, which, as banks scale back retail operations, are becoming the daily banking vehicle for an ever greater proportion of the population; and housing co-ops, of which there are several successful examples, and for which there is a large unmet demand. In the past, retail grocery co-ops have had some success: the Neechi Foods and Mondragon restaurant worker co-ops continue to survive, if not thrive. To me, this suggests that co-ops are seen to be a suitable organizational form for social enterprise in Winnipeg[2] and that there is interest in having the goods and services of daily life provided by social enterprises, in the form of co-ops. Perhaps a major concern of the planned CED social enterprise facilitation vehicle could be not just to foster participation in mega projects, but also to encourage the provision of cradle-to-grave goods and services, such as child care facilities, housing, transport, consumer-durable goods, groceries, cafés and funeral parlours. Perhaps also, some consideration could be given to help meet the technical needs of existing CED organizations through the creation of self-supporting, non-profit social enterprises in the fields of finance or human relations.

THE ABORIGINAL CHALLENGE

Some fifty thousand Aboriginal people currently live in Winnipeg: by the year 2016, one in five children in Winnipeg will be Aboriginal (Loxley and Wien 2003). An atrociously high proportion of Aboriginal people in the city live in poverty: this proportion is almost two-thirds and that rises to over 80 percent in the inner-city (Lezubski, Silver and Black 2000). If this outrageous situation is to be addressed, CED must also play a part. Solutions will call for early childhood interventions, education reform, improved housing and recreation, and greater neighbourhood stability, a larger training and apprenticeship initiative and training geared more directly to future employment needs. CED can play an important role in many of these areas and the Aboriginal factor must be built into all CED approaches and recognized in the opportunities for the promotion of social enterprises. The issue of whether Aboriginal needs should be met through separate Aboriginal institutions or through integrated ones is a difficult one. The needs are so great that a mix of both is probably needed. This will require changes in the way several CED institutions operate. It will require greater attention to recruiting, training, advancing and retaining Aboriginal staff as well as a greater say by Aboriginal people in the definition of their priorities for and strategies of CED (see Chapter 6 in this volume by Silver, Ghorayshi, Hay and Klyne). It will also require a greater Aboriginal presence on boards of directors. Each CED institution probably needs to develop an Aboriginal advancement plan in order to meet these challenges.

THE COMPLEXITY OF
POVERTY IN WINNIPEG

While the specific needs of the Aboriginal community in Winnipeg require special attention, because of its unique historical and cultural origins, care must be taken to recognize that poverty in the city is multi-ethnic, multi-dimensional and non-static. Thus, most Aboriginal people living in the inner city are poor, but most poor people are not Aboriginal. Indeed, recent inflows of refugees come from a diversity of backgrounds: many are African. Unidimensional anti-poverty strategies that do not take into account the varied backgrounds, problems and culture of the poor are, therefore, unlikely to be successful.

HUMANIZING THE MANAGEMENT
OF CED ORGANIZATIONS

If CED is to truly offer a more socially acceptable, people-centred, alternative approach to development, then we must address the issue of management of CED institutions of all types. We cannot replicate the top-down autocratic management styles of the private sector, driven by the bottom-line pursuit of profit. We must demand the highest standards of honesty and integrity, financial or otherwise, by managers. We must allow and encourage democratic structures of management with genuine worker input and horizontal decision-taking structures. We must seek out and promote democratic, participatory, management styles. We must change the way several of our organizations deal with staff — governing through intimidation, unilateral direction, arbitrary control and the threat of dismissal. Even where union agreements are in place, they are often unilaterally abrogated. These approaches promote insecurity and fear. They should be replaced by a more nurturing and supportive style of management: staff difficulties should be addressed more compassionately and more constructively. There should be clear, representative structures for dispute resolution with provision made for mediation. Staff should be encouraged to join trade unions.

Autocratic management behaviour should be condemned wherever it occurs. In this respect, Aboriginal organizations or those with Aboriginal leadership have, on occasion, been as guilty as non-Aboriginal ones.

Now that CED has reached a degree of maturity in Winnipeg, we must begin to pay more attention to these issues and be more demanding of management. We should also begin to pay more attention to the provision of adequate salaries, benefits and terms and conditions of service. We should pay particular attention to working hours and pension provisions. We cannot allow CED to become just another source of cheap labour. We should also judge CED workers by what they accomplish and not just by the hours they put in. This points to encouraging flexi-working arrangements.

RESPONSIBILITIES OF BOARDS

Boards of directors have a crucial role to play in CED organizations. That role must be clarified and board involvement must increase if the other challenges outlined above are to be met. Boards have a responsibility to ensure that organizations are managed efficiently and that funds are spent wisely and as approved. They must ensure management honesty and accountability, whatever management system is in place. In relatively small organizations they must also maintain contact with staff to ensure that all is well. Ideally, this could be done through having staff representatives on the executive committee and/or board. The issue of management accountability is a complex one which, potentially, can be made more difficult with participatory management structures, but it needs to be addressed. The fact that managers often play an important role in recruiting board members also complicates the accountability question and helps explain why arbitrary management styles are sometimes not held in check by boards. Ultimately, it is the board which is accountable to funders and clients for the performance of CED organizations: we need to rethink the role of boards in Winnipeg to ensure that they are performing this function satisfactorily. This may, necessarily, lead to constraining the influence of some executive directors.

IDENTIFYING WHAT WORKS
AND WHAT DOES NOT

We need a forum in which honest assessments can be made of experiments tried in CED, both in Winnipeg and elsewhere. We need to know, more clearly, what works, why and at what cost, and what does not work or can be improved upon. There is literature on this, based on other Canadian experiences, but it is not used widely (see, for instance, Ninacs and Favreau 1993; Lewis and Lockhart 1999; Community Resilience Team 1999; Richard 2004). These lessons must be made available to all those who are active in CED: CED activists and workers need to draw on them in their daily work. We must apply the same analytical frankness to our own experience in Winnipeg, and in

Manitoba generally. This means being brutally honest, even if some people are upset in the process: only in this way can past errors be rectified and avoided in the future. Such lessons should be drawn not only from projects but, more importantly, from policies and strategies that have been attempted.

CED MUST GO BEYOND POVERTY

While the immediate concern of much CED activity in Winnipeg is that of poverty alleviation, this must be considered only a necessary attribute of CED and not a sufficient one. CED is about much more than poverty, especially in its transformative version. Other goals of CED are a more equal distribution of income and wealth, greater gender equity, the sensible use of resources between generations, a more balanced spatial pattern of development and greater social inclusion. CED also furthers democratic decision-taking and participatory empowerment. Achieving these goals will require transforming the nature of the state: it will also require political mobilization of both the poor and the non-poor. In such a scenario the CED movement would become part, therefore, of a much broader movement, not only for economic and social change, but also for political transformation. While poverty eradication would remain an important element in the CED agenda, it would be but one element. This would necessitate CED activists becoming involved in broader social movement politics and mobilization, integrating the values and insights of these movements into the CED movement, while promoting the fundamental values of CED to the broader movement, and pressuring the state to be supportive of the principles.

These are the main challenges as I see them. They can and must be addressed if the remarkable progress of CED in Winnipeg is to be sustained and if the alternative vision of society that CED offers is to be fully realized.

NOTES

1. This chapter is based on two public presentations: the keynote address to a Workshop on CD/CED in Winnipeg: Maintaining the Momentum, held at the Freighthouse, Winnipeg, November, 17, 2003; and an introductory presentation at a symposium of CED activists entitled "Which Way Forward for Community Economic Development in Winnipeg's Inner City?" held at the University of Winnipeg, April 11, 2006.

2. In principle, there are numerous organizational forms through which social enterprises can be operated and, if the situation is right, any one can be as effective as any other. If co-ops have an edge at all, it would lie in the clear legal framework, including that of democratic decision taking, profit sharing and taxation, in which they operate. See Loughran 1985 for a detailed comparison of community development corporations versus cooperatives in CED.

Chapter Three

THE TOWN THAT LOST ITS NAME

The Impact of Hydroelectric
Development on
Grand Rapids, Manitoba

Peter Kulchyski and
Ramona Neckoway,
with the assistance of Gerald McKay
and Robert Buck

HISTORY OF GRAND RAPIDS

Grand Rapids is a community divided and, for too many years, silenced by hydroelectric development. It is comprised of two distinct political entities, which are located across from one another where the Saskatchewan River empties into Lake Winnipeg. The Cree community of Grand Rapids First Nation has a current population of close to 600; the Town of Grand Rapids has 751 residents. These communities are located approximately 400 kilometres northwest of Winnipeg. Passers-by who stop at the gas station on the Grand Rapids First Nation and then breeze on northward see what appears to be a typical northern reserve. A close look might lead one to notice the sign pronouncing the existence of a hydroelectric dam there, one of many built by the provincial utility during its expansionary glory days of the 1960s and 1970s. Upon even closer inspection, some sad and ugly truths about development in northern Manitoba are revealed.

The dam built at Grand Rapids can be considered the last great dam of a first phase of hydroelectric development in Manitoba, following, for example, dams on the Winnipeg River at Pine Falls/Powerview and at Pinawa, and an early dam on the Nelson River (called the Kelsey Dam). The Grand Rapids project was started with great fanfare: Premier Duff Roblin visited the community in 1965 to announce the great future that hydro development would bring. By the time of his announcement, however, the local First Nations and Métis peoples had already had a strong taste of the consequences of dam construction, and these were not to their liking. Prosperity did come to the utility, to the rest of the province, to the buyers of the relatively cheap power and to just about everyone who mattered — but the local people at Grand Rapids were not included in their number. The Misti Bistihk, meaning grand rapids, along which their community was situated, were suddenly silenced and the town of Grand Rapids "lost its name."

A decade later, the Churchill River Diversion, a far more massive hydroelectric development, was completed in northern Manitoba. By that time, circumstances had changed somewhat. After the national debacle over the Trudeau government's proposed *White Paper* (1969–70) and the Supreme Court of Canada's first moves toward recognition of Aboriginal rights (Supreme Court of Canada 1973), it became harder to ignore Aboriginal peoples.

In response to hydroelectric development in the northern Cree territories, a Northern Flood Committee was formed in Manitoba consisting of the five Cree communities most affected by the proposed project (a sixth community was at the time a sub-band of one of the five). Although the Committee wanted to prevent the project from taking place, it settled for a modern treaty called the Northern Flood Agreement (NFA) in the hopes of gaining, at least, appropriate compensation for the damage caused by the project.

Grand Rapids, on the other hand, received next to nothing in terms of compensation; no special attention was paid to the community until 1991, when the First Nation finally managed to negotiate a compensation package of approximately $5.5 million. The Town of Grand Rapids has yet to receive monetary compensation for the disruption to the livelihoods of its residents. Other communities that are not a part of this research project but that were affected by the Grand Rapids Generating Station, particularly Chemawawin-Easterville and Moose Lake, negotiated compensation agreements in 1990.

This story is of intrinsic value to the people most affected, and also contains lessons for the province of Manitoba and its public utility, Manitoba Hydro, as they contemplate a new phase of expanded hydroelectric production. The mentality that pervaded the Grand Rapids project subsequently pervaded the Churchill River Diversion Project and the negotiation of Implementation Agreements, and now saturates the new round of hydroelectric development proposals. This perspective treats local peoples, mostly First Nations and Métis, as *obstacles* whose support should be purchased with the minimum possible expenditures, and it treats the hunting and fishing economy as a residue from the past with no significant social or economic value in a contemporary context.

METHODOLOGY AND
RESEARCH APPROACH

This project was inspired and aided by the energy of two members of the municipal council of Grand Rapids: Mayor Robert Buck and Councillor Gerald McKay. Along with local teacher Blaine Klippenstein, they approached Peter Kulchyski in the fall of 2003 with an interest in securing financial resources to research and write an independent local history of the community. The two local leaders, mired in negotiations for a compensation package over the Grand Rapids project, felt that the story of their community needed to be told.

A graduate student from the Cree community of Nelson House, Ramona Neckoway, was hired to conduct interviews with local community members. Although an agenda of interview questions was established by Buck, McKay, Kulchyski and Neckoway, in general an open-ended format was used.

By the spring of 2005, twelve individuals had been interviewed, most of whom had been introduced to Neckoway with the support of Buck and McKay. Respondents included local Métis and Cree citizens, both men and women, as well as non-Aboriginal people who, in one capacity or another, were involved in the community at the time of the hydro construction. Neckoway also engaged in a modest degree of archival research, where possible correlating research findings with archival documents; as well, Kulchyski and Neckoway reviewed secondary literature and used official Manitoba Hydro documents to explicate the general features of the project.

This research deploys qualitative approaches combined with a strong degree of community-participation, action-based techniques. The action research component is, in part, due to the study's orientation toward documenting claims made by the municipality in support of the ongoing negotiations. No doubt the work will also be of value to the First Nation as it reopens similar negotiations.

GRAND RAPIDS AND
THE GRAND RAPIDS DAM

Today there are three communities sitting at the site of the former location known as Grand Rapids near the mouth of the Saskatchewan River at Lake Winnipeg. The Grand Rapids First Nation consists of descendents of the original Cree occupants of the territory. The community sits on reserve lands on the south side of the Saskatchewan River. Today it looks like most reserves in north and western Canada: gravel roads, run-down government housing, a few public buildings and attempts at "community development" are visible. Many residents of the Municipality of Grand Rapids are of Métis descent, are Cree who have lost their legal status and are therefore not entitled to live on the reserve, or are non-Aboriginal. Finally, a small "hydro community" — which this chapter calls by that name — with no more than 100 people has been created, away from the Municipality and the First Nation, behind the hydro generating station. With suburban-style housing for families, paved roads, and a large housing complex utilized by a modest number of hydro employees without families, this community lives in luxury in comparison to the Town and the First Nation. The story of Grand Rapids that follows will uncover the stark disparity in the qualities of living of these three communities.

It is important to note that the "Town of" and Grand Rapids "First Nation" are recent designations, introduced after the construction of the Grand Rapids Generating Station. Mayor Robbie Buck asserted in a recent interview that "there were [are] three separate, communities. One of the things that Hydro did was it separated the community. It made the reserve the reserve, it made the town, and then Hydro was a separate entity in itself."

Construction of the Grand Rapids Generating Station began in 1960 and was fully completed in 1968, at a total cost of $117 million to the utility. According to Manitoba Hydro Web site, in

> 1965 [the] Grand Rapids Generating Station, located on the Saskatchewan River about four kilometres from Lake Winnipeg, was officially opened on November 13. Its three units produced a total capacity of 330 MW. The generating station was re-rated to 339 MW in 1966, and to 354 MW in 1967. In 1968, the final unit was placed in service bringing the total capacity to 472 MW. Grand Rapids operated with a 36.6-m head, or waterfall — the largest in Manitoba. The giant Kaplan turbines and generators at Grand Rapids were the largest installed in North America for this size of operating head.

In a summary of the history of hydro development in Manitoba, the Web site goes on to note:

> One of the most challenging problems in developing the forebay at Grand Rapids was the prevalence of limestone and dolomite in the region. To prevent water from seeping out of the storage area through numerous crevices and separations found in limestone, it was necessary to form an underground seal beneath the dykes. Over 99,909 tonnes of cement were used in the sealing or "grouting" program, one of the largest of its kind ever attempted in the world.

It is significant that no mention of the local people is made in this brief overview of hydroelectric development, which treats the project as a problem and feat of engineering alone. The development included "spin-off" tasks that had significant impacts, including the construction of a road that, for the first time, connected the community to southern centres. The presence of the first liquor outlet in the community also had significant consequences, as did the sheer numbers of migrant workers required to physically construct the dam and its "spin-off" projects.

The actual hydroelectric project involved construction of a dam, a dike, transmission lines and a spillway dam. The dike, basically a huge pile of gravel that runs a distance of 25.7 kilometres, was built out of material dug from the earth in the vicinity. Cement was poured every few feet adjacent to the dike, which served as an "underground seal beneath the dikes" (Manitoba Hydro Web site). The dike and the hollowed-out landscape are the largest visible reminders of the project. The dam itself is a large, concrete facility situated very near to the community at the southeast corner of the dike. A few kilometres from the main dam, also on the dike, is another concrete dam, but its purpose is not to generate electricity: rather, it allows another outlet of water onto a spillway — the former riverbed — when the backup is too high. The ever-present hydro transmission towers, both from this project and from the more northerly dams, are other unavoidable physical reminders of the presence and impact of hydro development. Five transmission lines were associated with this project.

Manitoba Hydro notes on its Web site that "when development of Manitoba's northern rivers was first considered in earnest in the 1960s, proposals and plans were drawn up with little community consultation," adding that, as a result, "in the 1990s, Manitoba Hydro made a concerted effort to work with affected communities to find resolutions for past effects and to build cooperative relationships for the future." The Web site then describes a variety of settlements reached in the 1990s with NFA and other affected communities. Pertaining to the Grand Rapids situation, it is observed that "in the early 1990s, five settlements were reached related to the Grand Rapids Generating Station, built on the Saskatchewan River. Agreements totalling $31.8 million were signed with Easterville/Chemawawin, Moose Lake, The Pas Indian Band, Grand Rapids First Nation and Cormorant communities." A total of $5.5 million of these funds went to Grand Rapids First Nation.

At the time of writing, the Municipality of Grand Rapids has not signed a compensation package and is in protracted negotiations; the Grand Rapids First Nation, unhappy with the deal that had been reached, has reopened negotiations surrounding the issue. A recent estimate, compiled using data from *Manitoba Hydro Annual Reports*, shows that, since 1982, the Grand Rapids Generating Station has created $1.08 billion in revenue.

FINDINGS

The testimonies of local residents provide a wealth of information pertaining to the "on-the-ground" impacts of hydroelectric development at Grand Rapids. For the purposes of this research, we did not distinquish between members of the First Nation and members of the Municipality, between Métis and Cree or between status and non-status interview subjects. We have divided the material into five parts: life before the project; material pertaining to the construction phase itself (the immediate impacts); impacts of the development over a longer term; a photo essay on contemporary circumstances of the communities; and recent efforts by the community to regain control of its future.

Before the Flood

A visitor to Grand Rapids in 1959 would have found a quiet, industrious fishing community, similar in many respects to the contemporary Ojibwa community of Poplar River on the east side of Lake Winnipeg. There was no direct road access to the community, which meant that access for local people was restricted to water craft when there was open water and to dog teams in the winter. Prior to the project, most local people were responsible for the livelihoods of their families and, with little in the way of a wage economy, relied on the local renewable resources and harvests from the land. Local residents were hunters and fishers, as their ancestors had been. The community boasted no significant infrastructure apart from scattered houses, many of which were built by their occupants. Elders knew of the ancient trails that ran along the banks of the Saskatchewan River, and the roar of the great rapids could be heard from afar. It was said that if infants could be taken by canoe to shoot the rapids, they would gain spiritual power and have strength in body, spirit and endurance.

People were not wealthy in the material terms of today's society, and they had little taste for the consumer products that were changing much of the rest of the world. Local people recalled the difficult transition from fresh country food to that which was purchased at stores and came in cans.

There were no local businessmen amassing fortunes; in fact, there was little interest in such matters. However, there was a pride that came from being self-sufficient. Other benefits came from following a way of life that had been practised, albeit with different technologies, for centuries. There appears to have been fairly close cooperation between the Cree, who lived on reserve lands, and the Métis and non-status Cree who lived across the river: intermarriage, work partnerships, celebrations and a host of mutual supports were common.

Siblings Valerie and Floyd Ferland live on the north side of the river. In an interview together they recalled what life was like prior to Hydro:

Before, we didn't have welfare and jobs and people always had things [with emphasis]. Say if one family didn't have anything, and this family had quite a bit, they'd give to the other family that didn't have anything. Now you don't see that. Everybody used to help each other before, now they… they don't.

Gerald McKay, who is a resident of Grand Rapids, was a child when the construction era was in full force. Prior to that time, many of the local people relied in large part on the harvests off the land:

before the flooding my Mom and Dad used to go up, everybody went up the river. That was where all the animals were and all the ducks and geese, rats, and they were in the marsh. But after that was flooded then we went out north on the road. We used to go to Buffalo Lake and camp there and after when we'd finish there, we'd move camps.

A local trapper, Angus, discussed the significance of the land and its harvest to the people of the community:

There wasn't a hell of a lot but fishing and trapping. That's all they did [hunt, fish and trap]. Dog was the transportation, canoes. They paddled all the way to The Pas if someone got sick. Yeah, there was a lot of hard times. People even stayed out there in cabooses fishing and all that. The good old dog team was the only transportation that time.

Former Hydro employee Oscar Olson has been a resident of the Town since 1961, when he began working for the utility. He discussed the thriving fishing industry that existed in Grand Rapids prior to the construction of the dam:

I have all the records from the '40s up 'til the late '80s. During the '60s, the community produced a million pounds of pickerel a year. That's worth a fortune. That's just Grand Rapids, including the First Nation, Grand Rapids produced a million pounds of pickerel a year: '60, '61, '62, '63. After '63, they [the fish] could no longer get through.

It All Went Quiet

Many of those interviewed discussed the changes they observed and experienced once the rapids had been silenced. This subject matter was especially difficult to navigate, as the local people were divulging harsh and personal stories of traumatic experiences and upheaval. Nevertheless, it seemed that many were eager to share their experiences and to expose the treatment they endured. Many talked of the rapids being "shut off" or "turned off," and described how some of the community people had gone down to the mucky river bottom to retrieve old guns, or how they themselves, as children, had gone to find and catch the fish that were thrashing in the pools left in the emptied river.

Joe Mercredi grew up on the north side of the river, and lived on what he described as "prime real estate." Mercredi also described the period when the waters were silenced:

> The explosions were hard to deal with. Like the blasting was hard to deal with. But the rest of the sound was actually not a whole lot different from listening to the rapids. The rapids were there twenty-four hours a day, except for really, really cold spells in the winter time, when it would freeze over for a bit. And then it would be quiet. But because of the way the river ran, there was always that rumble, so the construction was basically more of the same. A little bit louder. All of a sudden there was no sound. It was exciting because they turned it off, "shut off the rapids," can't remember exactly what day it was, but we got to walk on the river bottom.

Robbie Buck, current mayor of the Town of Grand Rapids, discussed his experiences and memories related to the era of the construction of the Grand Rapids dam:

> [H]ome was along the Saskatchewan River, in the community of Grand Rapids... down river from the power dam.... Right beside our house there [was] where the river [was] the deepest. And so that's where Hydro put their dock up for the big barges to come in because there was no roads to Grand Rapids yet.... [T]hey used to bring everything in by barge.... So there was always things going on there twenty-four hours a day when I was a kid, eh. And in fact, when they moved in they tried to take over my Mom and Dad's land, and they tried to buy it off them, but my Dad refused to sell it to them so, regardless [of] whether it was sold to them or anything, they went ahead with their [Hydro] fence on to our land anyway... they were told "no," they went ahead anyway regardless of what they were told.

Buck went on to talk about how Hydro displaced and literally evicted people off their land:

> Until the sixties, Grand Rapids was what you called an "unorganized

territory," there was no what you call a "municipality" today. When Hydro came, they're the ones who organized… what was called Local Government District at that time, "LGD." They incorporated it… like a municipality I guess… with that came taxes and… they planned towning and everything. And people whose houses didn't fit into their plans were asked to move, eh, 'cause they were squatters and things like that. One of my aunts was living right next door to us, where they [Hydro] had… their warehouses and everything… she came to Winnipeg, cause she's sick, she's in the hospital for a while. She came home, and her home was gone. They had bulldozed it down… in the time that she had been gone.

Buck talked about the impacts of the project on his parents, who, at the time, were young parents coping with the introduction of a system unlike that to which they were accustomed, in addition to the overwhelming presence of migrant workers. Several of those interviewed mentioned the substantial change in population, which occurred nearly "overnight":

[F]or my Mom… there was always lots of that fear… because… there was a lot of people who came, who didn't get jobs, eh… they'd get hungry sometimes and they'd break into homes and everything like that… there's some stories where kids were just about stolen and things like that, and that was one of my Mom's big fears.

McKay recalled the transition from the subsistence economy, or the hunting and trapping lifestyle, to the wage economy, and the impact of this on his family:

There was five of us, five little kids and my Dad got put out of work. There was no training, nothing provided for them, and there was no welfare at that time, or else they refused it. We were never on welfare. So we went through some pretty tough times, like, for, actual hunger, you know. You don't think people go hungry in the land of plenty but we went hungry.

He also discussed the impact of the project, that is, the arrival of authority figures in the community who had the ability to enforce provincial and federal legislation, and what this meant for his family:

I can never remember ever being hungry before the dam, but after the dam we were hungry. What happened was, when they'd built the highway, all of a sudden there was police there and the resource guys… My Dad was not Treaty, his Mother was Treaty… but he wasn't. He was Métis. So he couldn't hunt, and he couldn't fish…

he had been brought up to live off the land, and then all of a sudden that changed over night. They couldn't... even set a net in the river for his own use. And he couldn't hunt. Only in September, or whenever hunting season was, that's the only time he could hunt. And he couldn't fish. Only when... sport fishing was open. Or when fishing season was on.

When they flooded it [Summer Berry Marsh]... there was no compensation. My Dad was just put out of work... He went from a qualified fisherman and trapper to an unskilled labourer. Just overnight... we never knew hunger until after that dam because my [Dad] would be working out of town, and there was no welfare; my Mom and Dad were never on welfare. So if we didn't have food, we didn't eat.

Community members discussed the physical displacement that resulted from the various projects in the community. Regarding the forced relocation of his family, Joe Mercredi had this to say:

One of the things that happened to us, which still bugs Mom to this day, is the fact that the house that my great-grandfather built whenever he moved there, in the late 1800s, where my Dad was born and where some of my brothers and sisters were born, was, well it was our homestead... Natural Resources wanted to have their compound right there, they ended up expropriating our land.

A Series of Entirely Explicable Social Disasters

One of the most compelling and blatant indictments of the Grand Rapids experience is the social chaos that occurred in the wake of hydroelectric development. All of those interviewed, at one point or another, discussed or reflected on the social disruptions they experienced as individuals or in their collective experience of the community. Regarding the impact on the social fabric of Grand Rapids, Pranteau had this to say:

You wouldn't believe the violence we saw man! Holy smokes! That was a horrible experience, boy! You know I wouldn't wish that Grand Rapids on anybody else — what happened to us. They turned our house into a bootlegging joint and a whorehouse. Yeah, that's what it was too. There was a lot of fighting going on... it was like an old wild west town, minus the guns... there was a lot of violence!... they used to watch and stare and make fun of us.

The actual construction phase of the project introduced the first of the social disasters that would follow. The construction camp, filled with strangers, transformed life virtually overnight: a powerful mix of alcohol abuse and racism fed tensions between the now outnumbered locals and the newcomers. This view is supported by McKay, who stated:

> When we were kids we didn't know any different. We just accepted what was here. We didn't know all of the problems that this stuff was causing, like all the influx of people looking for work. There was a lot of crime and after, when, I guess, almost right away when the road came, the alcohol [came]. And all the violence, you know, like I bet you we've seen more violence in those four years than most people will see in a lifetime. Violence in the community and violence between the workers... they were just harassing the local people.

Many horrendous tales involving the experiences of local people in Grand Rapids were documented. All are significant, but a story told by a retired nurse, who worked in Grand Rapids, especially stands out, and perhaps exemplifies the treatment experienced by local people. Some prior explanation is needed. Betty Caylin worked at the Grand Rapids nursing station: the doctor she refers to in the following story was her supervisor. A separate medical facility had been built to serve the Hydro employees. Caylin's story is compelling:

> [W]hen I came... first of all, I came to The Pas. I lived in The Pas and then I worked in Moose Lake, Cedar Lake and Grand Rapids. But... my doctor said "Don't spend any time in Grand Rapids, because there's a hospital there." But... those Hydro people didn't want to look after the people.
> [M]y impression always was that... it [the hospital in Grand Rapids] was for the Hydro employees... I had some experiences that were really bad... my impression was they... didn't want to look after people, really. It was for Hydro employees... that's the only people they wanted to look after.

To illustrate her assertion that Hydro was not in the business of looking after locals, Caylin told a disturbing story about a pregnant woman who was turned away from the Hydro hospital:

> [O]ne case... really, really upset me. There was a lady that came from the bush... well she was gonna a have a baby, but she didn't know how many months she was pregnant; she was bleeding and all that. And she said that she had gone to the Hydro hospital but they had said, "You don't belong here, you go to the station!"... I didn't know her... and I didn't know what to do with her. So I phoned my

medical director in The Pas and I said, "What am I going to do with her?" [He replied], "Well, hasn't she got some friends in town?"... [She replied], "well, I know the Leask's." And so she went there and by now it was colder, very stormy, it was in November or December when she was here and then all of a sudden, eleven o'clock at night, the guy pushed her into the nursing station and said, "She's your problem now!"... and then he took off... So anyway, he took off... I didn't have any facilities. Hydro had given me a bed and it was in the reception room, it was there if we were ever gonna set it up... But then, when I realized that she would have to stay the night, I went and got my own bedding and put it, tryin' to make the bed. And I guess I was mumbling to myself and she said, "But nurse, you do know I need help"... I said, "Yeah, I'm sorry." I said, "the reason why I'm upset is because I have a feeling I can't look after you... I don't know how to look after you." And I said, "But I'll tell you... if I would have been you, I would have gone in the bush and had my baby and died there," because she had been turned away at the hospital, and I was upset because I was supposed to look after her. Here she was... all alone and she's gonna have a baby. And then I said, "But I'll tell you one thing, I'll do what I can... and I'll help you as much as I can," and all night long I was with her, and she was having stronger pains. I was getting more worried and more worried. And I phoned... I just had that sense or that feeling that this was a case I could not handle... then I phoned the doctor in The Pas. I said, "Can't I phone Dr. Wal?... like Dr. Walton was a doctor here then, and he was very good. So he says, "No you don't! You look after her yourself." And then I waited and waited. Five o'clock... and I went against all my teaching. Like you never went against the doctor's order or stuff like that. So, I phoned Dr. Walton. I said, "Look Dr. Walton, I know this lady had been turned away from your hospital and my doctor said I wasn't supposed to call you, but I need help; do you mind coming and helping me?" He said, "Certainly not! I'll come right down." And then he examined the lady, and he looked awful worried and he said for me to go and lie down. I said, "No, I can't lie down." Then she had the baby... she bled a lot, and the placenta didn't come out after birth... he was terribly worried because she bled so much... had already passed out... and I was there with the baby. I didn't have a box; I had nothing. I had to get one of those zinc tubs... I put a pillow and that's where... I put the baby. Doctor Walton was really worried, he thought she was gonna bleed to death because she was already passing out. And then he said, "Why don't you phone the hospital and tell them to come and bring anesthetic and then I'm going to try and remove the placenta." And I was gonna say, "Oh! Just take her to your hospital! Never mind doing that in the nursing station!" You know with all the infection and stuff like that stuff. And then... it went through my mind and then he said outside, "On second thought, [I] just have a station wagon, tell them to come and get this woman," and he wanted to go to the hospital. So what they did then is load her up on that station wagon and took her to the hospital, and then he took her into the operating room, and he tried to remove the placenta. And the whole uterus was inverted, it goes inside out... And then afterwards, Dr. Scott said to me (that's the doctor in The Pas) he said, "You're lucky she didn't die because usually the shock of that kills a woman." I felt like saying, "You're lucky she didn't die! Because it was your fault!"... But if I wouldn't have gone against the doctor's orders, and if Dr. Walton would've refused to help me, that woman woulda died!... Dr. Walton was good... he didn't always do what Hydro said... But you know, they discharged her the next day and she went back into the bush!... That poor woman! I thought it was just terrible the way they treated her... the uterus had inverted so that's no small thing... so she went back into the bush... her baby was alright... today maybe you wouldn't get away with that.

While this section has focused on the unpleasant experiences of the residents of Grand Rapids, it is important to remember that the local people are "survivors" who have developed strength to face and adapt to difficult changes.

Following the dam's construction, the Métis and Cree communities were left to their own devices. A variety of social problems that had already emerged took hold, as citizens moved from a self-reliant, isolated "bush" lifestyle to a welfare-based lifestyle at the side of the road. Alcoholism and substance abuse started to have a real impact on families — an impact that was to become intergenerational. Grinding poverty with no outlet or hope replaced the "poor in things but rich in spirit" lifestyle which had formerly existed. Many people simply left town, giving up on finding a meaningful future there. All kinds of social divisions emerged between Hydro employees and non-employees; between the Cree and the Métis; and between status and non-status Cree. Nonetheless, a few people continued, against the odds, to hold their families together, to live off the now damaged land and to dream of somehow, some way, fighting back.

On a Dry Riverbed: Fighting Back

In the spring of 2005 councillors from the Municipality of Grand Rapids asked Manitoba Hydro officials what their plans were in the coming summer for the spillway. A good deal of brush had grown on the dry riverbed.

Suburban style housing provided for Manitoba Hydro employees at Grand Rapids (Ramona Neckoway)

The dual hydro meters on Hydro employees homes; their power bills are subsidized while Aboriginal and municipal residents are expected to pay full rates (Ramona Neckoway)

Housing for people in the municipality and on the reserve, meanwhile, are typical of low income Aboriginal families across the north: 'development' Hydro style has done little to improve their lives (Ramona Neckoway)

The Manitoba Hydro facility for single employees, dubbed the "Taj Mahal" by local Aboriginal peoples, in a wry comment on its lavish amenities (Ramona Neckoway)

The playground for the children of Manitoba Hydro's employees (Ramona Neckoway)

The playground on the "other side" of the dam; the social and racial division will be seared into the memories of the next generation (Ramona Neckoway)

Local people were concerned that if the spillway were opened, the brush would end up in the rivers and lakes. Distracted officials reassured them that there were no plans to open the spillway, no reason to hire a few locals to clear the brush. Then, in August, an impersonal fax arrived from Manitoba Hydro announcing that the spillway would be opened in two days. Newly elected Chief Ovide Mercredi and Mayor Robert Buck set up a camp on the riverbed to prevent the opening of the spillway.

What followed was an opening, a glimmer of hope in a place long denied such an important emotional resource. Most strikingly the community, which had developed its own share of divisions as a result of the project, began to come together in a show of solidarity. People provided the leaders with food and logistical support, came out to sit and chat and visit. About a week after the camp was established, a fiddle- and guitar-based, somewhat spontaneous music festival took place at the camp, with, at various times in that one evening, about eighty people coming out under a stormy sky to dance, listen or play music with the leaders.

Others dropped by the campsite. Indigenous people from communities as far away as Wabowden, Nelson House and Cross Lake came to show their support. Momentum grew as word got around. Within a week the President of Manitoba Hydro, Bob Brenner, visited the camp and listened to the leaders. A week later the Premier, Gary Doer, visited. It was the first time since Duff Roblin's ribbon-cutting visit that a sitting premier had come to the community. Formal presentations were made in the community. Senior members of the Manitoba government were shown around the project and the communities. The environmental and social damage was made clear. The Premier, clearly moved by what he had seen and somewhat shocked at the patent injustice, made a commitment to restart negotiations with the First Nation and to deal fairly with the municipality. Whether the commitment will be respected is for the future to determine, but it seemed clear at the time that desperately needed change was at least going to be discussed.

CONCLUSIONS, RESULTS AND LESSONS

The sad history of Grand Rapids is a cautionary tale. Often, conflicts with Aboriginal communities around land use are portrayed as disagreements between the needs of the general public and those of one small sector of society — indigenous people. We reject this way of understanding such conflicts, and certainly reject it in the context of the Grand Rapids Generating Station. Our society as a whole is deeply injured when intergenerational misery is inflicted on one of its very important segments, the First Peoples. The general public's well-being is not aided by the construction of a "legacy of hatred" — a deeply divided world of rich and poor, where one community is left without the resources even to hope for a better future, while right next door another community is thriving. Such a situation creates a time bomb in the midst of the general public, who must live as bearers of an injustice created in their name. The social and economic costs of such forms of development — not to mention the human costs — must be understood from a long-term perspective: this is what an overview of the current state of Grand Rapids urgently calls to attention.

The Municipality and the First Nation of Grand Rapids are currently in negotiations over claims regarding the impact of hydroelectric development on their communities. A just settlement will not include a one-time cash payment, however large. A just settlement will include a revenue stream that will continue to flow as long as does the power. Such a settlement should be made in the interest of paving the way to a meaningful new relationship between First Nations and Manitoba Hydro. Instead of the current logic, which will lead to many more situations like that of Grand Rapids, an approach is called for which understands that First Nations citizens deserve to live at least as well as employees of the public utility, and that First Nations communities deserve the same quality and kind of infrastructure that the public utility believes its own employees need. A just settlement might also lead to a mentality change on the part of Manitoba Hydro, such that it might begin to see that consulting local communities about apparently small matters, such as when to open a spillway, is a better way of doing business. The many other initiatives the public utility could undertake — for example, Aboriginal executive training programs that do not consider the only Hydro jobs appropriate for Aboriginal peoples to be those at the bottom of the employment hierarchy — will almost certainly spring from such a mentality change.

We offer this chapter in the spirit of respect for the treaty relationship; in the spirit of hope that change will come; in the spirit of gratitude to the people of Grand Rapids who have shared their often difficult stories with us; and in the spirit of admiration for a people who have suffered and survived to struggle on and to rebuild their community.

Chapter Four

GOVERNMENT POLICY TOWARDS COMMUNITY ECONOMIC DEVELOPMENT IN MANITOBA IN THE 1960s AND 1970s

Lynne P. Fernandez

EARLY YEARS OF CED IN MANITOBA

This chapter examines provincial policies towards CED in Manitoba's north in the 1960s and 1970s. The evolution of CED policy during this period merits study by those working in the field for two reasons. First, CED as it is known today began to take shape during these years. Practitioners will find it useful to understand how the ideas of the period continue to influence policy developments today. Second, the lack of continuity in program delivery resulting from policy swings produced inefficiencies and disappointing results. From learning about these episodes, policy-makers at all levels of government can gain insight into the importance of investing in long-term program stability. As the major source of funding for CED projects, governments must be informed of conceptual and practical developments in the past in order to continue to improve current policies and activities.

The working definition of CED one selects when writing a critical review of CED policy is of great importance, since it sets the standard against which results are to be compared. The most common source of variance in interpretations of CED is found in the relative weights given to economic and social progress. When too much attention is paid to the economic, CED becomes business development; when social amelioration is overemphasized, CED can turn into a form of self-defeating welfare delivery. The importance of finding the right balance between social and economic objectives is also stressed in development economics, a close relative of CED. Mainstream theorists in this field insist that the three objectives of development are: 1) to improve the distribution of basic sustenance, including food, shelter, health and protection; 2) to improve standards of living by way of improvements in income, education, cultural and humanistic values; and 3) to increase the number of social and economic choices to individuals, thereby releasing them from servitude to others and alleviating human misery (Todaro 2000: 18).

The definition of CED used in this chapter is informed by the above interpretation, proposing that meaningful CED considers each of social, cultural, ecological and economic indicators, while emphasizing community initiative. Accordingly, it is through the following lens that government policy and CED in the 1960s and 1970s in Manitoba will be analyzed:

> CED is a community-based and community-directed process that explicitly combines social and economic development and is directed towards fostering the economic, social, ecological and cultural well-being of communities. (BC Working Group on CED)

In the Aboriginal context, CED policy must be attentive to the preservation of traditional ways of life. Loxley (1985: 3) points out that the marginalization of Aboriginal peoples has been a sustained, historical by-product of Canadian economic development and that, therefore, Aboriginal communities are not likely to turn to mainstream society for solutions to their development issues and priorities. In fact, mainstream consumption culture, along with widespread racist discrimination, stifle the Aboriginal tradition just as much as the deliberate institutional repression of the past. In order to ensure that Aboriginal traditions are not reduced to historical curiosities, strategies for the development of Aboriginal communities must conserve and respect the natural resources upon which Aboriginal culture is based. Further, they must work within traditional social structures rather than superimpose the western system of social relations upon them. A CED approach, which concentrates on activities such as hunting, fishing, trapping, outfitting and forestry work, organizes social relations along communal lines and emphasizes the opinions of elders, can help communities regain self sufficiency, dignity and a renewed place in the Canadian landscape.

The Introduction of Community Development Services

According to McEwen (1968: 7, 16), the provincial government set up the Manitoba Community Development Services in 1958 in cooperation with Indian Affairs. As Director of this new Department, Jean H. Lagasse introduced CD to Aboriginal communities in Manitoba via a three-year investigation into the living conditions of Manitoba's Aboriginal people. Lagasse believed that CD in Manitoba should focus on two problems: "[T]he main emphasis of community development in Manitoba is economic development and social organisation because it is in these two areas that former government services have been most delinquent" (Lagasse in Lloyd 1967: 39). In accordance with Lagasse's recommendations, a community development officer was assigned in 1960 to each of Norway House, Grand Rapids and Camperville, and an economic liaison officer was appointed to Winnipeg. In 1961, Berens River and The Pas were included in the new operations (Lloyd 1967: 39).

Social and economic conditions in these areas at the time of the introduction of the community development officers varied significantly. The construction by Manitoba Hydro of a hydroelectric plant in Grand Rapids had overturned the community's traditional economic and social structures, causing its residents enormous hardship (see Kulchyski and Neckoway, Chapter 3 in this volume, for a detailed discussion of the socio-economic impacts of hydroelectric construction at Grand Rapids). Norway House, which had not experienced any hydroelectric development, still relied heavily on welfare payments. In 1961, a successful pulpwood cooperative was established in Berens River, and, for the first time in many years, no social assistance had to be paid. An effort to alleviate the problems facing Aboriginal people was launched in The Pas in the same year. Government hearings allowed the public to express concerns over housing, employment, job-training, education, the building of a Friendship Centre and transient and jail services. In the Camperville region, a six-month period of data collection was necessary before the government could even begin to understand the needs of the area (Lloyd 1967: 40).

Under the auspices of the new Community Development Services in Manitoba, the provincial and the federal governments began to coordinate their community development activities. Since Indian Affairs contributed financially to the new Services' initiatives, projects had to receive the approval of its supervisor for the region in which the CD work was to take place. Community Development Services also had to maintain close ties with various other federal departments, such as the Department of Mines, in order to coordinate services and avoid duplication (Lloyd 1967: 42). Coordination was further enhanced when Manitoba, along with the other Canadian provinces, signed an agreement in 1961with the federal government's Agricultural Rehabilitation and Development Administration (ARDA) that included Aboriginal communities. Included among the services offered were soil and water; research and development of rural resources, including industry, education and training; and community development for rural areas, as designated by federal-provincial agreements (McEwen 1968: 15).

In 1964 Professor J.G. Dallyn of the Department of Welfare, Winnipeg, prepared a report, titled "Community Development Service Evaluation," on the state of community development in Manitoba. He believed that although Community Development Services had been successful, its reach was insufficient. In order to deliver benefits to all of Manitoba's Aboriginal people, the Department would have to be greatly extended. He also recommended that CD officers work in more than one community, forcing them to standardize their procedures in order that they would be applicable to more than just one setting (Dallyn in Lloyd 1967: 43). Dallyn argued that arbitrary methods were being employed to deal with community problems and that a more systematic approach had to be established for real progress to be made (Lloyd 1967: 44).

Structural Weaknesses of CD Services in the 1960s
McEwen outlines some of the weaknesses in the delivery of CD services for Aboriginal people in the 1960s. On the one hand, he believed that the lack of legal authority, administrative skills and training among band councils prevented them from acting effectively. In his opinion, the civil servants of the provincial and federal governments were often in a conflict-of-interest position — once a provincial community development officer had educated Aboriginal people on the extent of their plight, he was accused by federal employees of unleashing discontent with government policy. As a consequence, many CD officers found it easier to conform to the status quo, acting as project officers rather than as agents for meaningful change (McEwen 1968: 29).

Other administrative deficiencies observed by McEwen were inadequate resources at the provincial level and the often meaningless, socially disruptive paper divide between status and non-status people. Poor coordination between provincial and federal agreements on the delivery of basic services further complicated CD initiatives: while the province controlled resources, roads, public health and wildlife, the federal government had legal responsibility for all matters concerning "Indians and land reserved for Indians" (McEwen 1968: 33). These failures in the delivery of CD services culminated in a feeling of profound distrust among Aboriginal people towards government officials, in particular towards employees of Indian Affairs. McEwen went so far as to suggest that career civil servants relied on the ongoing marginalization of Aboriginal communities to keep their jobs (1968: 33).

McEwen also criticized the design of regional development schemes, noting that those not considering the availability of local resources would probably fail. He highlighted cases where industrial development was proceeding without the participation of local Aboriginal communities, allowing pockets of poverty to exist within thriving regions (1968: 32). Moreover, he was concerned about the need to incorporate the traditional values of Aboriginal communities into CED initiatives.

To address these weaknesses, McEwen recommended the adoption of the following principles: that CD belong to the people, with the CD officer acting only as a catalyst; that the community obtain access to resources;

that there be complete and effective coordination of government services in regional settings; that the need for pilot projects to initiate the movement be recognized; and that CD begin within the culture and value system of the community (1968: 31–38). Overall, his insights and recommendations were very progressive for their time.

From this brief overview of the state of CD in Manitoba in the 1960s, we see that CD was beginning to appreciate many of the tenets of today's CED, but lacked the policy capacity to implement them. For example, CD recommended that the community itself take control of change, but no serious attempts were made in this regard. Some CD advocates, like Lloyd and McEwan, were well-informed and insightful, but governments failed to appreciate their expertise and did not put their recommendations into practice.

PROVINCIAL CED POLICY IN THE 1970s

The FRED Interlake Agreement

The Fund for Rural Economic Development (FRED) Agreement, a bipartite (provincial-federal) program bridging the CD policies of the 1960s and 1970s, was implemented in Manitoba's Interlake region between 1967 and 1977. The combined investment of the two governments totalled $85.1 million, with spending divided between resource management, human resource development and infrastructure. According to Decter and Kowall (1990: iii), authors of an Economic Council of Canada report titled *Manitoba's Interlake Region: The Fund for Rural Economic Development Agreement, 1967–1977*, the FRED Agreement was a clear example of a successful effort to improve the social and economic fabric of a region, since the Interlake was transformed from "a severely disadvantaged rural area of poverty and widespread underemployment to a region with sustainable economic development."

Developments achieved under the FRED Agreement included the establishment of a Seagram's Company distillery in Gimli and of a goose-processing plant and promotional-wear company in Teulon, and the expansion of the Harbrook Cheese plant. Agricultural production was diversified under the program, and demand for the region's rye was bolstered by the new Seagram's distillery. Managerial and technical training was provided to farmers and fishers, as well as funding for farm management and improvement proposals. Also, fish marketing arrangements and fishing equipment were upgraded (Decter and Kowall 1990: 33). Improvements to the region's infrastructure not only enhanced the growth of local industry, but also greatly improved the quality of life for those who lived in areas with poor roads and little access to water (Decter and Kowall 1990: 31).

The Economic Council of Canada report also notes that, whereas before-and-after economic indicators were well-documented, other ingredients of the program's success were not. In an attempt to address these omissions, the authors (Economic Council of Canada 1990: 40–41) emphasized the following lessons from the Interlake experience:

- that community participation is a necessary step in successful CED programs;
- that CED planning must include robust analytical work in order to efficiently link funds to strategic investments;
- that human resource development plays an important role in CED (FRED included a large education and training component);
- that a minimum time frame of at least ten years is required to realize meaningful CED;
- that a federal-provincial agreement may best be used as an underpinning and funding source for a project, with community-based initiatives providing the planning and control.

Again, these insights and recommendations were very progressive.

It is also important to note the Interlake Agreement's implementation structure. The Agreement was designed so as to allow stability and continuity in spite of changes in governments, ministers and departmental organizations at both levels of government (Decter and Kowall 1990: 20). Since government line departments took their mandates directly from the Agreement, the policy swings usually resulting from changes in government could be avoided.

The Economic Council of Canada (1990) report highlights how differences in the priorities of the various levels of government involved in the Agreement created tensions between them. While the federal government was concerned with economic adjustment and labour mobility, provincial administrators were focused on intra-regional economic development. At the community level, local advisory boards called Area Development Boards were established by the province to ensure that residents of the Area could participate in planning (Agreement Covering a Comprehensive Rural Development Plan for the Interlake Area of Manitoba, Appendix 1, Decter and Kowall 1990: 48, 49). The priorities of the Area Development Boards were education, agricultural development, land drainage, recreational development and infrastructure improvements. Levels of government correlated negatively with local development: the higher the level of government, the more emphasis was put on broad economic indicators and the greater was the commitment to labour mobility rather than local development that would encourage residents to stay in the region (Decter and Kowall 1990: 43, 44). Nonetheless, the localized success of the program demonstrates that the influence of the provincial government and Area Development Boards was great enough to overcome the federal government's disregard for improvement at the community level.

CED Policy of the NDP Government

The Progressive Conservative party, under Premier Duff Roblin, had represented the province during the initial FRED planning as well as during the introduction in the 1960s of CD initiatives in the north. However, in 1969, the province elected the NDP government of Edward Schreyer: this party held office until 1977. Provincial CED policy in the 1970s, therefore, would be most heavily influenced by the NDP.

The NDP's CED policy can be extrapolated from the Province of Manitoba's *Guidelines for the Seventies* (1973a; 1973b), premised on four principles:

1. maximization of the general well-being of all Manitobans;
2. greater equality of the human condition for all Manitobans through a more equitable distribution of the benefits of society;
3. implementation of an effective 'stay option' which would prevent Manitobans from being coerced by economic forces to leave their province or to leave the region within the province in which they prefer to live;
4. promotion of public participation in the process of government, and more particularly, in the development decisions which would affect all Manitobans in the years ahead. (Province of Manitoba 1973a: 13)

The *Guidelines* are organized into chapters explaining the government's policies on a range of issues, such as the economy, housing, social goods and services and regional development: the four underlying principles are woven into each of these areas. With this document we begin to see a more coherent CED focus with discussion of "vehicles for community economic development"; this is, in fact, the first time that the full term "community economic development" is used by provincial policy-makers. The four policy principles contained in the *Guidelines* were better articulated than its strategies for their realization, since, unfortunately, most of its promising policies were never implemented. This may be because, as with a provincially designed CED plan of the 1970s seen above, the province was too entrenched with the business community to dare to use the non-market policy tools the *Guidelines* prescribed.

Although the *Guidelines* do not have a chapter dedicated specifically to CED, it is possible to extract enough information from the document's general content to reformulate the Schreyer government's CED approach. This information is presented under the subheadings of: the stay option; policy towards the north; and the creation of "community development vehicles."

Stay Option

The depopulation of agricultural areas had already emerged as a problem in the 1970s — particularly in the north — due to a lack of employment opportunities. In the rural south, it was argued that farmers did not receive an equitable share of income because they were not able to control the prices of their products. The stay option intended to make it easier for northern and southern farmers to remain on their land, and to allow towns servicing farmers' needs to retain jobs and a tax base. Proposed changes to agricultural policy included the channelling of aid to low-income farmers, as well as the reorganization of agricultural production through the establishment of cooperatives and land banking and by encouraging farmers to switch to more profitable methods. Higher expenditures on rural health care and other provincial services were also suggested to help farmers stay on their land. Through this new policy direction it was hoped that the encroachment of large corporate farms would be discouraged, and that migration to larger urban areas, where social and economic problems were growing, could be slowed (Province of Manitoba 1973a: 14).

Northern Policy

The *Guidelines* focus more on northern Manitoba than on urban areas and the rural south, perhaps because of the community development work that had already been done in northern Aboriginal communities in the 1960s. The *Guidelines* acknowledged the dangers of relying on economic indicators as measures of well-being, highlighting the importance of qualitative factors such as environmental conditions. The document also recognized that rapid economic development in the north had occurred alongside deteriorating socio-economic conditions for Aboriginal people, who had not been given the opportunity to participate in projects exploiting northern resources (see Kulchyski and Neckoway, Chapter 3). In the context of this growing north-south divide, the stay option aimed not only to curb the migration of northerners to the south, but also, by improving northern services, to convince southerners, who had travelled north for high-wage jobs to stay.

Among the progressive policies concerning the north was the attempt to increase local participation in political structures and processes. The *Guidelines* acknowledged that the provincial government was perceived by northerners as remote and disinterested in the issues that concerned them. As such, the document proposed changes to local government that could empower northern communities and bridge the schism dividing them from the capital. This process was already underway in Aboriginal communities through the election of local band or community councils to positions of responsibility for issues that had previously been handled by Indian Affairs.

The *Guidelines* noted the need to address the duality of the north: comparatively high living standards in urban centres stood in stark contrast to the poverty-stricken living conditions confronted in remote communities. Details of a strategy for attacking this problem are provided sparingly, although the recovery of economic rents (which arise when a company with a high degree of market power earns profits exceeding the "normal" level of profit required to stay in operation) and the diversification of the economic base received mention. These strategies would reduce the poverty of remote communities by slowing the exhaustion by multinational corporations of Manitoba's non-renewable resources, and by enhancing employment opportunities. To address the need for economic diversification, government policy offered employment with Manitoba Hydro to locals and encouraged the development of new enterprises (such as a house prefabrication plant in Churchill).

The *Guidelines* also provided a critical review of past CED policy and its consequences for the relative underdevelopment of the north. It acknowledged that training, education, intensified liaisons with industry, counselling and other support services should be offered; that the development of northern resources should have proceeded at a more "orderly" pace; that the lack of public goods, such as transportation, communication technology and electricity, was hindering progress in the north; and that any economic rent created by resource development should have paid for the provision of social programs to benefit northerners and all Manitobans.

CED Vehicles

The *Guidelines* introduced the concept of "economic development vehicles" and discussed potential methods for their implementation. The formation of cooperatives, Crown corporations operating with local participation, and municipal development corporations was encouraged. Other provincial government vehicles for CED were the Manitoba Development Corporation and the Communities Economic Development Fund (CEDF). The latter, still in existence today, was formed as a provincial Crown corporation in 1971, with a mandate to provide financial and technical assistance to small businesses and community development corporations in northern Manitoba. Also, programs promoting economic development and providing support to the fishing industry were funded by the Manitoba Agricultural Credit Corporation, which operated under the Department of Aboriginal and Northern Affairs. The *Guidelines* recommended that these vehicles for community economic development be strengthened and more closely integrated. Hence, new legislation and the provision of support services would be required (Province of Manitoba 1973a).

The Great Northern Plan

The Northern Manitoba Development Strategy represents a landmark in the evolution of CED theory in Manitoba. The Northern Plan took a leap from the more loosely articulated policy proposed in the *Guidelines* to a tightly organized and coherent strategy for implementing CED. Essentially, the Northern Plan was meant to help northern communities reach their economic and social potential by attacking the very root of underdevelopment—the negative, lasting effects of colonialism. The Northern Plan provides us with one of the first examples of CED as it is known by today's practitioners. Not only does this policy demonstrate that economic theory, when suitably adapted, can be an innovative source of CED thinking; it also shows how to make the crucial move from theory to practice. It is unfortunate that the ideas of the Plan met a fate similar to those contained in the *Guidelines*: they were never implemented.

The Northern Plan was premised on the economic theory of convergence, put forward by development economist C.Y. Thomas (1974). Thomas had studied the economies of small nations, such as those found in the Caribbean and balkanized Black Africa. His analysis revealed that these economies were dependent on exports of unprocessed resources (or staples) and that few internal value-added linkages for their processing had been formed. As a result, these countries had never realized opportunities for industrial development and were heavily dependent on imports to meet their consumption needs. Thomas classified these economies as divergent. In other words, these economies were not using their own resources to meet their needs.

Thomas's solution to the problem of divergent economies was a convergence strategy, by which he meant the formation of an economy that produces what it consumes and consumes what it produces. Thomas's strategy proposed the creation of industries producing basic goods, meaning those goods used for the manufacture of a large range of items for consumption. Basic goods were thought to be a useful investment because they establish many backward and forward linkages and demonstrate high growth elasticities (increases in per capita value added in a given sector relative to changes in per capita income).

This approach to economic development lends itself well to CED because of the attitudes they share. First, convergence theory does not assume that existing patterns of demand reflect the true needs of a community, since demand for adequate housing, nutritious food, health care, education and recreation often does not register in markets in the communities that need them the most. A convergence strategy would undertake development of local industries to meet these needs, and the backward and forward linkages created by these enterprises would provide spin-off benefits to the community (Loxley 1985: 53). Second, a convergence strategy does not just lend itself to community participation—it demands it. It assumes that enterprises are community-owned and/or controlled in order to ensure that the direction the community has chosen for production and distribution can be adhered to. As such, democratically based community structures must be in place throughout the planning and implementation cycle (Loxley 1985: 52).

A Convergence Strategy for Manitoba's North

Thomas's strategy was formulated for small economies and was premised on small-scale production and the decentralization of economic activity. The market mechanism would continue to function within these restrictions. This emphasis on small-scale production means that convergence theory lends itself well to CED. This is because small-scale production allows a more personal work environment, a more "spatially balanced economy," more community participation and control, and the ability to fashion technology to the skills and level of employment existing in the community (Loxley 1985: 59). As Loxley points out, in many Aboriginal communities even a hundred-person work force is considered large scale. This being the case, a convergence approach would require interaction and cooperation between two or more communities in order to maintain and sustain a critical minimum level of production (Loxley 1985: 61; see Loxley and Lamb, Chapter 16 of this volume, for further discussion of the critical minimum level of production).

Thomas's strategy is further premised on two political assumptions. These were that the economy be that of a sovereign nation and that the society of that nation be in transition to socialism. Clearly, neither of these was true for northern Manitoba communities at the time. In fact, the Canadian economy in general does not provide a friendly environment for a convergence strategy. This is because the convergence approach will only work where there exists enough state representation — such as the ability to tax and take public control of land and resources — to simulate aspects of a socialist economy. (Loxley 1985: 57).

It was thought that the strategy could work in Manitoba's north, in spite of the lack of compliance with these conditions, for the following reasons. First, the identification of the various possibilities for production linkages in the north would put to rest the entrenched idea that the resource base is not adequate to support the population. Second, it was believed that the participation of Aboriginal people in strategic planning would precipitate the development of political consciousness, thereby eradicating one of the causes of underdevelopment. Third, it was hoped that state representation would act as a reasonable proxy for social ownership of the means of production, since state funding, coherent government policy and community-owned economic development conveyances such as community development corporations and cooperatives are reasonable substitutes for the proposed economic system (Loxley 1985: 57). The private ownership of mining and forestry enterprises and the leaking of surplus from the community were, therefore, not challenged because the state was heavily involved in these activities, as well as in hydro and land ownership. Finally, there was a perception that the NDP government of the day was truly interested in a sea change in the nature and role of the state—a perception reinforced in the *Guidelines*—and that this would allow past patterns of development to be reversed.

Planning for the implementation of a modified convergence strategy reached very advanced stages by March 1976, when the first attempt at concrete proposals was submitted to cabinet (Loxley 1985). All major sectors were covered. For example, the scheme for the forestry sector envisaged the creation or revival of fifteen sawmills which were to provide lumber for local construction and mining. Thirty-two community harvesting operations would supply the sawmills and would replace workers from outside the area, once they had quit or retired, with previously unemployed workers from the community. Forestry resources within twenty-five miles of the communities would be destined for use by the community. A particle board plant and a small thermo-chemical process pulp and paper mill would purchase and process sixty-five percent of the wood wasted by the sawmills, thereby establishing forward linkages to the furniture and home construction industries. In turn, the creation of a home construction industry would hasten the need for factories producing windows, doors, stairs etc., creating yet more (backward) linkages to forestry and other industries. A complex plan for the implementation of agricultural production — which would have complemented the industrial planning — was also drawn up. Overall, it was estimated that the strategy would create 2,300 jobs directly, with the 20 percent minimum employment of Aboriginal workers for existing industries adding an additional 3,000 jobs for Aboriginal people by 1981 (Loxley 1981. 172).

The Northern Plan was not implemented for a variety of reasons. First, state-owned machinery in the north could not be adapted to the requirements of the strategy as easily as had been predicted. Second, cuts by the federal government in 1976–77 meant that the province would receive only half of the funds it had requested, and politically challenging projects such as the Northern Plan were relegated to the back burner as a result. Finally, the idea that the (mildly) social democratic party in power would be able to—or would even want to—change its role from facilitating capitalist accumulation to implementing a convergence strategy was, in retrospect, not realistic. Loxley (1981: 172) claims that "the planners failed to comprehend the political coherence of capitalist development, and the extent to which their proposed strategy challenged both the ideology of capitalist accumulation and the political institutions which serve it."

In spite of the defeat of the Schreyer NDP government in 1977 and the dissipation of its CED policy upon the arrival of a new Conservative administration, the NDP's tenure provided fertile ground for the development of CED theory in Manitoba. Under the auspices of this government, the loosely articulated ideas of community development of the 1960s evolved into the more cohesive CED theory that continues to take shape today. In fact, much of the work of the 1970s, including the Great Northern Plan, has greatly influenced current CED initiatives, such as the principles of Neechi Foods (see Chapter 1, this volume), which were later adopted in the Province of Manitoba's CED policy and by CED practitioners throughout Manitoba.

CONCLUSIONS

Today's CED policy-makers and practitioners can learn much about the importance of intergovernmental coordination and cooperation from Manitoba's history of incongruent policies and programs. It is impossible for policy to be holistic when fundamental differences exist in interpretations of CED across government departments and between levels of government. In the 1960s and 1970s such conceptual differences led to the ad hoc delivery of programs by various government departments, each entrenched in its own agenda: this situation produced inefficiencies and poor results. There is a strong need to better coordinate the delivery of CED programs in rural and northern Manitoba through the sharing of information on successes and failures.

Enshrining CED principles in legislation and ensuring that practitioners take their mandate from it—as in the FRED Interlake Agreement of 1967–77—will prevent goals from being overridden when governments unfriendly to CED gain power. Further, all levels of the civil service must be educated on the tenets of the CED paradigm, and this education must be consistent across policy-making levels, to avoid periods of policy drought which can set communities back for decades. Not until all political parties embrace core CED principles will communities cease to suffer from destructive policy swings premised on ideology and political goals rather than sound CED theory.

There is tremendous hope for northern communities to make sustainable improvements to their living conditions once CED philosophy becomes genuinely ingrained in policies for northern development. For these goals to be achieved, however, government must act as a facilitator, rather than an administrator, of community-based initiatives, offering programs that provide a framework within which communities can work on an autonomous basis. This is important because a participatory approach can empower communities by encouraging self-sufficiency and creating positions of responsibility for community members. Community participation is particularly important in the Aboriginal context, given the dispute over Aboriginal self-government. Until the dysfunctional, distrustful relationship that Aboriginal communities have with the federal government is resolved, CED efforts will continue to be complicated and delayed by political barriers.

Chapter Five

CED AND SOCIAL HOUSING INITIATIVES IN INNER-CITY WINNIPEG

Ian Skelton, Cheryl Selig
and Lawrence Deane

Residents of Winnipeg's inner-city neighbourhoods have reason to be concerned about the deterioration of their housing stock. Ten percent of Winnipeg dwellings are in need of major repair, which significantly exceeds the national average of 7 percent and is the highest percentage among Canada's twenty-five metropolitan areas (Carter, Polevychok and Sargent 2005). Further, Winnipeg has one of the highest proportions of older dwellings among these cities, as well as poverty levels for households and individuals that are above the national average (Carter, Polevychok and Sargent 2005).

Winnipeg's experience of neighbourhood decline is being combated through programs that aim to rehabilitate or stabilize the housing stock. A number of Winnipeg neighbourhoods have received the designation of Housing Improvement Zones, meaning that they qualify for housing program funds through the provincial "Neighbourhoods Alive!" program. During the summer of 2004, when the research for this chapter was undertaken, five neighbourhoods were receiving funding. This funding is generally administered by community development corporations (CDCs) or neighbourhood associations that have been developing their capacity to bring about social and economic change in their neighbourhoods.

Housing has special significance for the social and economic development of communities. Housing is used to motivate community members because they can see the results of their efforts (Green and Haines 2002). The replenishment of the housing stock can "stabilize the population, restore the functioning of the housing market and re-establish the market for commercial activity that [will], in turn, support new businesses to fill vacant lots and boarded-up storefronts" (Vidal 1997: 432). Further to this, housing can increase investment potential, making residents, businesses, developers, banks and insurance companies more inclined to invest in the community (Riggin, Grasso and Westcott 1992). This makes it easier for residents and businesses in the neighbourhood to obtain insurance, secure loans and finance commercial projects. Finally, "relatively high labour content in the housing sector and linkages to domestic manufacturing make housing investment an attractive candidate for governments wishing to stimulate output and employment" (Jackson 2004: 4). In these ways, housing production can stimulate a local economy and foster social cohesion. Once built, however, these positive effects may be diminished by tenure arrangements that favour homeowners.

Inner-city revitalization strategies for Winnipeg have focused on owner occupation over recent years, with the expectation of promoting neighbourhood stability. At the same time, the Manitoba government has given priority to community economic development (CED), prompting local organizations to adopt revitalization practices that are compatible with its principles. This chapter examines the social housing component of neighbourhood revitalization in Winnipeg, assessing and supporting its involvement with CED. Social housing approaches to neighbourhood revitalization are described, followed by a theoretical review of CED and CDCs. This analysis is then complemented with the results of interviews with government officials and neighbourhood workers involved in Winnipeg revitalization efforts.

GOVERNMENT POLICY
TOWARD SOCIAL HOUSING

Housing prices in many of Winnipeg's inner-city neighbourhoods have fallen to levels so low over the recent period that the private sector has ceased to invest in these areas. This has prompted communities to address their housing needs through various affordable housing initiatives, which rely on government funding. By convention, housing costs should account for no more than 30 percent of pre-tax income. Along with adequacy of structural conditions and suitability of occupancy standards, affordability is one of three tests for core housing need according to the Canada Mortgage and Housing Corporation (CMHC 1991).

Canada has seen two major, though brief, periods of federal social housing programming. Centrally planned public housing was developed from the mid-1960s to the early 1970s; decentralized cooperatives and non-profit organizations then held the balance of responsibility from the early 1970s until the 1993 federal funding freeze (Skelton 2000), which had a devastating impact on social housing provision. While there has been some federal re-investment in housing since 2002 under the Affordable Housing Initiative, this program provides one-time capital for acquisition and renovation rather than ongoing subsidies, and therefore does not target the same low-income population as the previous funding schemes. The federal government's actions over recent decades reveal its reluctance to take responsibility for core housing needs.

Winnipeg is currently experiencing a proliferation of local organizations involved in developing and maintaining social housing. These housing initiatives have been spurred by highly visible neighbourhood decline, as well as by the provincial government's adoption of CED as a policy lens (see Sheldrick and Warkentin, Chapter 17, this volume, for an in-depth discussion of the Manitoba government's CED lens) and its focus on comprehensive development in declining urban communities.

COMMUNITY ECONOMIC DEVELOPMENT

The research for this chapter relied on the set of CED principles adopted by the Manitoba government in 2001 under its CED Framework. This list is derived from *It's Up to All of Us*, developed by Winnipeg-based Aboriginal worker cooperative Neechi Foods Co-Op Ltd. (1993), and can be found in the introductory chapter (see also Neighbourhoods Alive! 2002b: 4). This CED model was chosen for a variety of reasons. First, it is specific and holistic: it addresses the social concerns that are essential for the success of neighbourhood-based economic development initiatives. Second, it incorporates community control, which has been identified as a foundational principle of CED activities: "(t)he organization or group of institutions responsible for implementing or coordinating the economic change should be involved in determining the process" (Blakely 1994: 65). Self-determination is necessary for there to be sufficient support and initiative to ensure that projects or programs are implemented after the initial enthusiasm subsides. Finally, this model focuses on the creation of intra-community economic linkages.

SOCIAL HOUSING AS CED

Housing initiatives connect well to a CED approach because they "[bring] about physical development within the neighbourhood and [create] assets among individuals, stimulating cycles of self-maintaining economic and social growth" (Rubin 1994: 410). CED approaches to social housing typically incorporate provisions for long-term affordability.

When social housing programs were originally developed in Canada, price restrictions were established under thirty-year arrangements. Currently, however, affordable housing is only restricted for approximately five to fifteen years, depending on the stipulations of grants used for housing rehabilitation. As a consequence, future renters or buyers with a need for units with lower prices than those dictated by prevailing market conditions may be edged out by those with greater spending power.

The Role for CDCs in Winnipeg Housing Initiatives

Under current arrangements, Winnipeg neighbourhoods must incorporate a legal entity in order to secure funding for housing programs. Where there is concern for physical and social conditions in addition to housing need (which is most often the case), the structure usually adopted is that of a community development corporation (CDC). These corporations are non-profit and community-based, with their mandates and visions being borne out of community processes.

FINDINGS

The following section analyzes, in the CED context defined above, current approaches to the provision of affordable housing in Winnipeg's inner-city neighbourhoods, with a separate focus on each of the following: decision-making; employment and training; disposition of housing resources; social capital; and flows of money. The goals of this exercise are to understand the challenges to more effective integration of CED principles into housing programs in Winnipeg, and to suggest possible ideas or models for improving application of the CED principles outlined above.

During the summer of 2004, semi-structured interviews were held with eighteen people involved in community development in Winnipeg, including government officials and representatives of CDCs and non-profit housing groups. The interviews consisted of roughly ten open-ended questions, and were intended to gauge the use of CED principles in the development of low-cost housing. The set of CED principles described above was sent to interview participants beforehand to allow respondents to prepare for CED-related interview questions.

Decision-Making

The organizations involved in this study engage in decision-making processes that are concerned with program types, funding and hiring. Informants highlighted that several levels of decision-making exist within neighbourhoods: decisions concerning non-profit organizations that are not community-based are made by those neighbourhood associations that have a direct impact on their work; and decision-making at the collective level occurs within a context of informal organization, which takes place at a relatively high level despite a lack of regular meetings among organizations. An unofficial consensus as to the areas and activities for which each of the various players is responsible seems to exist.

Many organizations have little jurisdiction over important aspects of their programming as a consequence of their reliance on government funding. Rental rates for social housing produced by many local organizations, including those for homes renovated with grants provided under the Residential Rehabilitation Assistance Program and placed in rent-to-own arrangements, are set by the government. Provincial regulations also stipulate the income levels at which those in need of housing qualify for occupancy, and restrict the receipt of government support for social housing to particular neighbourhoods. In these ways, the funding structures dictated by the government have great influence over program formats.

Several informants indicated that they would rather not or do not access government funding because it inhibits their freedom in decision-making:

> The benefits of being independent give us more freedom in making choices, allows us to act quickly if we want to do something one way we can go in that direction.

However, a government official voiced his perceptions that policies do in fact support local decision-making, and that this emphasis has arisen from the recognition of its importance for CED:

> Local decision-making I think is important too. And one of the things we have been doing is funding local organizations in the community to do housing for us. So that is sort of a community process, that we are not part of but are supporting the community organizations to do that.

Disagreements over the effects of funding structures on local control suggest a need for improved communication between government officials and organizations implementing housing programs. Further, organizations should recognize that these stipulations are intended to ensure that funding addresses the housing problems of lower-income earners.

All of the neighbourhoods designated by the City of Winnipeg as Major Improvement Areas, which are the top priority Housing Improvement Zones under the Neighbourhoods Alive! program, have locally active development corporations. One of these serves several neighbourhoods, working in conjunction with neighbourhood associations. Development corporations have a high level of power in decision-making, in the sense that housing groups operating in their neighbourhoods must seek their approval for new projects (housing groups must sometimes also seek the approval of neighbourhood associations). Some respondents perceived this control to be pervasive when, in fact, it is not exercised in all localities:

> All of the neighbourhood renewal corporations have actually generated some sort of sub-committee of their board or residents' committee that's actually looking at projects that are being proposed for their neighbourhood, regardless of who brings them forward and making decisions of how well they fit into their plan, whether they have merit and they make that recommendation.

In some localities, the relationships of non-profit housing developers with their overseeing CDC are merely collegial.

While respondents discussed the importance of community decision-making a fair amount, many development corporation employees do not live in the neighbourhoods where they work, and as a result residents' positions on boards of directors were sometimes devalued:

> What we do try and do is to have the community development approach which means organizing block parties or something, in which case people on the board can more easily participate in something like that.

While the above comment is indicative of the opportunity for this organization to increase decision-making at the community level, another already does include residents in much of its decision-making. This organization intends to turn their challenges into learning opportunities:

> Dealing with a construction company, a larger construction company, it [local decision making] is lost because you are constantly begging for them to come back and do the details, and they have power to some extent. Although, then the local decision-making comes in and you can pull in residents and say at what point do we take this to the insurance company or the new home royalty program. There is a learning process there.

This comment shows how a focus on local decision-making can result in a transfer of knowledge, local empowerment and social development, in addition to the achievement of economic development goals.

Employment and Training

For inner-city residents, employment opportunities with housing organizations are limited. This was exemplified by the following comment: "We employ a local person to do some custodial work, like shovelling walks and things of that kind." In other cases, locals were given work as apartment superintendents or maintenance employees. While several of the organizations employ local residents in an administrative capacity, non-inner-city residents are, generally speaking, in charge of the management of development corporations.

One exception to this trend is an employment-creation initiative which was initially conceived as a joint venture among four housing organizations and two employment-creation initiatives: it works to combine CED principles with housing redevelopment. This program has created construction employment for twenty to twenty-five residents of the inner city, hiring not only labourers but tradespersons as well. The initiative pays higher wages than the construction industry average, provides benefits, subsidizes training and apprenticeships, and allows employee ownership and participation in management. While the largest housing organization involved made use of the initiative for all of its renovation work, other partners had done so on only one or two occasions.

The Winnipeg CED company hiring the greatest number of inner-city residents takes on both commercial and residential rehabilitation projects. It combines the creation of employment for inner-city residents with training, thereby increasing their current incomes as well as their future earning potential. Other training programs combine housing rehabilitation with crime prevention by hiring gang members and youth-at-risk:

> It's a training program where we have taken a number of ex-offenders and they're all ex-gang members or actual gang members. What we've done is that we've teamed them up with a couple of carpenters. There are ten trainees and it's very much a hands-on learning experience.

Some training programs take place in the form of workshops for neighbourhood residents. Topics included were describes as follows:

> We did a couple on how to buy a house, what you need to do, what you need to look at, are you ready for that, and all those kinds of things. We did financial workshops on very basic budgeting, things that you need to keep in mind because you now own a home. We did workshops on foundations, fence building and all different things.

The last comment was made with reference to the most extensive training or information workshop, apart from employment training, that any of the organizations provided. However, the informant also said that most of the workshop participants live in rent-to-own homes: this indicates that they have not been successful in engaging the wider resident population.

Overall, employment and skill-development initiatives involve a limited number of residents, and efforts are aimed almost exclusively at knowledge transfer. A huge need remains for quality, well-paid employment, so that residents can afford the housing being provided.

Disposition of Housing Resources

The five inner-city areas of Winnipeg that were receiving housing funding from all three levels of government at the time of the interviews did so through a tri-level agreement known as the Winnipeg Housing and Homelessness Initiative, which provided a single window for access to housing restoration resources. The results for these neighbourhoods have been a visible improvement of the housing stock, an increased sense of safety, improved access to decent housing, and an increase in housing values.

The goal of owner occupation, toward which housing resources have been more often directed, is, however, neither attainable nor desirable for all residents of inner-city areas. One study participant expressed the difficulties this strategy shift has created for people with modest incomes:

> That is really hard for families that had renter mentality... They don't have the technical, banking, financial and even if they are told this jargon/babble, they are confused.

It should be noted that, in one case, an organization and a financial institution brought a test case to a mortgage regulator to set a precedent for the qualification of people on social assistance for mortgages, a practice that had not been adopted because it would provide capital for recipients. As owner occupants, many households would pay much less in principal, interest and taxes than they previously paid as renters.

The owner-occupant approach reduces the affordability of housing for low-income families in two further ways. First, it does not stipulate that housing remain price-restricted forever: "After ten years they are allowed to sell on the market for whatever price they want." In this way, long-term provision of units that are affordable for lower-income earners is sacrificed in the interest of stimulating the local housing market. Alternative approaches incorporating longer-term price restrictions, such as building homes for rental or under a land trust agreement, could be taken instead. Second, the home-ownership model may undermine affordability if the preservation of older housing becomes too important an objective: "I would say that there is a secondary objective and that would be to save older housing stock that is beginning to deteriorate." This focus on saving the housing stock is useful because it places a check on neighbourhood decline; this objective, however, must not overwhelm consideration of the financial constraints of residents. If the housing stock is being saved under the auspices of affordable housing programs, it is essential to ensure that residents can in fact afford the housing these programs produce.

The importance of providing a variety of housing tenure types to balance the assaults on affordability that result from home-ownership is recognized by some program administrators: "(S)hifting and broadening the focus to include rental could really have a huge impact and it could also help these community organizations to develop an asset base, if they continue to own these buildings in the inner city." However, non-profit organizations may find the cost of maintaining rental units, as well as their dispersion throughout a neighbourhood, to be too prohibitive to supply them. To address these concerns, funding could be directed toward long-term subsidies for rental units, and also toward the creation of multi-unit rental housing so that properties are located in closer proximity to each other.

Government funding can also be used for repair projects and the hiring of housing coordinators. The role of housing coordinator was defined by one respondent as: "the person who works with the developers and works with the residents to keep the plans updated, finds tenants for the houses that are being renovated, and generally oversees the whole thing to make sure it fits in with the neighbourhood plan." Housing resources are directed towards a variety of initiatives, from housing rehabilitation to educational workshops. Nonetheless, the predominant use of funds remains the pursuit of activities related to home-ownership, with the goals of stimulating housing demand and increasing private investment.

Flows of Financial Resources

Determining the patterns of financial flows within the social housing sector proved a complicated process which produced relatively general information. Organizations are not required by funders to keep detailed financial records of the use of their resources; hence, accounting practices vary greatly. Those organizations working through subcontracting make little analysis of the relative costs of material and labour components, because the funding they receive is simply not sufficient to manage and track projects closely enough to ensure the most efficient use of resources.[1] Therefore, in the absence of the requirement to keep records, they have little incentive to do so. This problem is compounded by the complexity of the structure under which funding is delivered: that is, since the amount of money made available for a project depends on the nature of the work being performed, poorly man aged accounting systems have resulted in discrepancies in record-keeping as to the exact amounts of funding received from each level of government. For these reasons, this study was not able to map out resource flows in detail. Nonetheless, it was able to identify basic trends and to characterize the broad social purposes to which resources are put.

For a typical project, organizations may access $10,000 per unit from the provincial government through the Neighbourhood Housing Assistance program, as well as $10,000 per unit from the City. These sources are specific programs to assist housing renewal administered through the Winnipeg Housing and Homelessness Initiative. Some then receive an additional $30,000 from the province through the Affordable Housing Initiative (AHI). One informant stated that there is up to $75,000 available per unit through AHI; however, $30,000 seems to be the maximum amount usually allotted. Therefore, from $20,000 to $50,000 in government grant money is available per unit to help bridge the gap between the costs of rehabilitation, including the initial purchase as well as renovation or construction, and the market value of the home. The remainder of the financing is provided by mortgages, which are normally equivalent to 75 percent of the eventual market value of the house. Generally, these are obtained from a credit union that has an explicit commitment to neighbourhood improvement; however, all regular safeguards are built into the mortgages to mitigate risk. The grants thus become a subsidy to the purchaser, which is then written off over a ten- to fifteen-year period, and the mortgage becomes a long-term debt.

In addition to grants for full rehabilitation, organizations may access neighbourhood-designated grants for various smaller maintenance or renovation projects. These small grants are primarily for exterior clean-up, and are provided to improve houses and increase the attractiveness of neighbourhoods.

Rehabilitation funds are used for several purposes: the acquisition of boarded-up or dilapidated homes or sometimes empty lots; the cost of materials; and labour costs, including payments for subcontractors, such as electricians and plumbers. One respondent gave an approximate breakdown of rehabilitation costs as follows:

> I would say probably a rough estimate: wages would be about 50 percent, materials about 25 percent, and subcontractors about 25 percent. It varies from job to job but it averages out to about that.

The government favours the production of units over administration, since it perceives little support among the general populace for the use of public monies toward the maintenance of program managers. Conflict over funding can also arise when renovation projects have a training component, since government departments often disagree over responsibility for their associated costs.

Resources are most often used for the reactivation of local property markets. The rationale for this funding orientation was put by a community worker as follows:

> If somebody fixes up the exterior of their house everybody in the community benefits. It raises property values and it gives the person next door the incentive to fix up their house.

Although a community's visual presentation is indeed important, interviewees did not seem to recognize the detrimental impacts on the poor of allowing the market to operate without intervention. One community worker said:

> The housing stuff, we figure we're only going to do [it] as long as public sector help is needed. Once it pays off for private sector to come in and do it we'll back off.

This is not to say that organizations are blindly faithful to free market ideology and therefore ignorant of its consequences for low-income neighbourhood residents. Rather, a number of respondents looked to the market as a means of stabilizing housing provision and reversing an accelerating spiral of neighbourhood decline. The problem with this view lies in the lack of strategies for overriding market forces if property values should rise beyond the reach of low-income residents, causing people to be displaced. One such strategy could be to focus on asset accumulation, which would be used as leverage for other resources. Properties that are retained for rental, as opposed to being sold to private owners, could be used to contribute to general program financing. Overall, findings point to a need for more explicit attention to progressive, CED-oriented housing principles in order for resources to be more firmly directed toward the material needs of low-income residents.

Social Capital

Results show that some programs attached to housing projects do in fact build social capital, but that there is significant underutilized potential for expanding social development activities as part of a CED approach.

Social capital creation may be challenged in CED processes because, as housing organizations grow, they may need to expand their operations in a way that compromises local involvement. One respondent explained:

> I think that with the infill houses that the human dignity part gets lost to some extent, because it's a larger corporation that is doing the construction and it is very difficult after the fact to get them to do the details. If there were larger amounts of money, and you could hire somebody to custom build, then you would have the personal relationship with the person doing the building, and the dignity aspect wouldn't be lost.

This respondent identifies organizations' loss of power in decision-making as a barrier to social capital creation in the transition from smaller- to larger-scale projects. Social capital creation may also be impeded if employees perceive it to hold relatively less importance than social housing work. This was observed among some interviewees who did not view the creation of social capital as inherent to social housing programs. One community worker conceptualized a separation between these objectives:

> We build houses but we like to think we look at the social and community development part as well, as an added feature.

Similarly, a government official expressed a sense of conflict between the social housing and the CED agendas:

> That is the struggle I think. CED is focused at fundamental lasting change, and it is easier to do housing without that.

Many organizations, on the other hand, did consider social development to be a key component of their housing programs. These groups experience difficulty in defining their roles in social capital creation: while they recognize that, to be most effective, the process should be initiated by residents, they are also aware of their responsibility to act as facilitators. Speaking about orientation sessions, one informant commented:

> We talk a lot about community and being good neighbours through-out the application process. We just try to promote the idea we don't feel like we should do it because we want them to do it so that it serves their purposes and not ours.

Social networks among those responsible for the delivery of housing programs must also be strong. Two organizations address this need by providing a social worker for their employees and by addressing their workplace needs in a holistic way:

> We have a social every month... When they come to work, it's not just work it's to meet their friends and buddies. We have these sweats and social evenings and because of that there is a lot of camaraderie.

By addressing the social and cultural needs of employees, organizations can create a more satisfied — and therefore productive — work force, which will contribute to a stable neighbourhood environment.

Interviewees had contrasting perceptions of the effects of owner occupation on community social capital. The attraction of owner occupancy as a strategy for neighbourhood development can be explained, at least in part, by its relative feasibility in the absence of a sufficient level of rent subsidies for the poor. Some community workers also rationalized owner occupation with regard to its empowering effects on individual buyers: "dignity [and] self-respect are impacted through home-ownership"; and "affordable home-ownership supports stability and human dignity." Others saw owner occupation as attracting desirable new residents to a community:

> [We] do home-ownership programs in order to get more home-own-ers in the neighbourhood and create stability that way.

In some cases, however, informants' rhetoric suggested a tendency to devalue renters as a group. Using a logic that is derogatory toward low-income renters, a government official explained:

> One of the biggest problems in a lot of these neighbourhoods is the high incidence of rental property in relation to homeownership... Renters are not bad people by nature [but] because they don't own the property they don't have a vested interest in maintaining that property.

Some community workers did see owner-occupation approaches as having a negative impact on social capital by creating income-based divisions between residents:

> When you start rehabbing a community it is amazing all of a sudden market values go up, neighbours start to spruce up their homes... Those are positive things but the negative is that it doesn't necessarily accommodate the low-income people because it starts to improve the neighbourhood and increase the values.

Respondents sharing this view appreciated that, along with units for home-ownership, programs must provide affordable rental accommodation to meet the needs of low-income residents. Moreover, proponents of the owner-occupant approach seem to exaggerate the differences, holding other factors constant, between the spending patterns of tenants and renters. Study participants appeared to be using tenure to signify some other form of marginalization, such as processes that operate through class, gender or race. Rather than eliminate the social cleavages that social housing programs (theoretically) exist to tackle, owner-occupation approaches actually exacerbate these divisions.

CONCLUSIONS

Interview results make it clear that, although there are many areas where the ideals of CED match with current practices in Winnipeg, there are opportunities for increasing both economic and social intra-community linkages. Economically speaking, a requirement of the leaky bucket theory of CED is that local purchases of goods and services should be increased, but organizations are only committed to such a strategy as long as prices are competitive. It is important that housing programs find a balance between the limits of funding and the need for spending efficiency with the positive indirect economic benefits of purchasing and hiring locally, since a commitment to this approach encourages long-term development and enhances the economic multiplier effect of social housing activities. In terms of social linkages within the community, limited resident participation in daily decision-making and in the management of CDCs and non-profit housing organizations must be addressed.

Specific recommendations for addressing the shortcomings in the activities of housing organizations identified throughout this chapter are the following:

- Training in CED should be provided for government officials and community workers in social housing. Greater awareness of CED is a precondition for broader, more effective adoption of its principles.

- CED should become a guiding principle in housing initiatives, so that purchasing and hiring decisions may be made on the basis of their impact on neighbourhood economies, and not simply in terms of initial costs.
- In the next round of social housing expenditures, funding should be specifically earmarked for tracking financial flows with the goal of measuring the multiplier effect.
- Social inclusion must be enhanced through provision for rental in addition to owner-occupation. Co-operative, non-profit, condominium and other tenure categories should also be supported.
- Owner-occupation strategies must be implemented in ways that do not enhance inequalities by affording privileges to owners.
- Social cohesion must be addressed through means other than owner-occupation. Social infrastructures where people can form bonds directly, rather than through the housing market, are essential.
- Social policy at all levels should be made tenure neutral.

Change is needed not only at the level of neighbourhood associations, community development corporations and housing non-profits, but also with regard to the larger policy framework that directs their activities and funding opportunities. The Manitoba government has expressed a desire to incorporate CED into projects, not just in the realm of housing, but for all programs directed at neighbourhoods or communities. There is a need for municipalities to adopt a like-minded ideology because they have the ultimate control over housing creation through the provision of land, processing of applications, and supply of funding. Thus, municipalities must take the lead in promoting and encouraging urban CED initiatives to ensure their success.

NOTE

1. The information obtained by the study team for organizations that work through subcontracting represents best estimates only.

Chapter Six

IN A VOICE
OF THEIR OWN
Urban Aboriginal
Community Development

Jim Silver, Parvin Ghorayshi,
Joan Hay and Darlene Klyne

ABORIGINAL COMMUNITY DEVELOPMENT:
PHILOSOPHICAL UNDERPINNINGS

In this chapter, urban Aboriginal people who
are respected, long-time activists in Winnipeg's inner-city community outline
an inspiring and holistic Aboriginal approach to community development
Rooted in the traditional Aboriginal values of sharing and community, this
approach to community development starts with individuals and their need
to heal from the damage caused by colonization. The process of healing, of
rebuilding or recreating oneself, is rooted in a revived sense of community
and a revitalization of Aboriginal cultures. This in turn requires the building
of Aboriginal organizations. All of this is rooted in an understanding of the
devastating collective impact of colonization, and of the need to de colonize.
The process of reclaiming one's Aboriginal identity takes place, therefore,
at individual, community, organizational and, ultimately, ideological levels.
This process is now underway; it is a process of decolonization which, if it
can continue to be rooted in Aboriginal values, will be the foundation upon
which healing and rebuilding are based. It is a uniquely urban Aboriginal
form of community development.

There are considerable differences among community development strategies, but, in general, CD involves a continuous process of capacity building.
It is about empowering people and incorporating the goal of social well-being into that of generating economic wealth. It is based on the premise that
community members need to gain control of their resources and of resource
allocation to generate economic wealth, which is to be divided among them
in an equitable way.

This chapter draws upon the experiences of Aboriginal people who have
been, and are currently, active in inner-city community development efforts
in Winnipeg's inner city. We use this case study to enter into the debate on

development in general, as well as to participate in the discussion on community development by and for Aboriginal people in particular.

THEORETICAL AND METHODOLOGICAL CONSIDERATIONS

We started this project believing that community development in Aboriginal communities works best when it is built on Aboriginal peoples' own understanding of community development. Too often, the recipients of "development" have been excluded from the shaping of that development; rather, development has been imposed upon them. Community development is much more likely to be successful than forms of development that have been imposed if it is rooted in the reality of, and is the product of, the conscious decisions of the community. Therefore, we sought to know what Aboriginal people themselves — and particularly those Aboriginal people who are active in Winnipeg's inner-city community — consider community development to be.

This chapter is based on open-ended interviews with twenty-six Aboriginal people who are or have been active in various community development initiatives in Winnipeg's inner city. These respondents were identified by means of preliminary interviews in May 2003 with four Aboriginal people (two women and two men) who are active, well-known and respected in community development circles in Winnipeg's inner city.

Interviews were conducted by two experienced Aboriginal interviewers, Joan Hay and Darlene Klyne. Open-ended interviews and a "life story" approach were used to gain access to the "informal," "inside" world of Aboriginal people: the attempt was made to create a situation in which Aboriginal people would share their "private" views with the interviewers.

The research sought to answer the following questions: What kinds of obstacles to community involvement did you personally face? How did you overcome those obstacles and become actively involved in the community? What do you consider to be appropriate forms of community development? What would you like to see happening in the future in Winnipeg's urban Aboriginal community, or what is your conception of an appropriate form of CD for the urban Aboriginal community?

CONSTRUCTION OF ABORIGINAL PEOPLE AS THE "OTHER": COLONIZATION AND ITS IMPACT

The Aboriginal people who shared their life stories with us use the notion of colonialism, or colonization, to explain what happened to them and their families, their identities, their spiritualities, their knowledge and their communities. They believe that various state apparatuses were systematically used to degrade and erode their way of being in the name of "civilizing" them. Residential schools, the education system, the police and legal systems and Child and Family Services stand out as institutions that played a central role in constructing them as the "other."

Residential schools were mentioned by Aboriginal peoples as constituting their most painful encounter with colonialism. Respondents described experiences that demonstrated that residential schooling was based on the idea that anything having to do with Aboriginal people — be it knowledge, education, family, community, spirituality, language or their very way of being — had to be transformed. Rather than prepare them for the outside world, residential schools denigrated their cultures, broke their family ties and, worst of all, instilled in them a sense of shame. In the words of one interviewee, Joseph (all names are pseudonyms), it: "produced individuals with new personalities"; you "never know who you are, there was a lost identity, and I speak really about myself. I didn't know who I was… consequently I was in no man's land when I came out of residential school."

Lack of Urban Life Skills

Whether they belonged to the older or the younger generation, and whether they had attended a residential or a non-residential school, respondents observed that they were not given the proper skills to live in an urban setting. Those who came out of residential schools were sent to a world that was not theirs and that was hostile toward them. Joseph states that residential school survivors: "came out and were set adrift, not really belonging in a White world, where it was full of tensions, full of competition, discrimination."

A lack of urban, industrial life skills continues to be a problem for Aboriginal people, and forms a material basis for urban Aboriginal deprivation. In this regard, Charles makes an insightful and powerful observation:

> the economy's always sort of playing around with who we are and what we're about… all issues, I think, are related to the economic relations we have in this society. But the economy has a way of turning that around and making the personal issues of oppression and… dominance, to be our own.

In other words, the poverty and poverty-related living conditions experienced by many urban Aboriginal people are the result of a ruthless economic environment, yet appear to have been caused by their personal faults and failings.

There have been few programs to help urban Aboriginal people make the transition from rural to urban life. In a recent study (Hanselman 2003: 5), the Canada West Foundation observed that "urban Aboriginal transition programs receive less than five cents for every dollar spent on immigrant settlement and transition." Without help, making the adjustment to urban industrial life with little education or other preparation has been tough for Aboriginal people: they had difficulty getting jobs, and, as a result, had to go on social assistance. A downward spiral began, whereby children grew up in families on social assistance and learned to take this money for granted — not unlike how Aboriginal children before them had been taught to take hard work for granted.

Destruction of Family Ties

The Canadian government's deliberate strategy toward Aboriginal people in the late nineteenth and most of the twentieth century was one of assimilation: their approach was to remove Aboriginal people from their traditional ways of life and absorb them into the Eurocentric culture of the Canadian mainstream. The residential schools played a central and destructive role, by deliberately attempting to separate Aboriginal children from their families in order to prevent them from learning Aboriginal ways of life. The strategy was an effort "to kill the Indian in the child" (Milloy 1999: 42). Many Aboriginal families were literally torn apart by Canadian colonial policy. Joseph states his views on how institutionalization affected Aboriginal families: "our family relations had to be repaired, they were… severed and almost unreparable… the bonds that tie parents and children were severed at the roots and there was no hugging, no loving, no closeness, no warmth."

Destruction of Culture

For assimilation to succeed, Aboriginal cultures had to be destroyed. This strategy of state-sanctioned violence against an entire people was justified by the false belief that Aboriginal cultures were inferior to European culture. Thus the attempt to destroy Aboriginal cultures was seen by the dominant culture to be a "civilizing" mission. Aboriginal people have resisted this process, and have struggled tenaciously to cling to their ways of life, but the damage to individuals and families of this state-sanctioned campaign of cultural destruction has been massive. Joseph, who attended the residential school north of Lloydminster for fifteen years, from ages three to eighteen, states:

> We were more or less orphans and we got punished if there was anything that we did that resembled Native spiritual culture or traditional practices. All these things were evil and had to be completely eradicated. An imposition of values on another culture, that's what it was… the havoc that Native people experienced in their early adult life… was very severe… two-thirds of my life have been severely affected, negatively affected, as a result of being a survivor of this system.

Destruction of Identity and Self-Esteem

The belief that Aboriginal cultures are inferior to those of mainstream Canadian society was constantly expressed and acted upon by non-Aboriginal people. Many Aboriginal people internalized not a positive, but a harshly negative sense of self, which has been constantly reinforced by the racism and segregation and social exclusion which make up a large part of urban Aboriginal life. The weight of the pain they carry is great, since a positive sense of self is necessary in order to cope with the world.

For some, the internalization of colonialism manifests itself in a lack of self-esteem and self-confidence. Ingrid describes her teenage years as feeling "very ashamed of who I was. I couldn't look anybody in the eye, you know. I walked half my life with my head down, very ashamed of who I was." A man in his forties sees how a combination of factors has affected Aboriginal people's self-perceptions: "our confidence has been whittled by the residential school experience, the reserve experience, the racism, the bureaucracy, they [Aboriginal people] don't have that confidence and that pride about who they are." These examples are typical of the difficulties that these exceptionally talented inner-city community leaders have experienced at different stages of their lives.

Rather than succumb to the weight of these challenges, they have confronted them and made remarkable changes in their own lives and in the lives of their communities.

DECONSTRUCTION
AND RE-CONSTRUCTION:
RECLAIMING THEIR LIVES

Each interviewee had her/his own particular story of overcoming barriers and achieving self-empowerment, but three important "paths" seemed to emerge: the importance of adult education for Aboriginal people; the importance of involvement in Aboriginal organizations run on the basis of Aboriginal cultures; finally, the role of parenting as a source of empowerment, particularly for women. A combination of these "paths" has helped Aboriginal people to reclaim their lives and build on their personal strengths.

Adult Education and Empowerment

Education has empowered Aboriginal people, transforming both them and, to a lesser extent, the education system. Certain forms of adult education — especially those with an Aboriginal focus — and, in many cases, attendance at university have played important roles in enabling Aboriginal people to place their problems and socioeconomic circumstances in the broader historical context of colonization. As Aboriginal people have begun to attend university in growing numbers, their consciousness has been raised by the experience, enabling many of the individuals we interviewed to see the bigger picture. Education has allowed many Aboriginal people to begin to decolonize: they have healed personally and developed the consciousness of self and of their surroundings that allows for effective involvement in community development.

The role of education, and particularly of post-secondary and adult education, in this process of personal transformation has often been dramatic. For example, Jack had come to Winnipeg in the mid-1980s for health reasons: it was there that he encountered the Métis Economic Development Program, run by the Manitoba Métis Federation. He observes: "it was a real positive experience for me. Really opened a lot of doors for me." The life-changing opportunities he would eventually take up included a bachelor's and a master's degree in social work and a senior position at one of Winnipeg's leading inner-city Aboriginal organizations.

There are three important considerations with respect to adult education as a source of empowerment for Aboriginal people. First is the sheer significance of pursuing adult education for Aboriginal people, since a large proportion, when compared to non-Aboriginal people, do not complete high school, and have often had very negative high school experiences. A second consideration is that education organizations need be run on the basis of Aboriginal cultures, which sets the stage for effective learning by allowing learners to regain their Aboriginal identities through education. Ethel said, in describing her experience in an Aboriginal adult education program funded by the Core Area Initiative of the 1980s: "it was at that point when I was thirty that I first started identifying with who I was as an Aboriginal person... so returning to the culture was huge... it was just, finally, a place of belonging." Doris, who experienced many difficulties as a teenager in Winnipeg, finally attended the Aboriginal high school, Children of the Earth: "That's where I started to figure out who I was and who my people were... that whole healing journey."

The third area of importance is that of public investment in the inner city. Ethel attended an adult education program created by the publicly funded Core Area Initiative, and subsequently played a lead role in developing a unique Aboriginal program at one of Canada's most innovative adult education institutions, in Winnipeg's North End. This program has had great success, since it has educated approximately a thousand Aboriginal students over the past fourteen years, and has, since its inception, been funded, at least in part, by tri-level urban development agreements. Therefore, the initial investment in the adult education program that Ethel attended has generated a remarkable rate of return, when one considers the benefits eventually enjoyed by a thousand families: this is particularly so when one considers that almost all graduates of her program find jobs (Silver 2006b: Chapter 3).

Aboriginal Organizations and Empowerment

For some of our respondents it was informal, rather than formal, education, gained from involvement in organizations created by and for Aboriginal people, that played a key role in the deconstruction of colonialism and re-construction of self, based on a renewed pride in their Aboriginal identity. Jean remembers attending an Indian-Métis conference with her uncle in the early 1950s, shortly after the birth of her third child. She was a woman who, after fifteen years in the residential school system, hardly ever spoke to anyone. She states: "My husband always said I was very shy and quiet, and I hardly said anything for the first three years we were married." But that was to change with her introduction to collective meetings of Aboriginal people dealing with their issues:

> I went with my uncle because he wasn't sure where he was going... and I got really interested, and you know the best part about that is I felt really good because here were my people. I'm talking to people that I know. I can talk to people that speak the same language, you know, and then I found out what they were going to be doing and I said, "I'd sure like to help." And that's how I got to be involved in the organizing of the first Friendship Centre in Winnipeg... I helped organize the whole Friendship Centre, get it started, get it off the ground, encouraged other Aboriginal people.

The opportunity to become involved in collective Aboriginal endeavours is an important building block in the processes of personal and community transformation. John states that there are now over seventy Aboriginal organizations in Winnipeg, built because urban Aboriginal people were committed to creating a means for reconstructing their lives. Some of these were mentioned, over and over again, as having had a tremendously positive impact on the lives of urban Aboriginal people.

Parenting and Empowerment

Many women who participated in this study became involved around issues that directly affected and mattered to them; of particular importance, not surprisingly, were their children. In many cases mothers' transformations began when children first attended school, at age five or six. They would be asked to volunteer in the lunch program or some other school program; would demonstrate — often without their previously having realized it — that they were talented; and would soon be offered further opportunities. This led them to find their real abilities, long buried beneath internalized layers of racism, sexism and lack of self-confidence — the product of colonization. When presented with opportunities to become involved in the community, and with the support of those who believed in them, those latent abilities came to the surface and remarkable transformations occurred. Verna describes her experiences of this kind, which have been frequent. She says to people in the community:

> "Why don't you get involved?" "Oh, no, not me," you know, they don't have that confidence, they don't have that self-esteem, but helping them get on board or learn or do things you can see them blossom, and to me that's community development at its heart.

COMMUNITY DEVELOPMENT BY
AND FOR ABORIGINAL PEOPLE

Aboriginal community development starts with decolonization; honours Aboriginal traditions, values and cultures; recognizes and builds on people's skills and empowers them; rebuilds a sense of community among Aboriginal people; goes beyond economic needs; and generates organizations and mechanisms for democratic participation. In these ways, Aboriginal community development is a holistic process that directly challenges western models of development.

Decolonization

Community development is a site where people learn the true value of their work and how the dominant system excludes them (Freire 1973; Morgan 1996). Teaching the history of the oppression of particular groups, so that community members can understand, articulate and recognize the forces that oppressed them, is essential (Okazawa-Rey and Wong 1997). This is decolonization; it raises political consciousness (Shor and Freire 1987; Freire 1973). For the participants in this study, Aboriginal community development requires, as a starting point, an understanding that colonization has had a devastating impact on the lives of Aboriginal people, and that much that *appears* to be the product of personal failings, is in fact the consequence of colonization.

By addressing the colonizing agenda and deconstructing the colonial discourse, Aboriginal people can reclaim their voices, and their post-colonial identities can emerge. Healing is an outcome of this process, since it requires an understanding of the historical process of colonization as well as an immersion in Aboriginal cultures. It is a necessary step so that Aboriginal people can contribute to the collective and participatory process of community development. Joseph advocates that "we have to get to know ourselves," because the process of colonization took away his sense of identity. Ethel adds that Aboriginal people cannot become involved in community development "unless they've done their own work first. Because why would they be concerned about community if they're just surviving?" Ultimately, the process of healing involves the promotion of Aboriginal cultures so that people can regain a positive sense of identity. Charles had observed this process at a recent conference where many Aboriginal people talked about their personal lives. "One of the things that… every one of them said in different ways is that it was our community and being with Aboriginal people and being included and respected and valued that made the difference in their lives." What was observed here, in fact, is community development in its truest sense.

Bringing Back a Sense of Community

Community development involves building social relationships (Shragge 2002; Silver 2006b: Chapter 2). This empowers individuals, strengthens social ties and can become the foundation for collective action. Aboriginal people need, Shirley believes, places and spaces where they can connect and talk: "a long time ago in our communities there were always… places in the community… where you could sit and talk and listen. So we need to somehow recreate that in a way that fits the urban environment." The opportunity to connect generates Aboriginal involvement in the community. Darlene says:

> I think where people miss the mark on involving the Aboriginal community is really creating those opportunities just to get together and talk. I've seen that on a local level, just with our community care centres — people coming to our centres, sitting around, having a coffee, getting to know each other and saying, "hey, wouldn't it be nice if we put together a summer program for kids," and [her organization] can do that, can support that.

Community development starts where people are; it values the aspirations of local residents for their lives and communities; and it makes a conscious attempt to identify and incorporate local knowledge in community development programs. By adopting such an approach, community development has the potential to foster cultural preservation and to weaken the exploitative power of outside forces (Voyageur and Calliou 2003; O'Donnell and Karanja 2000).

Residents of Winnipeg's inner city have deep grievances about non-Aboriginal people delivering services to and for Aboriginal people, since they earn a good income from jobs built on the impoverishment of many Aboriginal people. Central to the emergent Aboriginal form of community development is the belief that this approach is exploitative and ineffective, and must be replaced by a strategy wherein Aboriginal organizations run by and for Aboriginal people take on the delivery of community development services in a fashion consistent with Aboriginal values.

Aboriginal Community Development Is Not Just about Economics

Aboriginal community development is a holistic process. It focuses on the individual, the family, the community, organizations and cultures. It addresses the spiritual and emotional aspects of people's lives, rather than economic development alone. As explained by Walter:

> For me, for Aboriginal people to truly succeed, and for the communities to get better… you need sort of a holistic approach to community development… community economic development is just a small part of it… When I talk about holistic we are not just talking about education, training, or employment, we are talking about supporting the individual.

While economic issues need to be dealt with, they have to be put in the context of the Aboriginal reality, and of the traditional Aboriginal values of community and sharing. As noted by Doug: "I have a concern that all too often community development moves to community economic development too fast." Another person adds: "But those economic issues also need to be framed inside of our own understanding of who we are and about our values and our sense of community and our sense of sharing and our sense of cooperation." Otherwise, "the values get removed from the initiative, right, and they simply then begin to act as corporations that make profit and they lose this notion of the sharing that needs to happen inside of any economic activity in the community." Most interviewees expressed the belief that the Aboriginal values of sharing and community must form the basis of Aboriginal community development. However, developing and maintaining a specifically Aboriginal community development grounded in these Aboriginal values is a challenge, because when one tries to maintain those values in an organizational form, there is a danger that they will "get caught up or get sucked into that whole, larger sort of capitalist economic development notion." The use of traditional Aboriginal values of community and sharing as a fundamental part of Aboriginal community development has nonetheless grown dramatically in recent decades, thanks to decades of work by Aboriginal people in Winnipeg's inner city.

Many of the Aboriginal leaders in this emergent form of community development are what Italian political philosopher Antonio Gramsci described as "organic intellectuals" (Gramsci 1978). Deeply immersed in the often harsh urban Aboriginal experience, they are able to theorize about, and to articulate in an analytical fashion, this sophisticated and inspiring form of community development. Their intellectual leadership in Winnipeg's inner city has been a central aspect of the successful development of this uniquely Aboriginal form of community development.

CONCLUSIONS

The authentic voices of Aboriginal community leaders in Winnipeg's inner city tell a story that is exciting and inspiring. They reveal that a process of decolonization is underway and is manifesting itself in a distinctive, Aboriginal form of urban community development rooted in the traditional Aboriginal values of community and sharing. The progression of this development process, however, requires that Aboriginal people can continue to heal. Their healing is not just an individual process, since it must occur in a community that is strong and healthy. Such a community must have an understanding and appreciation of Aboriginal cultures and knowledge, the achievement of which requires support from empowering Aboriginal organizations. All of this depends on the development and promotion of an ideology rooted in an understanding of the historical effects of colonization and the necessity for decolonization, developed and articulated by Aboriginal organic intellectuals. Once these links are in place, meaningful Aboriginal community development can occur, offering enormous promise not only for Aboriginal people, but for all.

NOTE

This chapter is an abridged version of Chapter 5 of Jim Silver, *In Their Own Voices: Building Urban Aboriginal Communities* (Halifax: Fernwood Publishing, 2006). A video based on this chapter, made by award-winning Aboriginal film-maker Coleen Rajotte and titled *In Their Own Voices: Urban Aboriginal Community Development* is available from the Canadian Centre for Policy Alternatives–Manitoba.

Chapter Seven

WOMEN AND COMMUNITY ECONOMIC DEVELOPMENT

Improving the Lives and Livelihoods of Women through Socially Transformative Practice

Sarah Amyot

Community economic development (CED) is a form of community development (CD) which is increasingly used with social groups that have been economically marginalized based on race, class, ethnicity, ability or, as this chapter shall attempt to show, gender. CED seeks to improve the lives of marginalized populations by utilizing the strengths and assets of a community to address the priorities it sets.

Despite the growing recognition that the application of CED principles with women is a viable CD strategy, relatively little research has been done on the theory and practical application of this approach. There are even fewer examples in the literature of successful models or best practices for the application of CED with women. Rather than view the relative absence of successful models or case studies as a sign of the failure of CED, this chapter sees it as a tool for addressing the economic and social marginalization of women, as well as its root causes.

This chapter seeks to add to the body of knowledge on CED with women by providing a critical examination of the potential of CED — as understood in the literature and practised by selected CD organizations in Winnipeg — to be a socially transformative practice for women. By analyzing the relations between the theory of CED and work performed in its name, this research reveals opportunities for improving the practical application of its principles with women. This chapter aims to meet its goal of improving the practice of CED with women through a clear presentation of the voices of women involved in CD and provision of ample space for their stories, priorities and concerns.

METHOD

Respondent Selection and Interview Methods

In total, eleven women representing ten organizations said to be engaged in CED work in Manitoba were interviewed: the comments of seven respondents are included in this chapter. During the interviews the women were asked to answer three sets of questions: what is the work of your organization and how was the need for it established; what have been the successes of the organization, and what are some of the barriers that you have overcome in order to achieve them; and do you think of your work as CED, and what does this term mean to you?

The interviews were conducted in an open-ended manner. Question sets were used primarily as checklists to make sure that all of the intended points had been addressed.

CED WITH WOMEN IN THE LITERATURE AND IN PRACTICE IN WINNIPEG

This section examines the ongoing discussion of CED with women, offering some insight into how the principal areas explored in the literature relate to the experiences of women working in CED in Winnipeg.

The Meaning of "CED"

The literature on CED is vast and includes a number of similar definitions of the term. The way in which this chapter understands the term is articulated well by Kuyek (1990: 118), who sees CED as a "departure" from the current economic system: it focuses on creating "self-reliant communities that are not dependent on outside investment."

Despite the diversity of activities undertaken by each of the organizations included in this study, most of the women interviewed understand the focus of their work as being on the creation of income-generating opportunities and economic development. For some, CED is a straightforward approach to community development that is about "providing community women with employment" or "providing them with skills." Others defined the concept as "economic development for women in the community"; "the money earned in the community stays in the community to help the community grow"; "helping the community develop some semblance of earning money"; and "being aware of possibilities the people in the community could take advantage of to earn an income." Other respondents, however, had a less tightly focused understanding of their work. For example, one respondent stated that "CED is the gestalt... what happens when you bring social development and economic development together, it's synergy, the sum of which is greater than the parts of those two things." Others rejected the term altogether, stating instead that their work was about "a community trying to rebuild."

Funding as a Limiting Factor to CED

One of the threads linking the women's perceptions of the relationship between the concept of CED and their work pertains to the factors that present a barrier to its achievement. All of the women interviewed explained that the character and direction of their work has been heavily influenced by the availability of funding. The problems associated with short-term project funding are well documented in the literature on the non-profit sector and are echoed by many of the women interviewed here (Gracey 1999; Shragge 1993). First, funding stipulations do not always coincide with the needs of a particular community. The ability of organizations to make their work meet the philosophies upon which they are built is severely constrained by the influence of funders and governments, as they are encouraged to take on more and more services that were once provided by government. According to one respondent: "It's hard to not become the institution." This problem is compounded in situations where funding is "cobbled" together from a variety of sources with different parameters and expectations. According to one respondent:

> the difficulty, I think, has always been the funding... each one [funding opportunity] had specific criteria around it that makes it difficult, and I think that there's not one group that you would talk to in this area that has not voiced the same concern, that funding is always an issue.

A related problem is that the ability of women's organizations to conduct their work in a way that directly meets the needs of the communities in which they operate is limited by the very process of obtaining funding. Despite variation in the particular nature of the problem, the lack of core funding remains the single most cited barrier to success among the women interviewed. According to one respondent, despite an organization's best efforts to listen to and actively address the needs of the community, no matter "how much people say that they listen to the people, there must be a certain level of money." This respondent also expressed the need to challenge the control that the struggle for funding may take over their work. For many organizations the struggle is to determine "where the funds are, and how you can adapt the funds that are out there [to your particular needs]." Also, attitudes are often affected when an organization has a history of unstable funding, which may contribute to a lack of trust in CED projects on the part of community residents. This was described by one respondent as a "once burnt, twice shy" syndrome.

In their study of women's CED initiatives in B.C., Alderson and Conn (1988) found that all of the projects had accessed funding at some point, and that most had remained dependent on some form of funding. Gittell,

Bustamante and Steffy (2000) support these findings in their study of women working in American community development organizations. In fact, according to Eric Shragge (1993) almost all CED initiatives are reliant on outside funding. At the same time governments' focus on deficit reduction has reduced the level of resources available to the non-profit and civil society sector (Zimmerman and Dart 1998).

The effects of these shifts were noted by respondents, one of whom observed that: "the government wants simply for us to do the things that they would do, only for fifty percent of the cost, and they don't want us to pay benefits to our workers." For some, the pressure to adopt more business-like elements in their organization has resulted in the development of programs that have been unsustainable and have even had a detrimental impact on the ability of the organization to function. The founder of the North End Women's Centre has explained that because funders were concerned with devising strategies to ensure the organization's sustainability, the Centre entered into a business venture that would eventually cause great difficulties and lead it to reconsider the types of ventures to be undertaken in the future (Gracey 1999: 8). Some of the women interviewed, however, advocate such policy changes as part of the role of CED in improving the lives of women. According to one: "Changes in policy are something that has to happen eventually and they've already been defined by the woman as a need, but you know, how do you get them in place?"

Feminist Perspectives on CED

According to Conn (n.d.: 2) there are four aspects that make up a "feminist perspective on CED: women's role in the economy, social accounting, the participation of women in the economic planning process and the potential for long term change." These aspects are discussed in turn below.

Women's Role in the Economy

Economic activity, as measured by conventional means, has generally been thought of as the exchange of goods and services for money. This definition of the economy marginalizes women, obscuring the fact that women are active in the economy not only as paid workers, but also as contributors to the invisible or informal economy. Women have traditionally been primarily responsible for the work of "domestic production," or caregiving, as well as for the organization and support of most community work, such as voluntary work, carpooling and ensuring the health and support of other members of the community (Conn n.d.).

Some feminist economists, such as Nelson (2000) and Rankin (2002), have suggested the need for a conceptual shift from an understanding of economics as involving market transactions to one that assigns an economic value to each of the acts that helps to provide for life for oneself and others.

Despite ongoing debate about how best to recognize the work of women, or even how to define the "economy," the recognition of the importance of women's unpaid and unrecognized labour forms the basis of most feminist CED initiatives. However, this is an element of CED that continues often to be overlooked in favour of larger-scale CED projects "that involve a transfer of power more than a shift in values" (Conn n.d.: 3).

Social Accounting

Social accounting considers all the benefits and consequences of economic decisions, including social, political and environmental factors. According to some, what has been thought of as women's role as caregivers has made them "quality of life experts" (Conn n.d.). It is argued that because women are most often the ones who are left to deal with the consequences of economic downturns and the side effects of economic strategies that have depleted resources, destroyed the environment or resulted in changing societal structures, they are best positioned to envision a new form of economics that includes a "multiple bottom line."

This concept refers to the practice of social accounting for economic decision-making, such that factors like social, environmental and political costs and benefits are considered rather than financial outcomes alone. Many feminist economists have long argued for a new vision of economics that takes the social costs and benefits of economic decisions into consideration. It is argued by this school of thought that, in addition to broadening the understanding of the field to include a real accounting of the costs and benefits of economic decisions, such a move would force the recognition that the "rational economic man" is not the sole existing economic being.

Women's Participation in Economic Development Planning

Feminist CED seeks to improve the participation of women in economic planning processes. Although numbers are relevant, this cannot be measured solely by numerical tabulation of the number of women who participate. A feminist model of CED seeks to examine the gender power dynamics that have traditionally limited women's participation in economic development planning. Attention to the meaningful participation of women in the economic development process is demonstrated in a number of ways, ranging from micro level strategies aimed at improving women's participation in meetings, to broader initiatives such as economic literacy campaigns that attempt to provide women with the tools to participate in the planning process. The commitment to meaningful participation means that feminist CED may rely on ways of organizing, such as collectives, which require patience and a commitment to the uneven development of projects. However, it should be noted that the focus on participation at the expense of broader change can limit the ability of CED to be a truly socially transformative practice.

Potential for Real Change

Conn (n.d.) notes that feminist CED has the potential to create real change in the lives of many people. For CED to meet its potential to create real change, we must reflect on the elements of this change and design CED strategies that can accommodate them. That is, to be a socially transformative practice, CED must take into account the systemic reasons for the marginalization of certain populations, and must avoid the tendency to undertake "micro development" that recreates the neo-liberal economic paradigm.

Feminist CED as a Socially Transformative Practice

The literature on CED focuses primarily on women's participation rather than on gender as the underlying cause of the economic marginalization of women. That is, discourses tend to deal with women as an isolated group, rather than explore the dynamics of gender and economics. In CED literature and in the practical application of its principles, the focus is primarily on improving women's access to resources and economic participation. Although these may improve the lives and livelihoods of women on an individual basis, they do not change in a meaningful way the marginalized position of women as a social group. For CED to be socially transformative, it must simultaneously address the marginalization of women and the underlying reasons for the marginalization of large groups of people, including, but not limited to, women.

Thus, the focus must simultaneously be on two interlocking dynamics that have resulted in women's marginalized status in society: gender and economics. This is because participation in a flawed system simply displaces the locus of marginalization to new ("other") groups in society. In fact, the marginalization of large groups of people is an inherent feature of the current economic system. For example, documented CED initiatives with women have tended to focus on ways of improving women's economic participation by providing child care subsidies and the like to women, or they have created work for women in fields such as catering and child care that are traditionally viewed as women's work and have, therefore, been socially and economically devalued. In viewing the issue of women's improvement in this way — as a matter of participation that can be measured numerically — CED initiatives have attempted to address one aspect of gender relations that has marginalized women (i.e., women's limited participation), but, in the process, have failed to challenge the system that requires the continuation of this marginalization in order to maintain itself.

The discussion of the practice of CED found in the literature represents only a limited view of feminism in which individual empowerment and access to resources are given precedence over change at the societal or community levels. Callahan (1997: 185) notes that feminist community organizing has remained on the periphery of community development because it raises questions about "the contradictory nature of communities and the gendered nature of community work."

For community economic development to be feminist, it must be informed by an understanding of the complexities of both gender and locality. It must be rooted in an understanding of its work as part of an attempt to create broad changes to the worldviews that cause the marginalization of social groups.

In practice, however, the women interviewed for this project seem to be constrained in their ability to implement feminist CED in their work. One of the organizations interviewed, for example, recognized that a catering program it runs will most likely never provide a sustainable income to the women involved. Nonetheless, the woman interviewed consistently expressed her desire to utilize this program to challenge the economic systems that ghettoize certain groups of people; for example, she saved a small amount of excess funds from the program each year and is using them to support some of the organisation's other programs that she considered to be more "challenging." The same organization runs other programs with youth that encourage them to explore sexism, racism and other factors that contribute to the devaluation of women's work through art and photography. For this respondent, programming that teaches critical thinking skills and challenges ideas about women's work was just as much a part of her contribution to CED as were other programs that have more traditionally been associated with it.

Funding for programs that challenge the dynamics of gender and economic marginalization was considered by the respondents to be more difficult to obtain than funding for programs that simply recreate them, such as job training or other skills-building initiatives. Much of the pressure to recreate pink ghetto jobs with low wages can be attributed to strict funding parameters that often allow for organizations only to pay the participants extremely low wages.

Overall, women's CED as currently practised in Winnipeg has the capacity to improve the lives and livelihoods of women, but only in some areas of their lives, and only in the interim. In this regard, local CED efforts with women can be seen as economic "coping" strategies, rather than socially transformative practices that can improve the lives of women and other marginalized groups over a sustained period of time.

CONFLICT AND CONSENSUS
APPROACHES TO CED

CED is rooted in two distinct conceptions of community work — the grassroots tradition of community organizing and, alternatively, an understanding of community work and community development as put forth by the state and by funders. The former has traditionally taken the form of advocacy and activist-based groups; the latter can be found in the proliferation of state-funded non-profit organizations and community-based organizations (Stoecker 2001). While none of the work of the women interviewed for this project fits neatly into one category or the other, a discussion of the two approaches will provide a necessary tool for the evaluation of the effectiveness of CED as a strategy for social transformation.

The Community Organizing vs. the Community Development Approach

As currently practised in Canada, CED combines aspects of both community organizing and community development. According to Stoecker (2001), these two perspectives on community work are anchored in two fundamentally different conceptions of how society functions. First, community organizing is based on an understanding of society as inherently conflict-based and as having a zero sum understanding of power. In the community organizing model, the strength of marginalized communities lies in their ability to work collectively to create change.

The community development model, on the other hand, has been characterized by the creation of organizations charged with acting as a broker for marginalized communities by providing them with access to government funds and support. Community development is premised on the belief that, if people are provided with adequate training and support, they will be able to improve their lot in life: this view has come to be identified with a consensus model of society because it works within, and does not challenge, existing social structures. Evidence of this model is found in numerous CED initiatives focusing on training, neighbourhood safety initiatives, housing and the like (Stoecker 2001).

Women, in particular, are prime targets for community development approaches. Women's CED often focuses on improving women's self-conceptions, such as self-esteem and relationship building, leadership training and the like, or, alternatively, on improving women's access to resources. This theory obscures, however, the fact that marginalized groups need access to power, rather than the opportunity to make life changes that serve to perpetuate existing power structures. The model defines the root causes of marginalization as lack of self-esteem, employment or housing without analyzing the reasons why these problems exist in the first place. This model focuses on improving the skills set or self-esteem of individuals or groups of individuals within the existing economic order rather than on changing the systems in which the lack of opportunities for certain groups exist. For CED to be an effective force for the improvement of the lives of marginalized populations, it must contain elements of both the community organizing and community development approaches.

"Women-Centred Organizing" in Winnipeg

According to Stall and Stoecker (1997; see also Stoecker 2001), "women-centred organizing" combines aspects of each of these approaches. Elements of this hybrid model are evidenced in organizations such as the North Point Douglas Women's Centre, which has been able to build successfully on a history of community organizing in order to create an institution that can support the needs of women. Many of the women currently involved in the Centre were previously united against the presence in the neighbourhood of a business accused of exploiting the poverty of the community's residents:

> Brother's Grocery store had been known to have a problematic impact on our community and had been picketed on several occasions for allegedly selling solvents. So replacing this store with a Women's Centre would not only rid the community of this problem, it would also send a very positive message to the community. (speech given at Point Douglas Women's Centre Fall AGM, 2003)

This history of community organizing provided the impetus for the women of the Point Douglas neighbourhood to come together to take advantage of funding made available to the community.

The respondents interviewed for this project also demonstrate some of the ways in which women involved in CED are combining the work of community organizing and community building. One respondent notes that "you could attribute all this [current problems in the community] systemically to some pretty clear times in history, especially in the Aboriginal history… so, it just starts with one community trying to rebuild." This respondent combines the analysis of systemic factors contributing to marginalization with a community (re)building perspective. Another respondent noted that if she could, "I would get rid of all this [the current economic system] and then we could go back to some type of thing where we really did work for the community." However, she also noted that her desire to challenge the current system is not reflected in CED as it is currently practised. Many of the other women interviewed also demonstrated the ways in which their work combines elements of both conflict and consensus models of society, thereby demonstrating the limitations of each of these models.

Limitations to CED as a Socially Transformative Practice for Women

The shifting role of government in the provision of social welfare and the resulting growth and professionalization of NGOs has affected the ability of women's organizations to continue the work of community organizing. For feminist organizations doing advocacy and organizing work, the shift has been felt as they are required to take on more elements of community development work (Stoecker 2001). As community organizations are encouraged to take on more of the work of community development, their ability to continue the work of community organizing, a practice that addresses the issues of power that maintain the marginalized position of certain communities, is constrained. When asked whether the CED currently being promoted by government agencies represented a challenge to the current economic system, one respondent stated: "they don't challenge capitalism, they don't challenge any of that... it's about how do we drive the economy so that everybody's off welfare."

Some of those interviewed also struggle with the ability of CED to create meaningful change in a society where power often lies outside of marginalized communities. Respondents discussed the struggle to define a place for CED in the "new economy," which is characterized, among other things, by the concentration of power in the hands of an increasingly small number of transnational corporations. One respondent said: "How can you compete with Wal-Marts? Big box stores?... You know it would have been better, long time ago when we had the community stores, people knew people in the community."

The potential for CED to effect social transformation is constrained by its hesitancy to challenge dominant ways of thinking about the creation and maintenance of marginalized communities. This hesitancy is a result of the adoption of a theoretical framework that promotes the belief among practitioners that one need only provide the opportunity for marginalized groups to succeed — an approach that overlooks the dynamics of power that affect a group's social position.

Another of the reasons for the pervasiveness of the community development approach, rather than that of community organizing, has been its popularity among governments and other funders. It has been particularly detrimental for women because in order for women-focused CED to be effective, it must challenge patriarchal social relationships that have been used to oppress and marginalize women. Nonetheless, the women interviewed for this project demonstrate some of the ways that women's CED both adopts and challenges these concepts, and the ways that women involved in the work of CED navigate some of the tensions that have resulted from complex relationships with funders and governments.

THE "INDIVIDUALIST COMMUNITY" IN CED

This section asks if CED utilizes, and therefore helps to perpetuate, a concept of community that is rooted in a "modernist, liberal framework" (Naples 2002). In this case community is conceived as an entity composed of autonomous individuals, each acting in a manner that satisfies her or his own best interest, who comprise the unit of primary importance upon which most social, political and economic institutions and relationships are centred. This section also explores the impacts of these constructions of the concept of community on the potential for CED to be a socially transformative practice.

The ability of CED to be a socially transformative practice depends on how it understands and employs the concept of community in research and in practice. Women and feminist scholars and activists have been among the first to point out that "the community" has not always been a good space or place for women. Geographic communities and communities of interest or identity all carry social norms that affect women's lives in a diversity of ways, both negative and positive. The concept of community is often employed in ways that can silence or censor women; for example, by keeping them from speaking out against abuse. Further, communities not only regulate behaviour between their members, but can also exclude "others" — one need only consider the tradition of the exclusion of women from academia. In looking at the concept of community in these ways we can begin to dispel the myth of community as a "warm, fuzzy feeling" (Mayo 2000), and begin instead to understand the concept of community as a political and epistemological creation that, in actuality, serves as a mechanism for punishment and reward at the level of the individual.

Much development work, at both the international and community levels, has adopted the "individualist community" as a framework within which the lives of women can be improved. Development literature has focused, by and large, on the importance of women's involvement in local decision-making processes, access to resources and empowerment. However, these goals all remain rooted in the concept of the woman as an individual. CED initiatives with women share this tradition and are replete with examples that demonstrate the adoption of an individualist understanding of community and community development. The majority of programs offered by the organizations participating in this project treat community development as something that can be accomplished by women as individuals.

As a result of its dependence on the concept of the individual, CED has not posed a challenge to the structural inequities that are inherent in the current socioeconomic system, thereby failing to challenge the underlying belief that poverty, and the escape from poverty, is the responsibility of the individual. Evidence of this approach in CED strategies with women is found in a predominant focus on job training, self-esteem building, access to credit and the like. If one accepts that an economic paradigm rooted in individualism has not worked, and inherently cannot work, to benefit all peoples, then it is clear that we need to develop strategies that, rather than attempting to bring more people into such a system, work to challenge it and create new forms of organization. Several of the respondents voiced a desire to confront the system in this way. One identified a photojournalism project that "put together a whole package looking at 'isms' and tried to figure out a way that they can eliminate those 'isms'" as part of the work of CED. This respondent also demonstrated her understanding of the repressive consequences of economic individualism in relaying a conversation with project funders: "economically independent of what? I'm dependent upon a paycheque."

CONCLUSIONS

CED is only one of many ways in which the sizable task of development can be approached. A recent personal experience of the author in Nicaragua serves as a reminder of this fact. While on the Atlantic coast of that country, the opportunity arose to meet with Elizabeth of the Indigenous Women's Movement (AMICA). When speaking about an ecotourism project of AMICA, the question was asked: "how many jobs had been created by this project?" The answer was that the goal of these projects was not to create jobs for individuals, but to create work for the community. The distinction here is that "jobs" are income-generating activities that belong to an individual, whereas "work" does not specify ownership of the benefits of the activities. The proceeds from this project are not paid out to individual community members, but rather are deposited into a community fund from which the community can draw for collective projects. In a community where necessity and tradition have resulted in communal ways of living, such an approach may be more appropriate than the conventional forms of development that have been criticized for imposing Western development ideas on communities in the developing world.

The tendency in critical development literature has been to condemn development as a practice that exports Western values, ideologies and models of community development and imposes them onto "non-Western" communities. However, when considering CED as one of the many possible forms of community development, it is important that we not limit our critiques to the ways in which development practice imposes values on "other, less developed" communities because CED may be doing the same in our very own communities. We must learn from different understandings of community and community development in order to challenge and improve upon our own perceptions and practices.

Chapter Eight

YOUNG WOMEN WORK

Community Economic Development to Reduce Young Women's Poverty and Poverty-Related Conditions

Molly McCracken, with Kate Dykman, Francine Parent and Ivy Lopez

Partners: Andrews Street Family Centre • Prairie Women's Health Centre of Excellence • SEED Winnipeg Inc. • Wolseley Family Place

YOUNG WOMEN'S ECONOMIC PARTICIPATION

Young women work: in their homes and communities, in schools, with other youth and in the labour force. Just like generations of women before them, they are working to improve their lives, and the lives of others, through everyday tasks such as helping a friend, caring for children and elders or finishing a homework assignment. However, young women who live in poverty continue to experience difficulty fitting into today's economic and social systems. They face many challenges: staying in school, working for low wages, teen pregnancy and insufficient access to child care. Facing a life in poverty, as well as the possibility of raising their children to encounter these same barriers, young women have a strong desire to work toward a brighter future and a better community.

How can young women be supported to achieve these goals? The answer is by believing in their capacity to learn, grow and thrive, and by providing them with suitable supports and encouragement. Community Economic Development (CED) is an emerging means of doing this in a sustainable and empowering fashion. This research project worked with young women in inner-city Winnipeg to define young women's needs, and to look at how CED can be used to build on young women's strengths and improve economic status.

Feminist development theorist Carolyn Moser (1989) conceptualizes women's needs as both practical and strategic. The former are short-term and immediate: food, shelter, child care and transportation; the latter are long-term and transformative: education, equitable wages, equal gender division of labour and reproductive choice. Fundamental to young women's full participation in CED programs are services available through the government-provided social safety net, such as adequate housing and child care.

Understanding young women's needs in the current economic context is important. The "new economy," with its emphasis on computer literacy, technology and innovation, provides an exciting, precarious and ever-changing environment. In order to find a place in the new economy, youth must have familiarity with computers, be educated and have job experience. However, among economically disadvantaged groups such as young women, the questions are: Are young women in the inner city participating in the new economy? Why or why not? What resources do young women require? The research set out to answer these questions.

This chapter describes the barriers and opportunities for young women in the new economy, and proposes CED approaches that support young women's participation in it, and that ultimately should reduce poverty and poverty-related living conditions. By focusing on young women in two inner-city neighbourhoods of Winnipeg, this research set out to examine the community supports that already exist for young women and the ways that CED can be built into the network of services that already exist.

This research project was conducted in the spring of 2004, and was guided by community resource workers who identified the need for information about young women living in Winnipeg's inner city. While people who work daily with young women have an understanding of their circumstances, documented evidence was needed on young women's life circumstances, to determine appropriate CED approaches for young women at risk of poverty. To accomplish this, the fifty young women aged fifteen to twenty-four were asked about their participation in our society, and their hopes and aspirations for the future.

This chapter is divided into four sections, beginning with a discussion of the world in which young women are growing up, a world in which there is a continuing gendered wage gap and other systemic barriers to their participation. The second section describes the feminist, participatory research methods used. Section three discusses the research findings, relating the inspiring and heart-wrenching stories of young women and their desire to build better lives for themselves, their families and their communities despite the very difficult circumstances they face. Section four presents possibilities for CED programs with young women, as suggested by the research findings.

GENDER, RACE AND POVERTY
IN INNER-CITY WINNIPEG

In Canada, for decades, women's average earnings have remained significantly lower than men's: among full-year, full-time workers, the female-male annual earnings ratio increased from 58.45 percent in 1967 to only 70 percent in 2001 (Drolet 2001; Statistics Canada 2001c). The over-representation of women among low-wage workers is prevalent in Manitoba, where 36.5 percent of women earned low wages in 2002, compared to 25.8 percent of men (Black and Scarth 2003: 1). Young women have not escaped this trend: eight of ten women aged fifteen to twenty-four earned lower wages than seven of ten young men (Black and Scarth 2003: 2).

In Winnipeg, with its high population of Aboriginal peoples, economic inequality is exacerbated by the legacy of colonization and residential schools: 45.5 percent of the Aboriginal population aged fifteen to twenty-four is considered low income, compared to 16.2 percent of the total population for this age range (Statistics Canada 2001b). Nearly half of young Aboriginal women (49.7 percent) and a significant proportion of young Aboriginal men (40.1 percent) aged fifteen to twenty-four live below the poverty line (Statistics Canada 2001b).

How Can Community Economic Development Benefit Young Women?

If young women are to benefit equally from CED, gender implications arising from the process and programs must be considered. A gender-based analysis — a process commonly used to review policies and programs in light of the differing needs and circumstances of men and women — of CED programs would likely find inequities in the types of CED activities in which women and men participate, since CED programs often start with the "assets" of participants, and gender socialization plays a strong role in the skills women and men have. For example, women are often found doing community catering and sewing; men often work in local home construction. Since the economy values these activities differently, CED that simply builds on participant's skills without an analysis of the economic implications risks perpetuating economic inequality.

The possible solution to the gendered nature of CED activities is two-fold. First, CED needs to support skills development in fields that are non-traditional for women. This may be achieved, for example, through an all-female training and construction crew: the absence of men in such a program would acknowledge the fact that women learn best in non-intimidating environments. Second, it remains important to work toward improving wages in occupations traditionally dominated by females. Both types of CED programming must take into consideration the importance of meeting both women's practical (short-term) and strategic (long-term) needs.

Practical and Strategic Gender Needs

Caroline Moser argues that efforts to achieve gender equality require reflection upon women's practical and strategic gender needs (Moser 1989). Practical gender needs assist women in their subordinate position in society (Moser 1989). Attempts to address these needs do not challenge the gender division of labour, but rather respond to immediate perceived needs within a specific context (Moser 1989). They are concerned with basic needs — health care and employment, for example.

Strategic gender needs are those required to transform, rather than support, women's subordinate relation to men (see Amyot for further discussion of socially transformative CED with women). Meeting strategic gender needs helps women achieve gender equality and changes existing roles (Moser 1989).

Programs with Young Women

To be fully effective for young women and young men, the design and operation of a program must consider gender — not in a manner that regards gender differences as innate and unchangeable, but in a way that explores the social construction of gender and invites young women and men to challenge gender norms, examine gender privilege and create a balance of power between genders (Ms. Foundation for Women 2001: 6–7). At its core, an effective program for young women provides a safe space in which to meet; allows for opportunities to develop leadership skills; fosters cross-generational relationships between girls and women; respects youth culture and community, and creates opportunities for community-building and social change work (Ms. Foundation for Women 2001: 6–7).

Some examples of young woman-centred programming can be found in Winnipeg. The North Star Girls' Club at Andrews Street Family Centre and the Girls' Club at Wolseley Family Place were created to provide safe spaces for girls aged eight to twelve. They have been funded on a temporary, project basis, by the Province of Manitoba through Neighbourhoods Alive!, a community development fund, and The National Crime Prevention Strategy of Justice Canada. The Laurel Centre also runs a girls' club: with funding from Justice Canada, it created "It's Our Turn: A handbook for youth role models," which encourages young women's leadership in Winnipeg's inner city. Both the North End Women's Resource Centre and the North Point Douglas Women's Centre have teen women's drop-in clubs featuring activities such as self-defence training and media literacy. All of these activities are important, and can be classified generally as Community Development (CD), because they do not include economic aspects.

SEED Winnipeg is one of the only agencies in the geographic region studied offering CED programming. One exception is Individual Development Account (IDA), a program that supports people to save money; however, this program is not offered to young women in particular because of resource constraints.

Programs with Young Aboriginal Women

Until colonization imposed patriarchal approaches to family and state, Aboriginal women traditionally enjoyed high status in their communities as leaders and life-givers. As a response to this, Aboriginal women are fighting for their rights and the rights of their communities. The Mother of Red Nations, for example, organizes and advocates for Aboriginal girls and women in Manitoba. Also, Manitoba-based Ka Ni Kanichihk Inc. has been developing and delivering programs that uphold Aboriginal culture and values with Aboriginal women. The organization launched a community-based training program licensed through Red River College, taking a holistic and Aboriginal-centred approach to computer training.

Ma Mawi Wi Chi Itata Centre offers many personal development and support services at various sites in central Winnipeg. The services they offer to the community's families are guided by a holistic, Aboriginal- and community-based approach. They recently opened a new safe home for teen women aged thirteen to seventeen, "Honouring the Spirit of Our Little Sisters," which provides education, employment, training, mentoring and life skills development. Further, they provide an Adolescent Parent Residential Learning Facility for pregnant young women, as well as Circle of Care, which provides emergency residential care for teen women aged thirteen to eighteen.

Other youth programs for Aboriginal young women include Boy's and Girl's Clubs, and "Ndinawemaagag Endaawad Inc." (Our Relative's Home), which is a safe house. Ndinawe, as it is commonly known, recently opened a youth resource centre in the North End that offers Aboriginal cultural programming, employment and a computer lab.

SURVEY OF PROGRAMS
AVAILABLE TO YOUNG WOMEN

This research project, which undertook a survey of organizations in the inner city offering programs, was conducted in 2004. Although there are a number of innovative programs for young Aboriginal and non-Aboriginal women in inner-city Winnipeg, as explained above, it is not sufficient to meet existing needs. Programs are scattered throughout the community and rely on temporary project-based funding, meaning that there is little continuity to the programs and services they offer. While there were programs geared to women under eighteen, there were no specific programs for young women aged eighteen to twenty-four. Moreover, only 11 percent of all programs offered employment skills and CED programming. The majority of programs focused on young women's health, status as mothers (i.e., Healthy Baby) and were responsive to challenges young women face such as sexual exploitation, behaviour management, crime prevention. There were very few programs with a focus on young women aged fifteen to twenty-four that were proactive in supporting young women's strategic needs for economic advancement, and that included the economic basis for CED.

METHOD

The research project on which this chapter is based is feminist and participatory in nature. Feminist participatory research is committed to the emancipation of women, valuing women's experiences and minimizing the hierarchical relationships between the researched and the researcher (Damaris 2001). The research process was built on the skills and knowledge of community-based organizations, local leaders and young women themselves.

The preliminary research question was developed in consultation with a number of community-based organizations working in the inner city. An advisory team with representatives from community organizations guided the research project. The principal investigator also met with several leaders in the Aboriginal community.

Two young women from the areas studied were hired as community researchers and were involved in shaping the interview and focus group guide, leading the interviews and interpreting the data. First, a survey was conducted to ascertain the types of programs that are available to young women. Second, interviews and focus groups were conducted with fifty young women from two inner-city neighbourhoods, West Broadway and the North End: twenty-eight young women participated in interviews; the remaining twenty-two attended focus group sessions.

The average age of participants was eighteen. Most of the young women self-identified as Aboriginal (72 percent). Two young immigrant women and another who identified herself as a visible minority also participated. Two of the young women self-identified as having a disability.

Participants included young women who did not have children (thirty, or 60 percent); young women who were mothers (sixteen, or 32 percent); and those who were pregnant at the time of interview (four, or 8 percent). Of the mothers, eleven had children under the age of one, with the average age of their children being two and a half years. The youngest child was one month old; the oldest was nine years old.

The Neighbourhoods

The inner-city Winnipeg neighbourhoods of the North End and West Broadway, where the young women interviewed for this study reside, have a high incidence of poverty and poverty-related characteristics. These conditions can deeply affect how young women perceive their own potential in life. Living closely with others who also suffer under poverty conditions may create a "culture of poverty" that feeds upon and reproduces itself (Silver 2000: 146). Coupled with structural changes in the economy, this has meant that inner-city residents often do not have the skills to take advantage of the changing demands of the new economy (Silver 2000: 147). Moreover, those women who are employed are often segregated into particularly low-paying and non-empowering occupations (such as the service industry).

RESULTS

Work

Unpaid Work

Unpaid work is done to sustain daily living, such as housework or caring for children or elders. One of the structural reasons for women's poverty lies in the greater likelihood of women to do unpaid labour, because unpaid work places demands and restrictions on women's time that can prevent them from doing paid work. Also, although women's unpaid labour is not valued in economic terms, it is valuable for the functioning of our economy: for example, women are raising the future work force. Unpaid labour is very important and valuable to the functioning of our society.

All of the young women participants did some sort of housework. Also, those who were not mothers often cared for other people's children in some way: nearly half (48 percent) of respondents "take care of any kids like sisters, brothers or cousins." When asked how often they did this work, their answers ranged from daily to a couple of times per month.

Paid Work

When approaching paid work, it is important to acknowledge and value unpaid work (for example, being a mother is a full-time job in itself). Paid work should always be a woman's choice and never imposed through policies such as "workfare." Paid labour can also cause disproportional burdens on women's time by creating a "double burden" of unpaid and paid labour that can have detrimental effects on women's health (Statistics Canada 1999). For these reasons, any efforts to support women to improve economic circumstances through paid work must also build in supports to alleviate and redistribute the responsibility for unpaid work — through increased access to child care, for example.

It is only by working for pay that women can lift themselves out of poverty: however, the jobs available to them may only pay minimum wage without benefits. Social assistance recipients receive benefits such as paid prescriptions and dental coverage that are not often available in low-wage jobs. An individual must earn at least $9.44 per hour to earn a living wage in Manitoba (Just Income Coalition 2004: 3): those working for minimum wage live at only 70 percent of the poverty line and rarely receive medical benefits.

Most of the participants in this study did not work for pay. Some worked casually as babysitters or cleaning homes for others, while a few had twice-weekly jobs with the Youth Opportunity Project, a school-based project which creates employment opportunities. A further two worked at fast-food restaurants.

Young women identified two specific barriers to entering the labour force: lack of work experience and discrimination. Making the transition from school to work can be difficult:

> I'm a medical assistant, I graduated a couple of years ago but because I don't have any experience, nobody will hire me. Which I think is crap, because how are you supposed to get the experience if somebody's not going to give it to you?

This young woman's experience points to the need for internships and work co-op programs to facilitate the transition from education to the work force.

Several respondents experienced discrimination as young mothers in the paid work force. One young mother said:

> They like me right up to the point that I said I have a kid. Well, all right, thank you for your time. And I've never heard from them. But I have all the skills; I have all the qualifications, you know, to do this job. But because I have a baby, they're not going to let me. And I know why, because emergencies, they happen.

Another expressed her desire for a workplace that understands her responsibilities as a parent:

> I wish there were more jobs that, like, helped mothers, like who understood what mothers needed, like when they needed to go to appointments... you need the flexibility because of other important things. Like your job is important but still your kids are number one on your list.

These young women are willing to work for pay, but, because they are single mothers, they require significant support and flexibility in their working schedules. CED can provide an appropriate response to this issue, since it takes a holistic approach which considers not only the need for paid work, but also for creating conditions under which young women can be successful in the workplace.

The jobs young women identified as ones they would like to have now were either in the service industry or in the caring professions. However, about half of the young women said they did not know what they could do to find a job right now. This underscores the need to teach young women job-search techniques and to help them make links to future career options. CED initiatives with young women could offer such career planning and job search skills.

The young women in the focus groups who had been to career planning and career fairs with their schools aspired to a much broader range of professions; those who said they had not had any career planning aspired to obtain work that is more familiar to them (for example social work, nursing or probation work). It appears, therefore, that the provision of career education and role models can broaden young women's horizons by exposing them to the range of paths they can choose to take. CED programming can address young women's need for information on career possibilities by offering skills development and career information sessions, and by providing them with mentors.

Motherhood

Parenting under Poverty

A young woman's experience with motherhood largely depends on the support she receives from her partner and/or family, and from the community. When asked what would make motherhood less overwhelming, basic supports such as transportation and access to healthy food were mentioned consistently. One respondent said:

> I went to Mom and Me. But other than that, I really don't think that pregnant women are given enough support. Like sure we get ourselves pregnant or whatever, but I mean, we have no means of transportation you know... I don't like how they keep raising the bus fares, that's going to make it even harder for women.

While they mentioned receiving government support to meet some of their practical needs through Healthy Child programs and the Child Tax Benefit, they did not refer to any support from government for their long-term needs of getting an education, improving their employment-related skills and entering the paid work force.

The Need for Child Care

Child care is a serious financial burden for young mothers living in poverty. Even those who are eligible for a subsidy pay $2.40 per day, or $48 per month per child. Mothers on social assistance who receive child care pay $1.40 per day, or $28 per month, out of their monthly allowance (Prentice and McCracken 2004). Most of the young women had difficulties finding child care. One noted:

> Yeah cause most of the young women in the North End have kids, and maybe that's why they don't want to go to programs... I have kids and I can't go.

For women, the cost of child care is directly correlated with the decision to enter the labour force. One woman notes:

> A lot of women who aren't educated, and even if you are, you can't find a job for at the very most for $7.50 an hour... and if you have two kids then you're paying for a babysitter... so you're going to work only to make like say ten dollars a day because the rest of the money that you have goes to child care.

Statistics Canada (1995) found that the presence of children rather than education, age or marital status, was the main reason for the wage gap between men and women. With child care, women accumulate longer, more continuous labour market experience, which opens up more opportunities and improves their abilities to save for retirement (Blau et al. 1998: 104).

The provision of child care was raised repeatedly and without prompt as the key to encouraging young mothers' participation in education, pre-employment training and paid work, and to improving their overall well-being. Providing on-site or otherwise accessible child care is therefore a fundamental component of any CED effort to support young women to improve their earning power.

Education

From a community development perspective, education is key to self-sufficiency and a higher quality of life, as well as a way out of poverty. Research has shown that the more education a woman has, the more likely she is to have a smaller family and the more likely her children are to be educated also (United Nations 1995). However, women's decisions to pursue education are influenced by what they expect in their futures. If a young woman anticipates that she will not be in the labour force because she will be caring for children, she will not find it as worthwhile to invest her time and money in education (Blau et al. 1998: 155).

Compared to the Winnipeg average, few young women residing in the neighbourhoods probed by this study attend school: 37.2 percent of females aged fifteen to twenty-four in West Broadway attend school full time, as do 38.5 percent of their peers in Point Douglas South. The Winnipeg average for full-time school attendance among this cohort is 50.9 percent (Statistics Canada 2001a).

When asked what they liked and disliked about school, the students expressed appreciation for respectful environments that provide personal attention and work at the student's own pace:

> I work at my own pace at my own time, you know it's not like pressure, and it's more like a one to one thing? So like me, I had trouble in math and I was doing way better, like I was having a tutor because I work better on a one-to-one… it's easier to do now, and I get a lot higher marks.

The importance of child care was again raised in response to this question, as exemplified by the following comment: "I like the fact that I don't have to pay for daycare!"

The barriers to school attendance identified by the young women were primarily financial. For young women living in poverty, a program's being low- or no-cost is essential. As explained by one young woman:

> Definitely would need financial support. In order to get a student loan you have to have great credit but once again if you've screwed up in the past well you're "S-O-L" now. Because with me I have a $200 phone bill and because I had that $200 phone bill which I'm not able to pay off right now I can't do my credits.

Other barriers to schooling mentioned included basic costs such as bus passes and lunches. Peers also influence school attendance, and several young women told us that drugs impeded them from attending or performing well in school. Court dates were mentioned by another young woman as a barrier to her attendance at school.

Many of the young women were taking steps to make sure they attended school and worked toward promising futures. This was exemplified by one young woman's comment: "I had a boyfriend. Dropped him because he was interfering in my work." Young women told us that success is connected to their identity, self-confidence and self-esteem. Young Aboriginal women appreciated having their culture reflected in their school curriculum and environment.

> I like my school because… our school's an all-Aboriginal school… [it's] all about respect and respecting other people and you'll get it back. Our school's very friendly, very supportive.

Young women told us they need support from others — family, friends, teachers and community people — to stay in school until they graduate. Motivation, encouragement and opportunities to apply their skills were mentioned repeatedly as keys to their success.

Using Computers

One of the key features of the "new economy" is its dependence on workers who are skilled in computer technology. Women, however, are under-represented in education programs and occupations related to technology. While male students are more likely to use computers and enter fields related to Information and Computer Technology (ICT), women who do enter ICT jobs exit at twice the rate of men, citing differential treatment as their reason for leaving (Looker and Thiessen 2003). This may be explained by women's relatively low exposure to computer technology: a study of university students entering computer science found there was a gap in prior experience with computers between men and women (Margolis and Fisher 2002). Economic and social class exacerbates the probability of lower computer use by young women, since the ability to afford a computer will obviously have an influence on use and knowledge of them.

Most young women we spoke to (89 percent) said they used computers, usually at community access facilities, community centres, school, friends' houses and the library. However only three had a computer at home. Whether or not they used them, all the young women agreed that familiarity with computers would be helpful in getting a job. However, young women said they could not afford computer training courses. Some mentioned the inadequacy of community computer facilities: one said she uses the computers at a local family centre, because child care was available to her there, but because this centre does not have printers, she could not print her résumé or job advertisements from the Internet.

The severe restrictions on young women's opportunities to use computers to improve their skills and knowledge will exclude them from high-paying jobs using information technology, such as, among others, engineering, graphic design and web design. One significant opportunity to respond to their interests and needs would be the creation of a CED program for young women aimed exclusively at developing skills for higher-paying positions in the Information Technology sector.

Visions for Their Futures

All the young women had strong visions of a better future for themselves and their families. When asked about their perceptions of future earnings, an extreme variety of responses was received. Few could pin down how much money they would need to earn in the future:

> As much as I can get.

> I don't really care about the money or anything. Because money comes and goes.

Hopefully $300 every two weeks.

Probably six or seven dollars an hour, something like that.

$7.50 an hour.

I don't know I'd probably want to make at least nine or ten dollars an hour.

Right now with Social Assistance yearly is like $10,000 a year. That's crazy… It's not even $1,000 a month really… So I think I don't know, $30,000 a year?

Just enough to live comfortably, you know. To live comfortably and be able to go out every once and a while and watch a movie or something, go to the bar, have some fun, stuff like that. Be able to get Internet.

It is evident from these responses that these young women do not aspire to high earnings, likely because they do not have a sense of how much money is required to earn a living wage and/or because they live in a "culture of poverty." The need for improving young women's economic literacy is starkly apparent.

CONCLUSIONS AND POTENTIAL CED ACTIVITIES WITH YOUNG WOMEN

This study has found a strong need for community economic development approaches to reducing the poverty and improving the incomes of young women in inner-city Winnipeg.

Currently a patchwork system of community supports exists for young women. Some of the biggest challenges were faced by young mothers, who faced formidable challenges, most notably a lack of available child care and access to education. Young women identified financing for education as a barrier and had limited knowledge of job-searching techniques

The research found that young women are eager to enhance their earning power through skills development programs; this interest, however, depends on programs' respect for their short- and long-term needs. This means that an approach to CED that meets young women's practical needs for food, housing, child care and transportation, as well as their strategic needs for education, equitable wages, equal gender division of labour and reproductive choice, must be taken. Since CED tailors programs to the needs of local young women through their participation in program design, it can be a highly effective means of understanding and targeting both kinds of needs. Further, programs must be culturally appropriate — in the Aboriginal context, this means that they must be Aboriginal-centred. In this way, CED programs addressing students' needs from a holistic approach are best equipped to ensure students' success.

CED offers the potential to support young women to gain access to the new economy by providing skills and enterprise development in sectors that are higher paying and by working to raise the status of traditionally lower paying sectors.

The following list of possible CED activities with young women in Winnipeg was devised as a response to such needs, as voiced by the young women who participated in this research. These activities should be undertaken at no cost to participants and should offer a living wage (where applicable): they must also incorporate elements of economic literacy and career guidance and mentorship. As a whole, they represent an attempt to integrate "the economic" into the network of community supports already available to young women.

Powercamp: Develop and deliver a two-week camp with young women based on the Power Camp model. Incorporate leadership development, violence-prevention and economic literacy. <www.powercampnational.ca> (accessed July 2007).

Young Women's Computer Club: Build a computer lab in a family centre or local community-based organization. Create a training program that teaches basic computer skills and marketable job skills for young women at no cost.

Young Women's Website and Graphic Design Worker's Cooperative: As a next step to the Computer Club, create a social enterprise (a worker-owned cooperative) with interested young women. Local organizations could contract with this cooperative for the design and maintenance of Web sites and graphic design work.

Young Women's Home Construction Training and Building: Provide young women with on-the-job training in home construction using an all-woman crew. This could start as a pilot with a single house in the inner city.

Young Women's CED Internship: Hire and train young women in CED practices. Connect them with a mentor, and place them in local organizations to run economic, literacy and CED programs with youth. This offers them the chance to develop skills and work with a range of local people and organizations.

Worker-owned Child Care Co-op: Provide loans for young women with low incomes to be trained as early childhood educators. Loans would be forgiven for young women who start a worker-owned child care co-op in the inner city and are working members for two years. Proper supports and infrastructure would have to be provided to train worker members and to help them to set up the centre, attain capital for building etc. Additionally, continuous work would have to take place to advocate for higher wages for child care workers.

Young Women's Leadership and Economic Literacy Program: Support existing leadership development programs, such as the Laurel Centre's mentorship program, to continue to offer leadership and mentorship programs where young women mentor younger girls in their neighbourhood. Incorporate economic literacy and career guidance into these programs.

Young Women's Individual Development Accounts (IDA): Currently offered by SEED Winnipeg, participants learn economic literacy skills and save toward a particular goal. Participant's savings are matched three to one, and can be used to start a business, toward education or for home-ownership. With further resources, this program could be expanded and incorporated into other activities offered to young women.

It should be noted that although the small CED initiatives listed here may not be able to offer high wages, programs can support young women to develop the skills that can be carried over to higher-paying jobs. A myriad of other possibilities exist for the multitude of young women who are ready and willing to participate in holistic programs aiming to help them build strong futures for themselves, their families and their communities.

Chapter Nine

MOVING LOW-INCOME, INNER-CITY PEOPLE INTO GOOD JOBS
Evidence on What Works Best

Garry Loewen and Jim Silver

THE PROJECT

This chapter is the product of a research project aimed at identifying ways of bringing members of low-income, inner-city communities into the paid labour force, and particularly into industries identified by the Province of Manitoba as growth industries. We conducted a detailed analysis of the literature on employment development strategies aimed at getting members of low-income, inner-city communities into "good" jobs — those that pay a living wage and offer benefits and opportunities for advancement. This review involved the examination of numerous well-documented projects aimed at getting members of disadvantaged communities into good jobs undertaken in various jurisdictions beyond Winnipeg in recent years; for many of these, we interviewed project managers, evaluators or sponsors. Employment development organizations in Winnipeg were also studied, and then compared to the best practices model derived from the literature review. Despite the multi-faceted strengths found to characterize Winnipeg's employment development landscape, our conclusions point to four areas in which the system can be improved.

Skill Shortages and Demographics
In Canada and across the industrialized world, evidence of an impending labour shortage is growing. Industrialized nations are generally facing the same demographic realities: longer life expectancies, falling birth rates and a large "baby boomer" generation that is reaching retirement age. With a smaller proportion of young people available to replace those who are soon to retire, shortages of labour are expected to arise soon (McMullin, Cooke and Downie 2004; Schetagne 2001; Gingras and Roy 2000). Manitoba and Winnipeg are particularly likely to be skill shortage "hot spots."

The Aboriginal community in Winnipeg represents a different demographic story. Manitoba has one of the highest proportions of Aboriginal residents in Canada (14.3 percent) and Winnipeg has more Aboriginal residents than any Canadian city, at 8 percent (55,755 individuals) of the population in 2001 (Mendelson 2004: 9). The Manitoba Bureau of Statistics projects that by 2016, one in every five labour market participants will be Aboriginal (1997: 3). Although Aboriginal children represent Manitoba's "economic future," Aboriginal people have been significantly underrepresented in the labour market. While Winnipeg had an unemployment rate of 5.7 percent in 2001 and was experiencing labour shortages, the city's Aboriginal population had an unemployment rate of 14.7 percent, or two and a half times that of the general population (Mendelson 2004: 29). Mendelson argues that "Canada cannot have a high quality of life if there is a significant minority forming an impoverished underclass," and that we must look to Aboriginal people to fill impending labour market shortages.

Nearly half of Winnipeg's Aboriginal population (44 percent) live in the inner city, which has been in decline for decades and has become an area with concentrated poverty, unemployment and social problems. There are twice as many low-income households in the inner city as in the city as a whole (40.5 percent compared to 20.3 percent). Labour force participation rates are lower in the inner city than in the rest of Winnipeg, and the inner-city unemployment rate, at 8.1 percent in 2001, is almost double that of Winnipeg overall. Almost one in five (19.2 percent) inner-city households rely on government transfer payments as their main source of income (City of Winnipeg 2004). Often disconnected from the mainstream world of work, disadvantaged inner-city residents — 19.2 percent of whom are Aboriginal, and another 20 percent of whom are visible minorities — represent a large population who are not benefiting from meaningful employment, and thus are not making the greatest possible contribution to Manitoba's economy.

BEST PRACTICES FOR EMPLOYMENT DEVELOPMENT INTERVENTIONS

The types of jobs that will need to be filled are not the entry-level, so-called "McJobs" into which disadvantaged job seekers are often shuffled. Instead, the impending shortages will occur in skilled sectors. The challenge of employment development initiatives, then, is to equip low-income, inner-city populations with the skills, education and training they will need to acquire, retain and advance into these "good" jobs. This will not be easy. Bob Giloth of the Annie E. Casey Foundation (AECF) "Jobs Initiative" describes the "disconnection between the hardest to employ and the mainstream economy" as two separate "worlds":

> One world is made up of business culture and expectations that hard work is rewarded. The other world is made up of people who have been marginalized by the mainstream over generations and face the labour market with cynicism, loss of hope, and few posi-

tive expectations. Bridging these worlds is an enormous challenge. (Giloth 2004b: 20)

In the U.S., a number of initiatives have been set up to take on this challenge. Based on a review of employment development literature, this section highlights the best practices of employment development initiatives over recent years in jurisdictions beyond Winnipeg. According to the literature, the most successful initiatives are comprehensive, networked and interventionist.

Successful Initiatives are Comprehensive

Some employment development programs focus only on basic education, developing low-income job seekers' skills in mathematics and literacy. Others focus on job-training, linking job-seekers with training programs that teach technical, or "hard," skills. Some programs focus on job search and job preparation activities, providing access to job kiosks, résumé writing assistance and interview tips.

Other approaches deliver supports to help job-seekers overcome their particular barriers to employment. "Job Readiness" programs teach the "soft skills" needed to adjust to the norms of the working world, such as appropriate language, punctuality and proper dress. Some programs help individuals overcome alcoholism or drug addiction, or offer counselling for victims of domestic abuse. Others offer support services, such as financial assistance for housing, transport and child care or help improving one's financial literacy.

Initiatives offering one or even a combination of the services mentioned above take the most traditional approach to employment development. Such programs are designed to respond to perceived employment "deficiencies" among disadvantaged populations. "Stand-alone" programs like these have had limited success in helping disadvantaged job-seekers obtain and keep good jobs. They constitute a "disjointed system" without a coordinated approach to training or employment preparation (Torjman 2000: 3).

Job-readiness training is similarly unsuccessful when on its own. "The low-paying jobs people generally find through such programs fail to sustain their commitment to work" (Dickens 1999: 421). Buckley (1992: 104) found that 1970s training courses for Aboriginal Canadians failed because they were not linked to jobs. A similar finding for U.S. government-led training programs notes that "they are disconnected from contemporary employer needs" (Clark and Dawson 1995: 5).

While these strategies are not likely to be successful when offered separately as "stand-alone" programs, the story is different when they are offered together in a comprehensive fashion. As Sommers (2000: 8) observes, "few organizations can provide the full range of training and support services needed to make an [employment] program work. As a result, [employment] programs often form as a partnership of organizations."

The provision of post-employment supports was identified repeatedly in the literature as a best practice which is critical to job retention. According to Fleischer (2001: 6), "[job] retention is even more important than placement," and, to achieve this, follow-up supports are critical. Examples of post-employment supports include mentoring, ongoing case-management, phone calls and continued financial assistance. A U.S.-based program found that "early and regular contact with participants was critical to job retention" (Torjman 1999a: 26).

Comprehensive strategies that provide disadvantaged communities with the resources they need to overcome the barriers they face fall into what we call the "traditional community development model." Its weakness is that it fails to look at both sides of the labour market — workers and employers. It does not build the networks that connect workers to employers, or initiate changes in the labour market to benefit low-income workers (Clark and Dawson 1995: 9–10).

Successful Initiatives are Networked

Networks, in employment development, are made up of relationships between actors in the labour market (Tilley 1996). The theory of networks recognizes that workers are not hired according to "what they know," but are hired through interconnected social and business networks; what really matters, therefore, is "who they know." Harrison and Weiss (1998: 35–37) explain that the job market is not a "queue," such that the next qualified worker in line gets the job. Rather, workers find jobs through networks that provide them with information about job prospects and connections to real employers, and that "teach young people about what is needed to find work" (Dickens 1999: 410).

The problem with low-income, inner-city neighbourhoods is that they tend not to have promising network connections. Wilson (1996) explained that in today's inner-city neighbourhoods, unemployment is very high and labour force participation rates low, and young people do not have connections or role models as did the youth of traditional working-class neighbourhoods.

Successful employment development initiatives form a network that links disadvantaged workers with jobs, training and education opportunities, as well as support services. The best networks, according to Harrison and Weiss (1998), are formalized connections between community-based organizations (CBOs) and employers. CBOs recruit, assess and possibly offer job readiness (soft skills) training to disadvantaged job-seekers. Located in inner-city neighbourhoods, CBOs act as "gateways" to employment opportunities for low-income people by bringing them into contact with the network.

A successful employment development network is a partnership among many different stakeholders. CBOs can recruit participants and offer soft skills training and career counselling; community colleges can provide training services; local and provincial governments can provide political and monetary support; adult education centres can provide basic education skills; and unions can be useful in helping workers navigate unionized sectors.

The most crucial partnership in a successful network, however, is that with employers. According to Sommers (2000: 7), employers should be involved in all aspects of employment development, "from design, to implementation, to ongoing evaluation and improvement." Employers make good partners in an employment development network because they can provide crucial information: they can identify what skills they want in a worker, help design a training program, provide labour market information and even provide instructors for training. The success of an employment development initiative relies on partnerships with employers who have really "bought in" to the program.

Building networks and creating partnerships characterizes successful employment development interventions, as does engaging employers in every step of the process. Partnerships among these various actors must be strong and formalized; however, building these partnerships and coordinating the efforts of so many actors are complex tasks.

Coordinating the Effort: The Labour Market Intermediary

Labour market intermediaries (LMIs) are organizations that "bring together a set of key players to create long-term pathways to careers for low-skilled workers and value added productivity for employers" (Giloth 2004a: i). Labour market intermediaries are described by Betcherman et al. (1998: 62) as "brokers," since they broker relationships "between consumers of labour and suppliers of labour, serving to improve the functioning of the labour market." The intermediary is responsible for brokering relationships with community colleges to provide training; with employers to provide jobs and guidance; with government and funding agencies to provide financial assistance; and with CBOs to recruit and deliver services to help clients find and keep jobs.

Examples from various cities show that many types of organizations and agencies can act as LMIs. The Annie E. Casey Foundation's Jobs Initiative, for example, is a multi-city project which has placed over nine thousand clients in well-paying jobs. In different cities the role of LMI has been taken on by groups of different kinds: cases were seen where a city agency, a state agency, a regional non-profit work force organization, a CBO and a community college assumed this function.

Although well-networked initiatives are successful in getting low-income workers into good jobs, they still do not address the root of the problem unless they attempt to change the structure of the local labour market. The most successful employment development initiatives are not only comprehensive and networked; they are also interventionist.

Successful Initiatives Alter the Structure of the Labour Market

The local labour market is the structure that produces employment in a particular area. Like any market, labour markets feature the exchange of a resource: on the supply side are workers who want jobs; on the demand side are employers who want labour. Markets do not promise to operate in a socially equitable way, and history has shown that disadvantaged, low-income people are not necessarily well-served by them. Interventionist approaches seek to change how the labour market functions so as to benefit disadvantaged workers.

One type of comprehensive, networked, interventionist approach is the "Sectoral Approach." Sectoral initiatives target a high-potential industry, intervene in its practices and create systemic change in the labour market (Fleischer and Dressner 2002: 10). Sectoral initiatives may attempt to influence employers' perceptions about their own needs, reform standard hiring policies and increase the quality of jobs.

Prepare Workers for the Workplace: Simulated Workplace Training

The transition to work can be a shock to those who have never retained a job, even if they have been given the most comprehensive soft skills, basic skills and hard skills training, and have been provided with counselling and support services. Many workers are not emotionally prepared for the workplace; becoming accustomed to time management and a highly structured environment can be difficult and stressful. Although post-employment supports are a successful way of easing the transition into work, steps taken during training can also be useful.

Researchers have found that highly successful initiatives provide training environments that closely resemble the real workplace environment. Jenkins (1999: 9) emphasized that "the best teaching method is applied training or 'learning by doing,' it is best to make instruction resemble the workplace [to] familiarize students with basic principles of how businesses operate." Since successful initiatives will have the involvement of employers, they can help make training as much like the actual job as possible by providing equipment, space or instructors.

Cultural Competency

In addition to workplace-simulated training, workers need to be prepared for the cultural differences they may encounter between themselves and the mainstream work force. Many clients assisted by the Annie E. Casey Foundation (AECF) Jobs Initiative, for example, were not only economically and socially isolated from the world of work, but were also minorities, and thus culturally different from the mainstream work force. Bob Giloth of the AECF Jobs Initiative knew that issues of race and ethnicity were important when he started the program, but soon found that "these issues had to be front and centre" (Fleischer n.d.).

Adjusting to the culture of the workplace was not only difficult for participants, but also for many employers, who were "unaccustomed to working with people of colour" (Fleischer n.d.). Fleischer (2001: 27) emphasizes that "disadvantaged job-seekers need to develop cultural competencies and work habits that will enable them to succeed on the job"; yet, employers also need to become more culturally aware.

One way to prepare workers for cultural differences in the workplace is to introduce the idea of "code-switching." The theory, developed by African American anthropologist Elijah Anderson (1999), is that people put on a "different face" and apply a different kind of behaviour when they are at work than they do at home, and a different face still when they are in other settings. To adapt to different situations, people have to be able to "switch codes." This is natural to those used to the mainstream world of work, but many disadvantaged workers have to be taught to "switch codes" when at work, and then "switch codes" back when they return home. Rhonda Simmons of the Seattle Jobs Initiative (SJI) realized that employers also need to "switch codes" and adopt "culturally competent behaviour" (Fleischer n.d.). SJI responded to this need by developing a course to teach soft skills and cultural competency to workplace supervisors.

Successful Initiatives Focus on Good Jobs with Opportunities for Advancement

Focusing on good jobs seems like a no-brainer, but is in fact a real departure from the "work first" mentality common in jobs programs, especially those in the U.S. The "work first" approach is a response to changes in the U.S. welfare system requiring that workers be moved off welfare and into work as quickly as possible (Brown, 1997: 5–6). This approach may succeed in getting people off welfare, but Jenkins (1999: 1) found that it does not succeed in "enabling most welfare families to become self-sufficient." A focus on poor-quality jobs does not benefit job seekers in the long term. Fleischer (2001: 10) found that AECF Jobs Initiative participants in cities focusing on higher-paying jobs had far better retention rates than those in cities where the Initiative placed workers in lower-paying jobs. A "good" job that pays a living wage, offers benefits and presents a career ladder provides a foundation upon which workers and their families can build better lives. Working in a good job makes people happier: it bolsters their self-esteem and self-confidence and improves their quality of life.

A Hierarchical Continuum of Employment Development Approaches

Based on the best practices revealed by the literature review, we have developed a hierarchical continuum on which different approaches can be placed and compared. The hierarchy of approaches can be used to highlight potential gaps in a given community's employment development landscape.

Figure 9.1

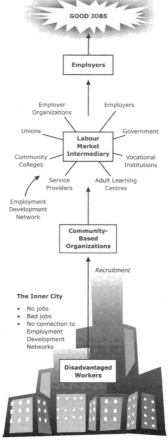

At the top of the hierarchy are approaches that are comprehensive, networked and interventionist, and that focus on high-quality jobs. Highly ranked initiatives also engage the employer at every step of the process, create training environments simulating the actual workplace and promote cultural competence.

An additional factor included in our hierarchy is whether programs address truly disadvantaged populations. Some of the most successful training programs, especially in knowledge-intensive industries, "cream off" the most "trainable" individuals from a wider selection of the unemployed. Although such programs still work with disadvantaged populations, they are attempting to ensure a high success rate by choosing candidates who are "almost there." From our perspective, "creaming" is not a holistic answer to the unemployment problems of disadvantaged communities.

We can compare common approaches to employment development — the "Work First" approach, the community development model and sectoral initiatives — by placing them on our hierarchical continuum. Not surprisingly, stand-alone programs (including job search, basic education programs and training programs) and the "Work First" approach occupy a low position on the hierarchy.

The traditional community development model may seem to be a very positive approach to employment development. It is comprehensive, offering a vast array of resources to disadvantaged workers, and may even feature partnerships between different service providers. The serious limitation of this approach, however, is that it focuses only on the supply side of the labour market.

Figure 9.2: A Hierarchy of Employment Interventions

Comprehensive, Networked and Interventionist Approaches

- Sectoral Approaches: Target a high potential industry and intervene in its practices to benefit disadvantaged job seekers.
- Customized Training: Short-term, intensive training for specific jobs in a given industry, designed in collaboration with employers.
- Bridge Programs: Training for disadvantaged adults to enter advanced technology trades.
- Apprenticeship Programs

Traditional Community Development Approach

Delivering a comprehensive array of needed resources to disadvantaged people.

Stand-Alone Programs

- Technical (Hard Skills) Training programs: Technical skill training at a college or vocational school.
- Basic Education programs: Teaching math, writing and reading.
- Soft Skills Training (Job Readiness): Teaching job seekers to adapt to the norms of the workplace looking at punctuality, proper dress, appropriate language, etc.
- Support services: Offered by service agencies, job seekers receive supports to help them overcome their barriers to employment (e.g., child care; drug, alcohol or abuse counselling; financial assistance for housing, transportation, health care, phone, etc.).
- Job Search Activities: Résumé-writing, interview skills, access to employment kiosks, help with job search, work experience placements.
- Post-Employment Counselling or Mentoring
- Motivation and Advocacy programs: Campaigns/career fairs to introduce job seekers to opportunities and motivate them to find work.
- Job Placement Activities: Job developers match job seekers with employment.

Best Practices

Focus on High Quality Jobs

Jobs alone will not help disadvantaged people out of poverty. They must offer benefits, opportunities for advancement and good pay.

Engage the Employer
Involve employers from beginning to end in designing the initiative. They can identify jobs, identify desired skills, help design training curricula, offer jobs to participants.

Build Networks and Create Partnerships
No group can do work force development alone. Neighbourhood community-based organizations, community colleges and vocational institutions, government, unions and especially employers need to collaborate to get people into jobs. A labour market intermediary works to bring these diverse stakeholders together.

Enlist stakeholders with clout

Offer comprehensive training with supports
The best initiatives combine not only technical (hard skill) training and basic education, but also soft skills ("job readiness") training and job search/placement assistance. Furthermore, they provide a range of support services (child care, transportation and financial assistance, drug/substance abuse counselling, etc.) to help clients overcome their barriers to employment.

Create training environments that simulate the real work place

Provide Post-Employment Support
Successful initiatives provide supports, mentoring, and/or follow-up counselling after a client is working to increase job retention.

Promote "cultural competence" for both employers and job seekers

Alter the structure of the labour market
Promote changes in the local employment system that will benefit disadvantaged job seekers.

Customized training and bridging programs are similar approaches that seek to link disadvantaged workers to good jobs. Their position in the hierarchy is elevated because they are not only comprehensive, but also networked, involving partnerships with employers, CBOs and training bodies. These approaches are also used to prepare workers for high-quality employment.

Customized training provides short-term, intensive training that prepares individuals for jobs in a targeted industry. Once an industry has been selected for an employment development initiative, an intermediary organization partners with employers and employer groups to determine what skills workers will need for jobs in the industry and what jobs are available. Training may be supplied by a community college, and designed in collaboration with employers and CBOs. Employers then use the intermediary as a "hiring window" because it has pre-screened and trained prospective workers (Torjman 1999b: 1).

Bridge programs offer disadvantaged job seekers a "bridge" to "employment as technicians and for post-secondary technical education in advanced technology trades" (Sommers 2000: 3). The point at which participants get on the training bridge depends on their individual attributes: "pre-bridge" programs can bring participants up to speed on basic education and soft skills. Bridge training provides technical skills in the same way as customized training, but it is typically a longer process.

The sectoral approach ranks the highest on our continuum. This strategy targets a high-potential industry, intervenes in its practices and alters the structure of the labour market to benefit disadvantaged workers. Sectoral approaches rank the highest because they aim to create a sustained change in the labour market, while providing comprehensive training and supports to participants and linking them to a broader employment development network.

EVALUATION OF WINNIPEG'S LOCAL EMPLOYMENT DEVELOPMENT CONTEXT AGAINST THE BEST PRACTICES MODEL

In Winnipeg, there are scores of CBOs offering a plethora of services to disadvantaged employment seekers: this is the real strength of Winnipeg's employment development system. Some of these CBOs help people to overcome barriers to employment by offering support services. Others, such as the Pathways to Alternative Tomorrows with Hope (PATH) resource centre in Winnipeg's North End, offer job search assistance, résumé help and career counselling. Others provide basic skills upgrading. Some, such as the Urban Circle Training Centre, provide a wide range of education and employment-related services, including technical skills training for specific jobs. Although the services offered are wide-ranging, and often overlap, a uniting feature of Winnipeg's employment development programs is that they are community-based efforts, attempting to meet the needs of disadvantaged populations in the neighbourhoods where such individuals are most concentrated.

There are many virtues to a community-based approach to employment development. Community-based employment service centres are located in neighbourhoods where disadvantaged people are most likely to live (mainly Winnipeg's inner city), and are thus more successful at drawing in disadvantaged populations than government training programs or employer-initiated interventions. It is also important that people feel comfortable walking into them, since they provide an informal atmosphere that is accepting, familiar and not intimidating.

Categorizing Winnipeg's Employment Development Agencies

We have developed three broad categories to classify Winnipeg's employment development agencies: these are "pre-employment" services; job search and placement agencies; and hard skills training agencies. As most organizations provide more than one service, we cannot hope to develop a categorization scheme with exhaustive and mutually exclusive categories. Instead, we have tried to come up with a general classification, in which we have placed different CBOs based on their principal employment development activities.

Pre-Employment Agencies

Pre-employment agencies are those that prepare people for work by helping job-seekers to overcome the barriers preventing them from entering the world of work. These barriers may include addictions, low literacy levels, family issues, lack of self-esteem and self-confidence, and lack of exposure to the world of paid employment and to the culture of the workplace. Consistent employment at a living wage is often not possible until these issues have been effectively resolved.

The Andrews Street Family Centre, for example, in Winnipeg's North End, provides "personal development" programming: services include parent and child, as well as single-father, drop-in groups; parenting classes; sharing circles to promote healing; and adult literacy and education upgrading. Although this type of CBO may not appear to be related to employment, these services can help members of disadvantaged communities begin to overcome their barriers and move closer to job readiness. Some of the many other organizations offering similar programming include the Native Women's Transition Centre, the North End Women's Resource Centre, Wolseley Family Place and the Ma Mawi Wi Chi Itata Centre.

Job Search and Job Placement Agencies

A second category of community-based employment development organizations in Winnipeg includes those that help job-seekers prepare a résumé, brush up on interview skills and search for a job. Some also provide post-placement support or counselling to smooth a client's transition into employment. Such agencies assist clients who are, essentially, ready to work, helping them to connect with employers and find a job.

The West Broadway Job Resource Centre is an example of this kind of agency. Located in the inner-city neighbourhood of West Broadway, the Centre has a job board, computers for job searching and offers résumé-writing assistance.

Some job search and placement programs are designed to help a particular disadvantaged group. Reaching E-Quality Employment Services, for example, offers help with job searches, résumé workshops, assessments and other services to unemployed job-seekers with physical disabilities.

Hard Skills Training Agencies

The third category of community-based employment development organizations offers training services that help job-seekers build specific skills. Hard skills training organizations often provide additional services, including pre-employment, job search and retention services, to complement their skills training programs.

Three examples of hard skills training agencies are described here. First, Opportunities for Employment (OFE) offers a number of courses, most of which include job readiness and soft skills elements, as well as job preparation, search and placement services. OFE offers two- to six-week courses certifying clients in air tools, food services, forklift operation and computerized accounting. For clients who need more job preparation, OFE offers an eight-week employability skills program, a self-marketing program and job search assistance. Second, the Aboriginal People's College offers training courses supplemented with employment counselling, job search assistance and retention services. Finally, the Aerospace Manufacturing and Maintenance Orientation Program at Tec Voc High School, which is free of charge, certifies students for employment in the aerospace industry while allowing them to finish high school at the same time. The training environment of this program simulates the aerospace industry workplace. Other hard skills training organizations in Winnipeg include Urban Circle Training Centre, Winnipeg Industrial Skills Training Centre Inc. and Red River College.

Some programs in this category are undertaken in collaboration with employers who offer jobs to successful participants. Trainees in the Manitoba Aerospace Human Resources Committee "New Hires Project," for example, have jobs waiting for them when they complete their training. This seventeen-week welding program is available to welfare recipients, Aboriginal people and women. The Manitoba Customer Contact Association is developing an Aboriginal Human Resources Strategy, and employs an Aboriginal Human Resource Liaison. The program emphasizes building networks between the Aboriginal community and the customer contact industry, incorporating a cultural component into training for both potential employees and employers, and providing post-employment supports to new Aboriginal employees.

Many of Winnipeg's employment development organizations provide more than one type of service, and some are nearly comprehensive enough to serve as best practice models. The Urban Circle Training Centre offers Aboriginal participants a range of supports, pre-employment and soft skills training, education upgrading, hard skills training and post-employment support services. The Centre's approach is holistic, and is rooted in an innovative, culturally empowering framework (Silver, Klyne and Simard 2003: 33–43).

COMPARING WINNIPEG'S EMPLOYMENT DEVELOPMENT SCENE TO THE BEST PRACTICES MODEL

Winnipeg's employment development scene has already developed the elements necessary to create a system that incorporates the best practices described above. Yet, when we measure it against the best practices model, we can identify four areas in which the system can be improved.

We Need Strong, Formalized Networks

Employment development organizations in Winnipeg are not networked in a strong, formalized way. The current employment development system is not so much a "system" as it is an assemblage of disparate parts. Many of these "parts" are strong; they are not, however, connected sufficiently to form a coherent whole. To build strong, formalized networks, organizations must sit at a common table and coordinate their activities. CBOs must formalize partnerships not only with each other, but also with employers, government, unions and education institutions.

We Need a More Comprehensive System

In its entirety, Winnipeg's employment development scene has all the elements of a comprehensive approach. Taken separately, however, no community-based employment development organization in Winnipeg offers the complete continuum of services. Therefore, organizations must partner with each other to ensure the comprehensive provision of services. Clients will attest that receiving all their services from a single, trusted CBO is better than taking referrals and having to make visits to various places.

We Need Initiatives that are More Demand-Side Driven

CBOs are the gateway to employment development networks, as they provide the crucial link to disadvantaged populations that other types of organizations simply cannot provide. In Winnipeg, this "supply driven," community-based side of the labour market system is well developed. However, more work needs to be done on the demand side. By this we mean that employers need to be involved in all aspects of employment development, from program design to providing work experiences, integrating the programs into their recruitment practices and, in some cases, performing the actual training and instruction. No amount of soft skills training, basic education, counselling or even technical training will guarantee success if employers are not on board to offer jobs to program participants.

We Need an Interventionist Approach

The approach to employment development taken by community-based employment development organizations is not sufficiently interventionist. That is, not enough effort is being made to change jobs to fit the circumstances of members of disadvantaged communities: the entire burden of change is placed on job-seekers, who are expected to fit into employment systems that have not been designed with their circumstances in mind. Some such changes could be made relatively easily, we believe, where the will to do so exists.

There are three kinds of demand-side interventions that could improve the employment chances of disadvantaged residents of Winnipeg. First, attempts could be made to change employers' recruitment criteria. By reassessing skills needed to do the job and removing inflated hiring standards, doors could be opened to disadvantaged job seekers. For example, in some cases where an employer requires prospective employees to have a Grade 12 diploma, Grade 12 may not really be necessary to perform the job.

A second such intervention would have major employers rely more heavily on CBOs to produce a supply of labour. If employers come to depend upon CBOs located in and drawing upon members of disadvantaged communities as a source of labour, they can tap into disadvantaged populations.

Third, jobs can be restructured so as to meet the needs of disadvantaged workers. The aerospace industry in Winnipeg, for example, uses relatively low-skilled workers to dismantle, clean, catalogue and store the parts of aircraft engines undergoing major overhauls. In performing this work, the workers learn enough about aircraft engines to prepare them for higher level functions.

BUILDING LABOUR
MARKET INTERMEDIARIES

How do we move toward a more networked, comprehensive, employer-driven, interventionist and culturally competent employment development system? The literature suggests this is best achieved with the creation of a work-force or labour market intermediary. Labour market intermediaries (LMIs) bring together otherwise diverse and separate elements of the community in pursuit of a common objective — moving significant numbers of low-income people from disadvantaged communities into good jobs. For an LMI to be successful, it is most important that employers, including those in the private sector, be actively involved, since it is they who have the ability to offer employment. But the involvement of other relevant actors, which includes governments, unions, CBOs and education institutions, is also absolutely essential. Employers have to be committed to hiring specified numbers of people who have met the agreed-upon criteria; CBOs must be committed to delivering specified numbers of potential employees who they deem capable of meeting the agreed-upon criteria; and education institutions have to be dedicated to mounting courses that employers and CBOs have designed and agreed upon, and which will lead to good jobs upon completion of training.

Pulling together the various actors constituting a work force intermediary is no easy task, since many of the parts of this kind of network are unlikely to be in communication with each other. The participation of the corporate community is considered to be an essential ingredient for success, as is the emergence of a "champion" — a community leader — to initiate the process and drive it forward.

The second condition involves a process of "issue definition." Since problems do not necessarily emerge as public issues, they have to be defined or constructed as such. Most important in this process is the construction of a problem as something that is "amenable to solution through civic or political action" (Stone, Henig, Jones and Pierannunzi 2001: 26). Forces in the community who are capable of bringing otherwise disparate elements of the community together around what they collectively define as a "public issue" — a problem that they agree is important, and for which they can agree on a common solution — need to play leadership roles in defining the issue and building a broadly based coalition to solve the issue.

We believe that in this chapter we have contributed to "defining the issue." We have demonstrated that the problem of a high rate of unemployment along with a low rate of labour force participation among members of disadvantaged communities — a problem which spurs many social ills — is one for which a solution can be found, and we have developed a model which describes that solution. It is also necessary that a broadly based coalition, in the form of a labour market intermediary, committed to putting in place a version of that model, be built. Building such a coalition is indeed possible, yet a strong community leader must emerge to make it happen.

Chapter Ten

CAN CALL CENTRES CONTRIBUTE TO MANITOBA'S COMMUNITY ECONOMIC DEVELOPMENT?

Julie Guard, with assistance from Myles Brown, Andrew McIsaac, Geoff Lloyd, Sara Stevens and Femi Sowemimo

CALL CENTRES IN MANITOBA

Call centres are a significant part of the Manitoba economy, employing at least 2 percent of the total provincial work force. According to an industry study prepared by Winnipeg-based market research company KiSquared (2004), over ninety call centres employ the equivalent of eleven thousand full-time Manitoba workers, most of them in Winnipeg. Since the employment calculations made in this report are based on "full-time equivalents" rather than actual employment numbers, and because many call centre workers — probably well more than half — work part-time, the total number of call centre employees in Manitoba is, in fact, significantly higher.

Manitoba call centres are actively supported by the province through an array of subsidies and other benefits. One of the principal ways in which the province supports the industry is by funding training for call centre workers. Although some of this training is provided through the public education system, in the form of university and community college programs as well as an internship program at a Winnipeg high school, most is provided through call centre employers. Representatives of Manitoba Advanced Education and Training and the Manitoba Customer Contact Association note that most of those who are trained for call centre employment are unemployed workers receiving Employment Insurance benefits, but special provision is also made for disadvantaged job seekers. These include First Nations, Inuit, Métis (including non-status Aboriginal) people, professional immigrants, disabled youth and people aged fifty-five and older.

The province is very reluctant to release information about its support for call centres, including training, and without complete disclosure it is not possible to determine the full extent of public support for the industry. Information concerning the number of people trained and their success in getting and keeping jobs is similarly partial. Based on figures for the 2003 to 2006 period, the available evidence suggests that the province allocates in excess of $1.76 million per year on training and related activities.[1] It should be noted, however, that because the data are incomplete, the actual numbers may be higher. Over this four-year period no less than 3,245 people received training, at least eighty of whom were classified as disadvantaged by virtue of being over fifty-five years of age, professional immigrants or youth with disabilities. In addition, at least thirty-one — and almost certainly more — of these trainees were First Nations, Inuit and Métis (including non-status Aboriginal) people. Roughly calculated, training for call centres represents a cost to the province of approximately $578 per person for a four- to six-week course. Much of this funding is transferred to the province from the federal government.

For development initiatives to benefit the entire community, and not just business, they must lead to good jobs that pay a living wage and build self-esteem. The experience of call centre development elsewhere, together with Manitoba's long-standing commitment to Community Economic Development (CED) (Fernandez 2005), suggest that the best way for Manitoba to ensure that publicly funded training for call centres contributes to the economic and social well-being of the community is to adopt a CED-oriented approach.

METHODOLOGY AND SOURCES

The research for this chapter is based on interviews with key individuals in the Manitoba government, Aboriginal community organizations and the call centre industry, as well as on data from government and industry sources.

Altogether, forty interviews were conducted. Interviewees included seven senior and intermediate level government officers; two Aboriginal liaison officers; five representatives of Aboriginal community organizations; six union staff and officers representing call centre workers; three call centre managers; and nine call centre workers. Some subjects were interviewed more than once. We obtained data on funding arrangements from the Education Training Services (ETS) and the Canadian Union of Postal Workers (CUPW), Prairie Region. We obtained data on the Manitoba call centre industry from the Manitoba Customer Contact Association (MCCA) in the form of two research studies. Specific data on Manitoba's work force, including data on Aboriginal workers, was received from Statistics Canada. We gathered information about provincial and federal funding for training programs from a variety of government Web sites, in interviews with representatives of Manitoba Advanced Education and Training, and during telephone conversations with various officials representing government and Aboriginal community organizations.

Officials representing the Assembly of Manitoba Chiefs and the Manitoba Métis Federation were also helpful, but explained that the complexity of their funding arrangements makes it impossible to provide specific data on the amount of funding allocated to training their clients for jobs in call centres.

CALL CENTRES IN THE
MANITOBA ECONOMY

Call centres in both the public and private sectors are a significant part of Manitoba's economy: the private, for-hire call centre industry hopes to grow even larger in the immediate future (KiSquared 2004). High turnover at the lower end of the industry and a tendency for low-end employers to recruit young workers means that a significant proportion of high school, college and university students will, at some point, work in a call centre (KiSquared 2004).

Both primary and secondary call centres can be found in Manitoba. Primary, or outsourcing, call centres sell telephone and electronic communications services to other businesses; secondary, or in-house, call centres are those in which the business or public service has not contracted their communications functions to a primary call centre, but has created a call centre within its own firm or branch. The operations of secondary call centres are performed internally by the business or public service's own employees. Most of the calls in secondary call centres are inbound — initiated by the customer, not the call centre worker — and mainly involve technical support or customer or public services rather than telephone sales.

Nearly half of Manitoba's primary call centres employ the full-time equivalent of over one hundred workers and, because so many positions are part-time, a great many more actual employees. The nine largest primary outsourcers in the province employ the equivalent of almost five thousand full-time workers. By contrast, more than half of secondary call centres have between eleven and twenty-five employees, and the nine largest employ the equivalent of three thousand full-time workers (Destination Winnipeg 2005: 10; KiSquared 2004: 11). Typically, the best jobs are in secondary call centres, where most calls are inbound: more of these jobs are permanent and full-time, they are more likely to offer opportunities for career advancement, and workers are more likely to be unionized.

Workers in primary call centres are more likely to make outbound calls — those that are initiated within the call centre either by the worker or, more commonly, by an automated dialler. These workers are generally among the lowest paid, and experience the least desirable working conditions. In 2004, wages in entry-level outbound telephone sales and market research positions started at less than ten dollars per hour and averaged thirteen to fifteen dollars per hour. Workers at outbound call centres are half as likely as those at inbound centres to advance within the company, and their employers are far more likely to report high turnover as a problem. It is typical for market research interviewers, whose calls are all outbound, to have virtually no chance for advancement within the company. This job category and that of telesales agents see the lowest average pay, as well as the highest rates of turnover — 54 percent for market researchers and 34 percent for telesales agents. Low retention rates suggest a high level of dissatisfaction with the lack of opportunity in the industry, with 43 percent of workers leaving the industry when they leave their jobs and only one-third moving up the job ladder within the firm (KiSquared 2004).

Workers in primary call centres who take inbound calls fare better than those whose work is mostly outbound, although their wages are often only marginally higher and many have limited opportunities for advancement. Inbound customer service representatives make up the largest category of call centre workers in Manitoba, constituting 63 percent of the call centre work force. Most earn between twelve and seventeen dollars per hour, with a minority comprised of mostly supervisors and senior technical support agents earning between twenty-two and twenty-five dollars per hour. Working full-time, all year long and at the top of the pay range, customer service representatives can earn a living wage; yet, many workers in this industry, including those working full-time and year round, fall below the poverty line (National Council of Welfare 2005: 94).

HOW DO CALL CENTRES
BENEFIT THE COMMUNITY?

Call Centre Unionization

Pay and working conditions at many call centres are consistent with their reputation as "electronic sweatshops" (Baldry, Bain and Taylor 1998; Guard 2003; Guard, Garcia-Orgales and Steedman 2006; Taylor and Bain 1999). But not all call centre jobs are bad jobs. Twenty-seven percent of Manitoba's call centre workers are unionized, a proportion that is only slightly less than the rate of unionization for the work force as a whole, which stands at 33 percent. Most unionized call centres are in the public sector, including Healthlinks, Statistics Canada and Veterans Affairs, to name only a few; however, a number of large call centres in the private sector, including Air Canada Reservations, CN Rail and Manitoba Telecom Services (MTS), are also unionized.

Unionized call centre workers earn more than their unorganized counterparts, regardless of whether the centre is primary or secondary, and whether calls are in- or outbound. In 2004, the average starting hourly wage in a unionized call centre was $17.88, compared with just $8.62 in a non-unionized centre. Moreover, workers in some of the top-flight unionized call centres in Manitoba currently make over thirty dollars per hour and receive full benefits and pensions. The union differential — the difference between the earnings of a unionized and a non-unionized worker — is particularly significant for market research interviewers. The average starting hourly rate of pay for market researchers in a unionized centre is over seventeen dollars, as compared to slightly under nine dollars in a non-unionized centre (KiSquared 2004).

All collective agreements negotiated in Manitoba include a dispute resolution process, which ensures that workers and employers have mechanisms for addressing conflict and for providing protection against unjust dismissal.[2] Most agreements also include pay schedules, which help to eliminate favouritism and to bar against incentive structures based solely on faster, stress-inducing job performance. Contracts protect workers' health and safety by providing for access to clean headsets and to safe, well-functioning computer screens and keyboards. As well, collective agreements in this industry typically address call monitoring, and try to ensure that surveillance is used as a means of helping workers improve their performance rather than as a way to intimidate, punish or harass them.[3]

PROVINCIALLY FUNDED CALL CENTRE TRAINING AS CED

In funding call centre training, Manitoba's provincial government hopes to maximize the industry's benefits to the community. Training is organized in collaborative arrangements described as "partnerships" with employers, community organizations and various government branches and offices. Generally, Manitoba Advanced Education and Training (AET), through the branch responsible for training (Employment and Training Services [ETS]), pays the call centre sector organization, the Manitoba Customer Contact Association (MCCA), as well as some call centre employers, to provide training. Training is initiated by a call centre employer with an immediate or imminent requirement for new workers, and courses are developed and delivered by the MCCA.[4] Community organizations such as the Assembly of Manitoba Chiefs, the Manitoba Métis Federation and, more rarely, seniors and youth organizations such as the Seniors Job Bureau and Youth Now, participate by nominating clients and purchasing seats in training courses for them. Several municipal, provincial and federal government offices contribute funds directly, or provide additional supports to clients.[5]

Because the province pays for training, ETS officials have some voice in the selection of trainees and the content of training programs. Proposals are ranked according to the number of new jobs they will create, as well as on their potential to generate a "multiplier effect" by stimulating the growth of related businesses in the region. While funding is sometimes used to retain footloose employers, most criteria favour job creation and the hiring of unemployed or underemployed local residents, especially when new hires include individuals who face multiple barriers and are thus hard to employ.

Relevant, Job-related Training

Even when employers provide training specifically to meet their own recruitment needs, as opposed to delivering training through public servants or professional college teachers, provincial funding can help ensure that training efforts advance community interests. Paying employers to train new workers may give them too much control over the design and delivery of the training process. But employment development experts point out that partnerships with employers may improve the outcome of training programs by ensuring that what students learn is relevant and by increasing the chances that graduates get hired (Loewen et al. 2005).

Though almost all call centres train new hires in the telecommunications equipment, protocols and scripts, products and services of their particular workplace, provincially funded training tends to last for a longer period of time and to impart transferable job skills — those that prepare workers for future jobs with other employers. Longer training times before workers "go live" on the telephone reduce stress and increase job satisfaction. Workers at a number of Manitoba's largest primary call centres report that new hires typically get two or three weeks of training. When the province pays for training, on the other hand, the process tends to be about twice as long — from four to six weeks — and includes transferable skills such as computer literacy, basic arithmetic, team work and communications (MCCA 2006b).

Training for Disadvantaged Workers

An important way in which employment development can contribute to CED is by preparing disadvantaged people for decent jobs that allow them to participate in the social and economic life of the community (Loewen et al. 2005). Involving employers in training may help keep training for disadvantaged workers on this track. In fact, many employment development experts advocate involving employers in training for disadvantaged workers, noting that initiatives preparing economically marginalized people for employment fail when they do not connect workers with the employers who will hire them (for an overview of this literature, see Loewen et al. 2005: 15–18).

Some call centre training is intended to help people who are economically and socially marginalized, or who are chronically unemployed or underemployed, to acquire basic job-readiness skills and entry-level job experience. When training is publicly funded, the curriculum is expanded to include transferable job-readiness and life skills that are not normally included in the in-house training provided by employers. Publicly funded entry-level training, for instance, addresses life skills, time management, dealing with conflict, problem solving, personal finances and punctuality. Training may also cover numeracy, enunciation, vocabulary and effective listening — basic job skills that help prepare disadvantaged workers for employment (MCCA 2006b).

Call centre training that helps disadvantaged Aboriginal people to prepare for and get entry-level jobs contributes to CED. Collaboration among various branches of the provincial government enables ETS to recruit participants from Aboriginal communities and to provide education upgrading for those who lack academic qualifications.[6] Drawing on funds allocated to them by the federal government, the Assembly of Manitoba Chiefs and the Manitoba Métis Federation pay tuition for Aboriginal and Métis clients and contribute the supports that disadvantaged workers need to participate in training programs (Manitoba Aboriginal and Northern Affairs 2006; IIRDC 2005).

Perhaps the most ambitious goal of a CED approach to employment development lies in changing the structure of the local labour market: firms across an entire sector must be persuaded to alter their hiring practices by recruiting workers who have typically been overlooked (Giloth 2004b). The province's Aboriginal Representative Workforce Strategy, initiated in 2004, is an attempt to address this obstacle, in part by training Aboriginal people for call centres (MCCA 2006a). The goal of the plan is to help call centres become "an employer of choice for the Aboriginal community," by "building relationships and… cultural awareness for employers and management." As part of this effort, according to Aboriginal Liaison Officers, ETS and the MCCA sponsor "cultural awareness events" intended to convey the message that "if you want to employ [Aboriginal] communities you must first learn about them and not just how we want to work from nine to five or eight to four… We tried to create that understanding."

Culturally Sensitive Training

The provincial government engenders cultural sensitivity and contributes to CED by funding Aboriginal Liaison Officers (ALOs) in ETS and the MCCA. This is a central part of its Aboriginal Representative Workforce Strategy, as it builds relationships with Aboriginal community organizations. Interviewees from AET and the MCCA report that, rather than only trying to fit Aboriginal people into the workplace, ALOs seek "to create an environment in which Aboriginal people feel a level of comfort." ALOs, in collaboration with ETS project managers, negotiate with employers to reduce barriers to disadvantaged workers by monitoring curricula for cultural sensitivity and tutoring managers to recognize and respect the specific needs of Aboriginal clients.

Interviewees from AET, the MCCA and ETS all suggested that ALOs advance CED by encouraging the development of cultural competency among employers and public servants (see also MCCA 2006a). Cultural competence, defined as the increased awareness of how race, ethnicity, language and power are expressed in the workplace and the development of interventions to deal with conflicts arising from these differences, can help workers cope with unfamiliar work environments (Annie E. Casey Foundation 2001). For example, employers often require new hires to have a completed Grade 12 or at least Grade 10 level of formal education, but, according to interviewees representing AET and the MCCA, ALOs "educate" them to understand that these academic requirements are systemic barriers for many Aboriginal people.

PROBLEMS WITH THE CURRENT APPROACH

While the aspects of call centre training outlined above serve to address community needs, some problems with the process remain. These issues are addressed in turn below.

Lack of Public Accountability

A lack of public accountability is one of the most serious shortcomings of the provincial government's current approach to call centre training. Both the federal and provincial governments promise transparency and public accountability in their programs; however, these commitments are contradicted by the extreme difficulty any member of the public experiences in trying to attain specific, quantitative information. The close collaboration between the province and the call centre industry constrains public officials from revealing information about how public money is allocated, where new jobs are created and how many people get and keep them. Public accountability is thereby reduced to the extent that it is almost impossible for community members to know whether the province is investing in good jobs through call centre training, or is supporting low-road employers who are not contributing to the social and economic well-being of communities.

The cost of training is shared between employers and the province; yet, while the latter contributes actual financing, employers are allowed to make "in-kind" contributions. In addition to obviously legitimate training costs such as curriculum development and trainers' salaries, employers are entitled to count general overhead, human resource and skills needs assessments and recruitment, as well as unspecified "business expenses," as their contributions to training. No information is available to the public about whether any employers contribute cash, or if all of their contributions are "in kind."[7] Since almost all call centres must acquaint new workers with their procedures and provide at least basic information about their products or services, in the absence of public scrutiny it is impossible to determine whether public funding for training is merely "money for old rope" — defraying a normal business expense without providing any benefit to the community.

Even with input from the province and ALOs, it is not clear that training prepares workers for jobs with dignity. Training videos and curricula outlines give evidence that training focuses on techniques for dealing with rude and abusive telephone costumers, and for "staying positive" while enduring angry or threatening calls. The heavy emphasis on training people to deal with abusive calls suggests that workers are being trained for the kinds of call centre jobs in which abuse is common — jobs that provide few opportunities for building self-esteem. The title of one training video clearly expresses the expectation of employers that, despite stressful and unpleasant working conditions, trainees should not expect better working conditions, but rather should "Take This Job and Love It!" (MCCA 2006c). Training does not appear to include information about employment standards, workplace health and safety, human rights legislation or the right to unionize, although the province is legally responsible for providing this information to workers.

Public Support for Low-Road Employers

Not all call centres provide good jobs, and Manitoba does not lack for these "low-road" call centres. Such call centres are those that exploit workers through low pay and fast-paced work regimes. Low-road call centres, as Good and McFarland (2003; McFarland 2002) have shown, target regions experiencing high unemployment, where they can hire desperate workers who have few other employment opportunities, frequently with help from local and provincial governments. Public money should not support these call centres; yet close, collaborative relationships between public sector actors and employers undermine transparency and public accountability, making it difficult or even impossible to track how the money has been spent. Collaboration with employers compromises the province's ability to restrict funding to those employers whose jobs pay a family-supporting wage, offer opportunities for advancement and build self-esteem.

Inadequate Results

The province refuses to disclose information concerning the outcomes of its training programs, and results are therefore hard to determine. Nonetheless, claims that publicly funded training will create opportunities for Aboriginal people and other disadvantaged participants in the local labour market seem exaggerated. Despite the province's much celebrated commitment to increasing job opportunities for Aboriginal people, a relatively small number have been trained for call centre jobs; further, the province is not willing to provide data on the number of individuals who have found and kept jobs.

Moreover, even if the provincial government had been more successful in its efforts toward job-creation, training disadvantaged Aboriginal workers for entry-level jobs does not address the fundamental social and economic relations that cause inequitable labour markets. Rather than focus on the underlying problems that perpetuate a situation of limited choice and unequal opportunity, the province sustains an insecure labour market by endeavouring to integrate already disadvantaged individuals into call centre positions that do not guarantee full-time, full-year employment, wages sufficient to support a family or a job that provides dignity and builds self-esteem.

For training to make a lasting contribution to CED, it must lead to secure, long-term employment. Employment retention in turn depends on ongoing support and sustained follow-up once people have found jobs. Employment development "research confirms that the more services [programs] offer, the better results will be" (Fischer 2005).

Failure to Include Unions

Community involvement in training is very limited, and has so far failed to include labour unions. Although they have been widely overlooked by CED advocates, unions are community organizations with an established tradition of advancing community social and economic interests (see Shragge 1997 for an example of CED literature that does not overlook unions). The province is under a legal obligation to protect workers' rights, and has a specific obligation to encourage collective bargaining. Unions protect vulnerable workers from abuse and exploitation, forcing employers to respect their basic rights and to ensure they are treated with at least a modicum of dignity; no other type of organization is solely concerned with protecting workers. However, as labour specialist Roy Adams (2006: 20–21, 44, 71) points out, Manitoba has failed to meet its legal obligation to support workers' right to organize. At the same time, as noted by a number of interviewees, the provincial government collaborates closely with employers who are widely reputed to have discouraged their employees from organizing (Adams 2006: 22). The province fails to meet its responsibilities to workers and the community when it implicitly condones the anti-democratic behaviour of these employers by continuing to provide them with funding.

A COMMUNITY ECONOMIC DEVELOPMENT
APPROACH TO CALL CENTRE TRAINING

To be consistent with CED principles, training must do more than provide businesses with a work-ready labour force — it must benefit the whole community. The following recommendations address the problems outlined in the preceding section by promoting the consistent application of a CED approach treating public expenditures as investments in the social and economic potential of communities.

Involve the Community

The collaborative arrangements under which training is provided must include more community partners. CED advocates broadly based collaboration, but distinguishes between real partnerships that involve the community and arrangements that involve only, or primarily, employers (Fontan and Shragge 1994). CED practitioners caution that "partnerships in CED are often used to disguise hierarchical relationships" in which business interests dominate (Bryant 1994). Partnerships between the province and the call centre industry are, in reality, public-private partnerships, and not media for CED. Public-private partnerships, also called P3s, have been widely criticized as poor vehicles for delivering public services and infrastructure (see Davidson 2002; Grieshaber-Otto and Sanger 2002; Robertson, McGrane and Shaker 2003, Sanger 2001), since employers' interests are not always compatible with the public good. These partnerships are typically asymmetrical, with public partners bearing most of the risk and private partners reaping much of the benefit. Indeed, there is compelling evidence to suggest that P3s have sacrificed public interests, transferred public money to private interests and undermined accountability. Even the business-friendly *Financial Post* published a stinging critique of P3s as "a rip off, a steal, a plunder, a legalized mugging, piracy, licensed theft, a diabolical liberty, a huge scam, a cheat, a snatch and a swindle" (Freeman cited in Robertson, McGrane and Shaker 2003: 4). The province has a responsibility to protect the public interest by ensuring that the costs of its partnership with the call centre industry do not outweigh the benefits. The best way for it to achieve this is to develop real partnerships that give a voice to representatives of the community.

Increase Transparency

The province's close relationship with the call centre industry sacrifices transparency to the interests of employers. The ability of public officials to protect the public interest is compromised by this intimate association, since it restricts the information they can dispense. A lack of transparency and accountability is a typical feature of P3s, which are notorious for narrowing policy options to those that are acceptable to the private sector (Robertson, McGrane and Shaker 2003). Secrecy, however, is the antithesis of CED, which seeks first and foremost to empower individuals and communities to participate in their own social and economic development (Manitoba Research Alliance on Community Economic Development in the New Economy; Shragge 1997). To meet its commitment to advance CED, the government must become more accountable to the community by making complete information available to the general populace, rather than to its business partners alone.

Protect Workers

Another negative consequence of the province's close collaboration with industry is that its ability to protect workers is undermined. This is reflected in the absence of mechanisms to protect workers' rights, and in the failure to ensure that all jobs for which people are trained are good jobs. Yet, CED is advanced only when people get good jobs in which they are treated with dignity. As MacKinnon (2006) observes, "Community empowerment and social justice must be at the heart of social economy and/or CED activities and policies." Workers who do not know their legal rights lack the basic tools necessary to demand dignity in the workplace. The province must use its influence to ensure that publicly funded training includes information about employment standards, health and safety and human rights legislation — and the right to organize.

Develop Partnerships with Unions

The inclusion of unions in training partnerships is consistent with CED values. Union involvement in workplace training programs improves outcomes for both workers and employers, and leads to higher wages, increased employability and job satisfaction for workers, as well as increased profitability for employers (Betcherman, McMullen and Davidman 1998). Unions bargain with employers to achieve good wages, opportunities for advancement, fair treatment and dignity for workers. Further, supporting workers' right to organize and involving unions in training programs would allow workers to participate in the decisions that determine the quality of their daily experience and their career chances.

Enlarge the Role of Aboriginal Liaison Officers

The creation of ALOs, who strive to foster cultural awareness and eliminate barriers for Aboriginal people, is perhaps the most innovative aspect of the province's current training practices. ALOs contribute to the promotion of CED in call centre training by monitoring the enhancement of social and economic equality, and by educating call centre managers to be more respectful of Aboriginal workers. Their success in encouraging managers to treat workers with greater respect has, most probably, had positive effects not just for Aboriginal, but for all workers. ALOs help transform bad jobs into jobs with dignity; because jobs with dignity contribute to CED, the province should expand their role and create more ALO positions.

Fund Only High-Road Employers

The province's current approach to training weights proposals from employers for publicly funded training according to their potential value for the community. Yet, despite this ranking system, a number of notoriously exploitive call centres have received funding. To be consistent with CED principles, the province must refuse funding requests from employers who do not respect workers' basic rights and whose management practices erode workers' dignity. Instead, the province should continue to support those call centres that have proven themselves to be high-road employers, and particularly those that have demonstrated a willingness to accommodate employees' decision to unionize.

NOTES

Funding for this project was provided by the Manitoba Research Alliance on CED in the New Economy, the University of Manitoba Centre on Aging and the Social Sciences and Humanities Research Council of Canada. Thanks also to an anonymous reviewer and the editors of this volume, whose suggestions have improved the paper.

1. "Manitoba Customer Contact Association/Industry Training Partnerships Management Report 2003–2006," "Employment Partnerships (LMDA) [Labour Market Development Agreement]." Received from Education and Training Services by request of author, October 14, 2005. Calculations made by the author.

2. Province of Manitoba 2005. *The Labour Relations Act*, updated to November 30. Queen's Printer. Available at <http://web2.gov.mb.ca/laws/statutes/ccsm/1010e.php> accessed July 2007.

3. Agreement between the Canada Post Corporation and the Public Service Alliance of Canada, expiry date August 31, 2008; Agreement between MTS Telecom Services Inc., (MTS), MTS Communications Inc., and the Communications, Energy and Paperworkers Union of Canada (CEP), October 5, 2001 to December 19, 2004; Union Agreement between UFCW Local 832 and the Faneuil Group, effective date June 1, 2004 to May 31, 2007; Union Agreement between UFCW Local 832 and Integrated Messaging Inc., effective date June 18, 2000 to June 17, 2003.

4. "Manitoba Customer Contact Association/Industry Training Partnerships Management Report 2003–2006," "Employment Partnerships (LMDA)." Received from Education and Training Services, by request of author, October 14, 2005.

5. "Employment Partnerships (LMDA)," 2005.

6. "Manitoba Customer Contact Association/Industry Training Partnerships Management Report 2003–2006." Received from Education and Training Services by request of author, October 14, 2005.

7. Manitoba Advanced Education and Training, September 2004. "Employment and Training (ETS) Labour Market Partnerships (LMP) Program, Program Guidelines."

Chapter Eleven

ABORIGINAL STUDENTS AND THE DIGITAL DIVIDE
Non-Formal Learning in the Inner City

Lawrence Deane and Sherry Sullivan

THE DIGITAL DIVIDE

There has been much discussion in the recent community development literature of a so-called "digital divide" (Norris and Conceicao 2004; OECD 2000). This term refers to a new form of social inequality that is based on the differential access of disadvantaged groups to information technology (IT). For example, it has been found that only 23 percent of female-headed lone parent families in the U.S. have Internet access, compared to 51 percent of all other households, and that African-Americans have fewer computers at all income levels than do whites (Norris and Conceicao 2004). In Canada, only 49 percent of Aboriginal households have a computer, compared to 73 percent of other households (Looker and Thiessen 2003).

Most proposals to address the inequality in access to IT knowledge involve initiatives to increase the availability of computers and Internet connections, or to increase teaching of the use of IT in formal education settings (OECD 2000; Norris and Conceicao 2004). Just as important as increased access to computer hardware and formal teaching in schools for disadvantaged young people, however, may be flexible assessment of their non-formal learning. Flexible assessment may also improve the employability of young Aboriginal people of the inner city by improving deflated self-perceptions. A recent study indicates that inner-city Aboriginal students tend to devalue or undervalue their abilities, and have lowered expectations of their opportunities for employment (Silver et al. 2002).

A deflated view of one's economic skill set and social position can also have long-term effects, given that success in the labour market depends on lifelong learning. Adult learning theories indicate that motivation, self-concept, perception of social roles of the learner and perceived usefulness of information are key components in the process of learning (Merriam 2001).

Also important is assisting students to make appropriate evaluations of their learning progress (Cretchley and Castle 2001). Therefore, if young Aboriginal people from the inner city are under-valuing their future prospects, the appraisal of their technology skills and the provision of appropriate feedback may make an important contribution to their employment potential over the longer term.

METHOD

This study sought to determine the level of technology skills acquired in non-formal settings by young Aboriginal people from the inner city, and to compare results to students' own perceptions of their learning. Results are based on work with ten inner-city high school students ranging in age from fifteen to eighteen years. Eight of the participants were Aboriginal, and all were residents of Winnipeg neighbourhoods at the lowest end of the income spectrum. Participants were recruited from an after-school program at an inner-city vocational school in Winnipeg. The program offers students job exposure, limited employment opportunities and skills development. Students volunteered at community clubs and non-profit agencies, sometimes being paid for their time.

Flexible Assessment

The study used a set of methods called flexible assessment, which formally, fairly and accurately assesses learning that students have gained through a range of learning situations (Wong 1996). Learning situations may be categorized as formal, structured and credentialled, such as a high school course; formal, structured and uncredentialled, such as a workshop; and non-formal, unstructured and uncredentialled, such as learning to use a computer program by oneself or with the help of a friend. Flexible assessment typically consists of portfolio assisted assessment, course equivalencies and challenge exams for standard courses. This study used the first and last of these methods.

A portfolio is a compilation of material that reflects the depth and breadth of a learner's knowledge and skills. It first collects information on learning from a wide range of settings, and then provides documentation verifying that learning has occurred. These documents may include letters of reference, certificates and descriptions of situations where skills were demonstrated. Most importantly for this study, not only is the portfolio product valuable to the learners, but the process of compilation allows the participants to become consciously aware of the skills they have developed. Mandell and Michelson (1990: 2) describe portfolio development as "a significant exercise in critical thinking." Wong (1996: 20) states:

The process of writing and organizing a portfolio is developmental; it can lead to a deeper understanding of personal strengths and weaknesses and assist the learner in prioritizing personal and academic goals.

Non-formal Assessment

All students completed portfolios assessing their prior learning during ten one-and-a-half-hour sessions, which took place over a three-month period. The process consisted of analyzing experiences in relation to a particular set of knowledge and skills statements and finding documented evidence for their statements of learning. All components of the portfolios were word-processed. Students were encouraged to be creative in their presentation, but to give the whole package a professional appearance so that it could later be used in obtaining employment.

Students then self-assessed their employability in fifty-two specific skill areas on a scale of one to five using a transferable skills checklist. Ratings were documented by concrete examples of how they had used the skills. For example, under the general heading of "organizing," they assessed themselves on the skill "keeping records." Students thought about a time when they had kept records, and then incorporated the experience into a statement beginning with "I can." One statement read, "I can keep records of money and objects. I have managed a canteen at the community club and kept track of cash and inventory." Students were prompted throughout this process by facilitators, who asked questions such as "When you worked at the community centre, what did you have to keep track of? What things did you have to write down?"

Students also made non-formal assessments of their computer skills. Participants' self-ratings were assisted by an IT self-assessment tool, which is part of the Prior Learning Assessment and Recognition (PLAR) package for computer skills developed by the Province of Manitoba for Adult Learning Centres (Government of Manitoba 2006). The tool was helpful in familiarizing participants with formal IT terminology in preparation for post-secondary challenge exams. Since it is common for individuals undertaking a self-assessment to underrate their abilities because they are not familiar with technical terms for tasks or skills, or because they do not associate these terms with tasks they already know how to perform, understanding the terminology was important. This was clearly demonstrated in many instances when answers to an "I can" statement changed from a "no" to a "yes," once unfamiliar terminology had been explained. For example, items such as "I can use a scroll bar" or "I can identify the parts of a URL" were initially answered "no." When the meaning of "scroll bar" and "URL" were explained, however, these answers often changed to a "yes." Many students made a breakthrough in self-perception once they saw their score change from a failing to a passing grade.

Formal Assessment

After the portfolios were completed, participants were taken to the campus of a post-secondary technical college where a number of standardized, challenge-for-credit examinations in two post-secondary IT courses were administered. These evaluated technical proficiencies required for the courses "Computers in Business" and "Word-Processing Theory and Practice," which are offered as part of the Business Administrative Assistant course at Winnipeg Technical College (Winnipeg Technical College 2006). These courses are offered for dual credit, meaning that successful completion is worth credit at both the secondary and post-secondary levels.

Interviews

Following portfolio development, and again following the challenge exams, students were interviewed about their perceptions of the range and level of their employment skills and their specific knowledge of IT.

FINDINGS

Results were produced in three forms: portfolios provided documentary evidence of general employment-related skills and knowledge; challenge exams gave formal evidence of non-formal IT learning; and open-ended interviews gathered participants' self-perceptions before and after assessment. The outcomes of these three measurements are discussed below.

Portfolios

Portfolios captured learning through experiences such as volunteering and organizing an annual general meeting for a non-profit organization; part-time work, for example at a fast food restaurant; and personal interests, including auto body repair work and playing a musical instrument. All experiences were related to action statements, such as "I can."

Interviews

During the interviews, students described the experience of creating their portfolios, and it was evident that they recognized and appreciated strengths, achievements and goals of which they may have been only vaguely aware. The comments of some participants capture this discovery process:

> Thinking about [job skills] I didn't even know that that tied in with this kind of thing. Like "supervision." I didn't know I was supervising. Never came into my head, "Oh, I'm the boss now."

> McDonald's asked [when I applied], "What can I bring to this job?" I'm like, "Um." [This] made me realize what I can actually do.

Table 11.1:
Scores in Standardized Exams in Post-Secondary IT Courses

Student	Computers in Business	Word Processing Theory and Practice
1		64
2		63
3	64	80
4	66	80
5	61	76
6		50
7	60	59
8		68
9		66

Source: Winnipeg Technical College

I learned I could speak in public more than I thought I'd be able to. I'm not really a public person. I'm usually shy.

I'm very good with remembering numbers and facts. I'm a human telephone book.

When I was reading through and reading the examples I was like, "Holy, I never knew I could, like, know how to do that... and it sounds so hard!"

Challenge-for-Credit Exams

Nine of the ten students were assessed using challenge-for-credit exams. On the standardized tests, all nine students obtained at least one post-secondary credit, and four students obtained two credits. Student grades are shown in Table 11.1.

DISCUSSION

This study was formative and exploratory. The measurements of primary interest were students' perceptions of their abilities before and after assessment. It was found that inner-city Aboriginal students did undervalue their general levels of skill, and in particular that they underrated their knowledge and skills in IT. The study also found that although many of the students did not have a computer at home, they had learned IT skills in non-formal situations to an even greater extent than in the classroom. The challenge exams showed that this non-formal learning was sufficient to earn at least one course credit at the post-secondary level and had significant relevance to their employability.

This study demonstrates the importance of making flexible assessment methods available to students who, because of minority status, racial stereotypes and economic disadvantage, are prone to devalue their own knowledge and abilities. It supports the position that flexible assessment is important in providing education and employment opportunities for disadvantaged groups. Although it can be argued that a majority of people undervalue or discount their non-formal learning, and that virtually everyone might be surprised by a formal assessment of their abilities, the evidence suggests that inner-city Aboriginal students devalue their knowledge to a greater extent than do non-Aboriginal inner-city students. In terms of equity, it is important that interventions creating an appropriate balance for these students are made.

Given the role of self-perception and the importance of making objective assessments of progress, access to flexible assessment can motivate students to engage in lifelong learning and encourage them to move on to subsequent stages of adaptation and employability. This type of intervention should be made a critical component of public strategies to address unequal access to information technology.

Chapter Twelve

ABORIGINAL LABOUR AND THE GARMENT INDUSTRY IN WINNIPEG

Raymond Wiest and Cory Willmott

For decades, the Winnipeg garment industry work force has traditionally been composed primarily of women, most of whom have been immigrants. As of 1982 there were eighty-one apparel firms employing a total of 6,468 labourers, with 82.9 percent of production workers being women (Ghorayshi 1990: 278, 282). Seventy percent of garment workers in the industry were reported in 1981 to be of a non-English speaking background (Ghorayshi 1990: 281). While the trend of garment work being performed mostly by immigrant women continued in the 1980s, their predominant ethnic origin had shifted relative to the 1920s and 1930s, when women in the Winnipeg garment industry were mainly of Eastern European background. By the 1980s, 60 percent of garment workers were from South Asian countries such as India, China, Vietnam, Pakistan and the Philippines; as well, a few were of Aboriginal background (Ghorayshi 1990: 281). From the 1990s until the industry downturn that began in 2004, garment workers have been largely of Asian origin, although they are increasingly from Central America and the Caribbean (Mossman 2006: 22–26, 42).

For a considerable period of time the garment industry benefited from government support for special immigration policies designed to attract investment and labour, and to give it a competitive edge. In many areas of the world (see, for example, Ross 1997), and to some extent in Winnipeg, the growing supply of immigrant workers has translated into wage concessions and work conditions generally not tolerated by workers who are not legally constrained by temporary worker agreements. These labour conditions have, undoubtedly, contributed to profit margins deemed essential by the industry to remain competitive.

In Canada, federal and provincial governments alike have made concessions and considerable investments in order to hold and expand the garment industry. They contend that this industry, well known for its special products and innovation, has generated and maintained important investment in research and development and local employment. In recent years, however, job creation in this industry has been systemically and systematically linked to offshore production opportunities designed to address rising labour costs at home and the phasing-out of protection under the long-standing Multi-Fibre Agreement. As Yanz et al. (1999) note, an industry once dominated by large manufacturers and unionized work forces has been replaced by large retailers bidding globally for low-cost production in countries where labour costs are exceedingly low. In effect, this means that women garment workers are competing on a global scale to work for lower wages and in poorer working conditions.

The Winnipeg industry defies the national trend by continuing to rely heavily on new immigrant labour as a cost-saving measure. This practice persists despite the presence of a relatively large and underemployed resident labour force, much of which consists of Aboriginal people. In this chapter, upon outlining the cultural, historical and political conditions that influence Aboriginal and immigrant views of employment in the garment industry, we propose that the tendency to rely on immigrant labour can be explained in part by the fact that Aboriginal people do not consider work in the garment industry particularly desirable, while new immigrants with limited livelihood options do, at least for a time. Moreover, we show that historically entrenched perceptions of Aboriginal workers as unreliable result in recruitment policies that systematically favour offshore over local hiring. We conclude that the recruitment of Aboriginal people into the mainstream garment industry is therefore not a viable answer to inner-city underemployment: as an alternative, we explore an example of a Small-Scale Entrepreneurial Economic Development — or S-SEED — initiative to show how this approach to Aboriginal CED may make economic growth possible for Aboriginal residents of Winnipeg in the secondary textile industries.

This chapter draws upon authored research papers published in the *Winnipeg Garment Industry: Industry Development and Employment* (Wiest, ed. 2005), a report on research undertaken between 2003 and 2005 that assesses the impact of new technologies on the composition of the labour force in the garment industry in Manitoba.[1] An explicit objective of this chapter is to recognize research-team members whose work contributed to the theme it addresses. Team members drew upon published and unpublished documents and Internet sources, as well as interviews with government personnel, industry administrators, labour leaders and garment workers (who were primarily sewing machine operators, or SMOs). Although explicit attempts were made to locate Aboriginal people working in the garment industry, these efforts — particularly those to contact currently employed SMOs — had little success, in part because of legal restrictions on disclosure of personal information by industry and government.

FIRST NATIONS AND WAGE LABOUR
IN HISTORICAL PERSPECTIVE

Aboriginal people are particularly poorly adapted to the exploitative conditions of low-wage employment, since the concept of selling labour in a cash economy was not present in North America until the arrival of the Europeans (Knack and Littlefield 1996: 4–5). As the colonizers reallocated natural resources to agricultural and industrial uses, "ethnic niche economies" — pockets of ethnic economic activities that are contained within the mainstream economy (Halter 1995:15) — occasionally emerged that were on or near the original land bases.

Aboriginal economies were based on reciprocity, and workers were not alienated from their labour or from its products. Rather, Aboriginal peoples upheld control of the production process from the beginning to the end, either individually or communally. Once forced to participate in wage labour, Aboriginal people often attempted to maintain control of production by working only under their own terms. This often meant working when, and for however long, they chose. The viewpoint that wage labour and urban residence are only temporary and provisional measures often led to patterns of "cyclical migration" (seasonal movement between reserve and city life) and "return migration" (permanent return to the reserve after extended residence in the city) (Fixico 2000: 77; Knack and Littlefield 1996: 22–23): this was interpreted by employers and government officials as "unreliability" and "laziness."

The cyclical economic patterns of many Aboriginal groups were also a basis for the assumption of European colonizers that Aboriginal people have a poor work ethic. Traditionally, an Aboriginal group's economic position moved from extreme abundance to absolute zero and back again. One did not exert oneself until the zero point had been reached, and one did not accumulate in perpetuity, but rather for immediate consumption and/or redistribution. Removed from the ecological context in which this pattern made sense, Europeans in "civilized" regions concluded that Aboriginal peoples were "lazy, unstable, incapable of settling down to an orderly existence" (Francis 1992: 215).

The perception that Aboriginal people refused to voluntarily submit to the alienation of their labour led government officials to introduce legislation that they hoped would achieve this aim by force. From the *Enfranchisement Act* of 1857 to the first *Indian Act* of 1876 and its 1951 revision, Canadian policy towards Aboriginal peoples has treated them as "children." As the Minister of the Interior, Arthur Meighen, told parliament in 1918, "[The Indian] has not the capacity to decide what is for his ultimate benefit in the same degree as his guardian, the Government of Canada" (in Francis 1992: 202). The *Enfranchisement Act's* supposed purpose was to "assimilate" Aboriginal peoples into Canadian society through a series of stages that absolutely eliminated their status as distinct societies. The mechanism for this process was "enfranchisement," whereby Aboriginal individuals and bands lost their Indian status through gaining Canadian citizenship. However, the all-encompassing powers of the Indian Act functioned instead to foster perpetual dependency on government handouts.

In addition to usurping control of the material resource base upon which the traditional Aboriginal economy depended, the *Indian Act* claimed control of Aboriginal human capital by means of job training provided through the residential schooling system. All Aboriginal children were trained for low-wage labour according to their gender: boys learned carpentry and the like, while girls learned sewing and other "domestic" skills (Milloy 1999: 34–35).

The transformation of Aboriginal economic strategies from indigenous patterns of reciprocity to varying degrees of integration into capitalism suggests that government policy toward Aboriginal peoples has had an inordinately profound and deleterious effect on their means of subsistence, causing not only high instances of poverty, but endemic social disintegration as well. Consequently, Aboriginal people often regard mainstream society with hostility and suspicion. Nevertheless, some Aboriginal people have found ways to subvert the oppressive restrictions of the *Indian Act* by working in wage labour only when and how it suits them, and by redirecting their industrial job training toward goals that are consistent with their traditional cultural values. Key objectives of Aboriginal CED are, therefore, self-determination in addressing poverty and social problems, and the development of support mechanisms for those individuals who are transcending the legacy of social and economic oppression.

ABORIGINAL VERSUS IMMIGRANT RELATIONS TO THE ECONOMY AND THE STATE

Aboriginal peoples differ from immigrants because they were the original custodians of this land whereas immigrants are, by definition, new arrivals. Not so obvious are the major past and present consequences arising from this fact. The conceptual framework of "multiculturalism" erases the fact that the reallocation of resources that accompanied colonization resulted in the loss of economic resource bases for Aboriginal Canadians, while immigrants gained new economic opportunities. The structural relation, in which First Nations' loss results in immigrants' gain, has remained entrenched in relations between these two broadly conceived groups throughout decades of competition for unskilled low income jobs.

Position in the Winnipeg Economy

The twentieth century was marked by a dramatic trend toward urbanization. In Canada, both immigrant and Aboriginal groups played an important part in this demographic shift. There are critical differences, however, between "migration" of Aboriginal people and "immigration" of foreign-born people to the city. Aboriginal people often migrate to cities because there are no jobs on reserves. Aboriginal communities have suffered chronic underdevelopment and dependency on government funds ever since, or before, treaties were signed (Lafond in RCAP 1993: 63–64). Whether urban or rural, Aboriginal communities suffer from "bungee economics." Since neither indigenous service sectors nor ethnic economies have ever developed, money flows out of these communities at least as fast as it flows in (LeDressay in RCAP 1993: 220–24). This legacy of "unjust conquest," and the continuing paternalism embedded in the Indian Act, provide the context in which Native peoples typically view North America as a "land of deprivation" rather than of opportunity (Nagler 1970: 24). The fact that Aboriginal migrants to Winnipeg fare little better than their counterparts who remain on reserves validates this preconception. A study conducted by the Institute of Urban Studies in 2003 (36) indicated that, among a sample of 525 Aboriginal, Métis and Inuit individuals who had recently moved to the city of Winnipeg, 75 percent earned less than $15,000 per annum.

Immigrants landing in Canada face different conditions. Whether having originated in a rural or an urban setting, they anticipate permanent resettlement, economic stability and the "benefits" of full citizenship in a "land of plenty." As Delwar Jahid (2005) notes, immigrants and refugees are "drawn to a society continually ranked as a destination of choice, a society that values their contributions not simply in the economic sphere, but in a social and cultural context as well." Although immigrants who are visible minorities may face the unanticipated racial discrimination, cultural and structural factors already noted above, their migration generally presents more favourable economic prospects for them than for Aboriginal people. A report by Citizenship and Immigration Canada based on 1996 Winnipeg Census data suggests that, although very recent immigrants (those who have landed since 1990) report a higher unemployment rate than individuals born in Canada or than those who immigrated earlier, the unemployment rate among persons who immigrated during the 1980s is comparable to the rate for people born in Canada, while the unemployment rate among immigrants who landed earlier than this time is actually lower. Similarly, whereas one-half of very recent immigrants report an income of $10,000 or less, only two in ten of earlier immigrants report their earnings to be at this level, while the average income of this group actually surpasses that of native-born Canadians (Informetrica Limited 2000). Due to the historical and present success of immigrant "integration" into the Canadian economy, politicians perceive immigrants as an economic asset (see Pat Martin for Winnipeg Centre Web site).

In contrast to the endemic underdevelopment of the Aboriginal ethnic economy, the structural and cultural influences on immigrant populations often stimulate the development of various types of ethnic economies among them. Some ethnic groups develop "ethnic web economies," in which there is a "clear pattern of interconnectedness despite geographic dispersal of participants" (Halter 1995: 16–17). Other groups develop "ethnic enclave economies," which are characterized by spatial clustering and many immigrant-owned businesses and service industries that employ immigrant employees (Light et al. 1995: 27). In many cases, however, these intense concentrations of people and services continue to trade goods with their countries of origin, which has the effect of increasing both imports and exports (Head and Ries 1998).

Unlike Canada's Aboriginal peoples, if colonization is involved in immigrants' lives at all, it is in their country of origin. Once immigrants apply to immigrate to Canada, their relationship with the Canadian state is governed by the *Immigrant and Refugee Protection Act* (IRPA). Submission to the IRPA is always an achieved — as opposed to an ascribed — status that only applies if and when one chooses. Moreover, it is only active in one's life for the transitional period between application for landed immigrant status and the achievement of full Canadian citizenship. Additionally, it governs only those areas of life that pertain to entry into Canada and Canadian citizenship. The IRPA regulates entry into Canada on the basis of a point system in the areas of education, age, work experience, language ability, economic assets and job demand (David Aujla, Immigration Lawyer Web site). Although this system does not apply to the Family Class under which most immigrants enter Canada, the government's ability to "weed out undesirables" results in the perception that those who successfully gain entrance are "worthy" of support and services. Once landed, citizenship depends upon three years of permanent residency, absence of a criminal record, knowledge of Canada and the rights and responsibilities of citizenship, and proficiency in either French or English. There is no implication of sacrificing one's ethnic and cultural identity, traditions or foreign citizenship in order to gain Canadian citizenship through IRPA and the *Citizenship Act* (Department of Justice Canada Web site).

RESEARCH TEAM FINDINGS

Our research team investigated recruitment strategies and job training initiatives; hiring criteria and industry predispositions toward the potential of certain groups as a source of labour; and the perspectives of inner-city residents, including Aboriginal people, on the industry. As may be predicted from the foregoing description of historical and structural differences, fieldwork and interviews confirmed a significant disjuncture in the characterizations of industry managers, Aboriginal people and immigrant workers regarding Aboriginal, as opposed to immigrant, participation in the garment industry work force.

Recruitment and Training

Dependence on New Immigrants
Drawing upon team interviews with garment industry and labour union spokespersons, training centre spokespersons and her own interviews with resource and employment centre spokespersons, research team member Sara Stephens (2005)[2] revealed that, among strategies for the recruitment of new workers, the garment industry has relied primarily on formal recruitment, with government support, of immigrant workers. While use of this strategy has slowed rapidly over the last few years due to factory closures and an increasing reliance on offshore production (in countries such as Mexico and China), Stephens notes that the industry has continued to rely on arrangements with both the provincial and federal governments in regard to recruitment of workers (Stephens 2005: 44).

The industry's predisposition toward hiring immigrant workers may, in large part, be explained by its perception of certain characteristics of immigrant workers, which are thought to enhance the stability of a low-cost labour supply: the required skills are often assumed to be readily available from prior experience, the social connections and common language among recruited workers facilitates communication and cohesiveness among workers, and immigration conditions entail constraints on movement and job mobility. Nonetheless, some industry personnel revealed during interviews that they believed that the technology used and the work performed did not require great skill: they thought that nearly anyone could perform SMO jobs (Stephens 2005: 48).

Other Recruitment and Training Initiatives
Stephens (2005) observes that, in addition to offshore recruitment, the industry has used other strategies such as placing newspaper ads, listing openings on government job banks and recruiting directly from the Manitoba Fashion Institute (MFI) and employment centres. Also, casual "off the street" hiring in the garment industry is used to deal with worker shortages and the need to fill positions quickly. She further notes that one plant utilized an Employment Insurance (EI) officer to determine when workers lost jobs with other companies. This particular strategy underscores the importance for job-seekers of having experience in the industry, because the industry is reluctant to

put resources into job training — including that which addresses changing technology (Mossman 2006: 32–34).[3] Indeed, one plant spokesperson said that, with plant closures and worker layoffs, it was getting easier to recruit experienced SMOs in the city (Stephens 2005: 45). It should be noted that recruitment for upper-level positions has drawn upon graduates from the Clothing and Textiles program at the University of Manitoba, which does indeed provide an avenue of engagement for Aboriginal persons who have pursued higher studies in this area.

Training centres such as the MFI, an initiative of Nygard Industries, have been targets for government funding. In January 2005, however, the MFI closed its doors due to industry changes brought on by Canadian international trade policies, the rise of the Canadian dollar and pressures to adapt to the information technologies created by the "new economy" (as reported by an industry training partnership representative and Mossman 2005: 54).

De Facto Exclusion of Aboriginal People
Stephens (2005) examined team interviews to shed light on Aboriginal recruitment initiatives in the industry. She also conducted telephone contact research to determine the extent to which Aboriginal people have been, and currently are, involved in the industry.

Staff of several employment centres reported that there was little, if any, contact from the garment industry. One resource centre which had been contacted by two factories upon its opening — one of which was specifically looking to hire Aboriginal workers — had had no more contact with the garment industry, as significant downsizing had taken place in the industry since its opening (Stephens 2005: 44). Stephens (2005: 46) concludes, "Aboriginal peoples in particular were not being specifically targeted for recruitment by the garment industry." However, the low level of engagement of Aboriginal people in the garment industry may be explained by "the decline in jobs in the industry [which] could also have had an effect on the level of recruitment and the number of channels or strategies required by the garment industry to attract new labour" (Stephens 2005: 46). Furthermore, one employment centre suggested "the lack of interest was mutual, and that their clientele did not find garment industry jobs appealing" (Stephens 2005: 46).

EMPLOYER PERSPECTIVES ON ABORIGINAL WORKERS IN THE GARMENT INDUSTRY

Sara Stephens and Kathryn Mossman (2005: 108) suggest that industry perceptions may explain why only 3 percent of garment workers are Aboriginal. Team interviews with industry personnel revealed confidence in Aboriginal workers' skills, intelligence, capacity to learn quickly and ability to do good work, but these generalizations were offset by the generally held interpretation of Aboriginals as being unreliable and not committed to the job.

Generalizations that only a small percentage of Aboriginal workers are reliable may contribute to prejudicial hiring practices and treatment of labour, but the nature of garment industry jobs and the opinions of Aboriginal people toward them must also be considered. Work that is tedious and repetitious is not particularly attractive — a fact acknowledged by industry spokespersons. Ironically, industry personnel tend to invoke cultural variation to explain differences in the reliability of workers. But as Stephens and Mossman (2005: 109) observed, from the results of one interview, the social dynamic of the workplace should be considered. With many Asian people working in the industry, there often are significant clusters of people who speak the same language, share similar experiences and even belong to the same community. In contrast, they note, with so few Aboriginal workers in a factory at any given time, the likelihood of the formation of social groups that would make this work more attractive to them is low.

Immigrant Perspectives on Aboriginal Workers

In-depth research carried out by Amena Khatun[4] with a small group of Winnipeg garment workers offers some insight into immigrants' opinions on Aboriginal garment workers and interrelations between immigrant and Aboriginal workers. In her interview sample were eight former short-term garment workers whom she identified as Aboriginal, although each of these individuals dropped out of the interview program at an early stage (Khatun 2005: 70).

When asked how immigrant workers relate to Aboriginal people, and whether they are unsympathetic or unfriendly toward them, Khatun (2005: 95) reports the following response:

> No, I saw just the reverse picture. Even though we often tend to become friendly with our new colleagues from among the Aboriginal people, they seem reserved and mistrusting; they appear nervous. In fact, they appear to be restless and inattentive to work. They also seem to dislike shop-floor discipline. [She smiled and added,] Don't treat me as a racist; this is just an honest delivery of what I have felt about them.

Another excerpt represents the views of a worker from China regarding the reliance of Aboriginal people on social benefits:

> Of course this [social benefits system] is good, because it helped me to secure my own prestige and dignity without any compromise. But you know, such provisions are counterproductive for some people, like Aboriginal people. They misuse this provision... Look, I know there are so many issues that discourage the downtown Aboriginal

people to work. One is this social security system. Since they could carry out their lives some way, especially through specialized government subsidy systems in everything, they do not work. If I were them, perhaps I would have behaved like them. (Khatun 2005: 98)

An interview by Asfia Gulrukh Kamal[5] with a Sri-Lankan refugee who had completed the MFI SMO training program during the summer of 2004 reveals a complex set of relations between the numerous Aboriginal participants and different classes of immigrants. In particular, business- and family-class immigrants tended to be critical of Aboriginal women. The interviewee was "afraid to socialize with them" due to perceptions that they [Aboriginal women] were "often pregnant, sick and prostitutes," had "scary male visitors," lacked "good family planning or a stable home life," and often quit because they "had recourse to welfare." Other refugees were more sympathetic, however. One Sudanese woman in the course attempted to persuade other participants that it was their "lack of interpersonal skills" that kept the Aboriginal women isolated, "not prostitution or welfare."

Although the above examples represent only a few voices among many immigrant garment workers, their observations provide interesting perspectives on how Aboriginal workers are understood — and misunderstood.

Aboriginal Perspectives on Garment Industry Labour

To achieve a broader understanding of Aboriginal perspectives on the garment industry, our research team drew upon interviews with Aboriginal people who had experience with employment centres, garment-factory work, design and small-scale sewing businesses. Their statements suggest that the attitudes of Aboriginal people toward the garment industry depend on the type of work in question, as well as its cultural relevance.

Negative assessments of garment industry work among Aboriginal people typically point to its reputation for offering low-paying jobs. Other Aboriginal people who commented on employment opportunities in the garment industry pointed to the industry downturn, which has made jobs scarcer and less secure, and consequently undesirable (Stephens and Mossman 2005: 111). Some Aboriginal people drew attention to the preponderance of immigrant workers, and to the climate of prejudice against Aboriginal people. Others pointed to the very low numbers of Aboriginal workers, which hinders the creation of an attractive and favourable work environment.

Positive assessments by Aboriginal people of prospects for work in the garment industry draw attention to the relative safety and ease of packing and order-filling in comparison to construction or lumberyard jobs. However, the most prominent positive perception of the garment industry was identified as its potential to meet the interest of many Aboriginal people in arts and crafts, as well as to satisfy the high cultural value attached to the ability to sew. Stephens and Mossman (2005: 110) noted, however, that Aboriginal people with an interest in arts and crafts have seldom found their medium of expression in the mainstream garment industry. Rather, they were more likely to express their interest through small-scale independent businesses operated out of homes or in community-based cooperatives. In order to gain an understanding of these alternative contexts, our research team investigated a sewing cooperative that produces First Nations' "star blankets" — a kind of quilt that resonates with cultural significance. The results of this examination are presented below.

Alternative Visions: A Case Study of Northern Star Co-op

The Northern Star Co-op had its beginnings in 1988 with a group of First Nations and Métis women who had common interests in the traditions of sewing and beading. Originally, it served as a place for Winnipeg North End women to learn rug-making and quilting skills (Winnipeg Foundation Web site). Using a room in the North End Women's Centre, the Northern Star Co-op recycled unusable clothing into colourful quilts, including their signature product, the Star Blanket. Star Blankets are quilts with a characteristic star motif that stands for the Morning Star, an important deity in Native American religious traditions. Demand for these quilts grew by 1996 even without formal marketing, although success was measured as a consequence of the single item theme initially used. Additional products and motifs were added over the years, with the common characteristic of adherence to traditional themes of significance for Aboriginal and Métis peoples.

The co-op eventually outgrew its original quarters, and in 1998 moved to its own production facility where, as Northern Star Collections, it initially employed some ten persons and provided learning opportunities to a considerable number of women. According to the Winnipeg Foundation Web site, "in 1999 the Northern Star Collection was asked to present Star Blankets to each of the countries represented at the 1999 Pan Am Games." Subsequently, it added the "Anamush" Parka line. In 2001, Northern Star had to discontinue a successful training program it had offered for a period of time due to financial constraints and the extra time required for interactive training (Mossman 2005: 57).

This Small-Scale Entrepreneurial Economic Development (S-SEED) initiative was originally funded by the United Way and the Winnipeg Foundation, among other contributors. Métis designer Jennine Krauchi was on the board of the co-op when it was receiving this funding. In an interview with team member Temperance McDonald,[6] Krauchi noted that her family background influenced the idea of Northern Star. She underscored the importance of tradition and her experience working with Fleece Line Co-operative in Brandon, Manitoba, upon which Northern Star was based. There, Aboriginal and Métis women from reserves came in to do beadwork, and the products — mukluks, moccasins and mitts — were marketed across Canada and the U.S.

During the interview Krauchi also noted the difficulties of having to work on quilts while simultaneously trying to coordinate the many organizational needs. She observed that, while some have argued Northern Star has not been a "business" success in the sense of large-scale commercial achievement in Canada, "it… did bring a lot of confidence, and some [women] ended up, maybe not working there full time… but they got other jobs. And they never would have done that if they would not have gone through the whole process at Northern Star."

Our research team conducted several interviews with Northern Star Co-op personnel that strongly support Krauchi's observations. One Aboriginal woman who was involved in Northern Star Co-op reported that she first began sewing for the co-op on a voluntary basis, and then stayed on because she enjoyed it. Sewing quilts with Aboriginal designs made the work relevant to her Aboriginal background. She noted that Aboriginal-style quilts were an important cultural symbol at major life events, such as births, deaths and marriages, as well as when a person was being honoured (Stephens 2005: 111).

The presence of this co-op in the community is seen in positive terms, so recruitment is often by word-of-mouth. Persons wishing to learn to sew often approached the co-op for learning opportunities, even with no promise of remuneration. At times, large numbers of women came in from reserves — in one case, as many as thirty women came in and were trained (Mossman 2005: 56). Stephens (2005: 40) notes that "some of the women trained through the co-op were eventually recruited by large garment factories, and the co-op workers appeared to believe this was beneficial, both for the women and the community."

Northern Star Co-op has a history of financial difficulty. After several years' worth of public and private agency funding dried up, "five employees boldly restructured themselves as an independent business in the hope of keeping their jobs and craft alive. Abruptly on their own, in less than a year the co-op was on the verge of insolvency" (Rothney 2003: 7). After a period of reliance on public and private funding and continual operation near insolvency, a Pilot Project operated by Assiniboine Credit Union (ACU) worked with the co-op from the fall of 2000 to the summer of 2003 (Rothney 2003: 1), identifying a clear product focus based on co-op members' desires, on market considerations, and on their willingness to work hard to achieve commercial viability (Rothney 2003: 8). Rothney told us that, during this period, Northern Star members recognized the need to develop a high end "cultural product" rather than market toward Wal-Mart.

In this process of financial reformation, co-op members opposed a "take-control style of assistance that seemed to be out of line with self-determination and cooperative development" (Rothney 2003: 9). With volunteer sales promoters offering help, new loans could be arranged. More effective processes for handling customer inquiries and orders facilitated a more organized approach to promotion. Management efficiency improved after a thorough reorganization of the office filing systems; and better marketing awareness has led to greater appreciation for marketing- and sales-skill needs, although in the meantime, sales have increased, even without specialized sales staff (Rothney 2003: 11, 10).

While the future of Northern Star Collections will certainly not be without problems, it is clear that this initiative has been a community success in terms of offering meaningful employment and of extending valuable training to women with few employment opportunities. Also promising is its growing reputation for producing creative, high-quality products, and its impact on the community as an Aboriginal organization that offers the opportunity to produce something with cultural significance. Nonetheless, the achievement of a balance between the personal involvement of workers and fiscal management that addresses basic requirements for financial sustainability will present challenges — in the collective decision-making process, in moving beyond heavy reliance on voluntary labour and in reaching a desirable level of support for its worker members. The organization is particularly vulnerable to the balance between labour supply and production runs, and the recent hiring of additional labour will highlight the critical balance between production expansion, provision of opportunities to work and responsibility to adequately sustain employees. External support will continue to be needed, for which great compensation will be received in the forms of social impacts and contributions to community economic development.

CONCLUSIONS

The active recruitment of immigrant labour has been at the heart of the garment industry, despite the presence of large numbers of under- and unemployed Aboriginal people whose traditions value design and production of apparel. Yet the mainstream industry has never developed a proactive policy to address employment needs in the inner city. Training programs arose among industry leaders for a time, but there have been no successful initiatives — outside of the effort by the Northern Star Co-op for a period of time — with the Aboriginal population of Winnipeg.

Our research confirms predictions derived from historical barriers between the mainstream garment industry and Aboriginal labour, and from structural reasons for the uncomfortable relationship between Aboriginal and immigrant workers. We found that, for many Aboriginal people, the garment industry environment does not nurture respect for different cultural values or individual creativity. Indeed, the mainstream garment industry has even been characterized as a form of colonial oppression. Since the lack of engagement of Aboriginal people in the mainstream industry appears to be a mutual inclination, we argue that S-SEED alternatives, like the Northern Star Co-operative, should be taken seriously as a viable and productive form of CED for Aboriginal people in the textile and fashion industries. These approaches not only provide opportunities for economic advancement, but also for cultural expression and pride.

NOTES

1. The research report, "The Winnipeg Garment Industry: Industry Development and Employment," was prepared for the Manitoba Research Alliance on Community Economic Development in the New Economy, Project #1. Available at <http://www.manitobaresearchallianceced.ca/Documents/4-GarmentIndustry-revNov22.pdf> (accessed July 2007).

2. Sara Stephens earned an M.A. degree in Anthropology, University of Manitoba, 2006. Her thesis, "Concepts of 'Community' in Community Economic Development: The Social Dynamics of Community-Based Development in Winnipeg's Inner City," was in part an outgrowth and extension of her work on the garment industry research team.

3. Kathryn Mossman earned an M.A. degree in Anthropology, University of Manitoba, 2006. Her thesis was titled "Experiences of Immigrant Women in the Winnipeg Garment Industry: Gender, Ethnicity and Class in the Global Economy." Mossman was a member of the garment industry research team from its inception, which provided a research and experiential background for her thesis research (see Mossman 2005).

4. Amena Khatun earned an M.Sc. degree from Asian Institute of Technology, Bangkok, with a thesis on women garment workers in Bangladesh (see Khatun 1998). She conducted extensive research among garment workers in Dhaka, Bangladesh, 1998–2002, under the supervision of R. Wiest (see Wiest, Khatun and Mohiuddin 2003).

5. Asfia Gulrukh Kamal, M.A. student in Anthropology, University of Manitoba, joined the research team for a short period of time at the end of the project to assist with data analysis and to conduct additional interviews.

6. Temperance McDonald, a student of fashion with the BHE (Bachelor of Human Ecology) in Clothing and Textiles, University of Manitoba, and a member of the Aboriginal community, participated in the project to assist Cory Willmott with interviews with fashion designers.

Chapter Thirteen

ABORIGINAL EMPLOYMENT IN THE BANKING SECTOR IN MANITOBA

Kathleen Sexsmith with Aaron Pettman

INTRODUCTION

This chapter investigates the effects of the increasing use of information technology on Aboriginal employment in the Manitoba banking sector. The overarching goals of the research were to determine the level of access Aboriginal people have to jobs in Manitoba's banking sector; to uncover how increasing reliance on information technology in the banking sector may have affected employment opportunities for Aboriginal people; and to identify the efforts that both suppliers and demanders of labour should make in order to achieve equitable rates of employment. This chapter seeks to contribute to the discussion on the effects of the "new economy" — the structural shift in the Canadian economy toward knowledge- and technology-based work — on disadvantaged communities, as well as to suggest how the principles of community economic development can be applied so as to help these communities share in its benefits.

Demographics of the Aboriginal Population in Manitoba

The 2001 census indicates that Aboriginal people comprise 13.6 percent of the Manitoba population, and that approximately one in three Aboriginal Manitobans were under the age of fifteen in 2001. Within Winnipeg, 8.2 percent of the population is Aboriginal, a proportion that is projected to increase by about 40 percent by 2016 (Statistics Canada 2001c). The young age and rapid rate of growth of the Aboriginal population means that the job market will soon see an influx of Aboriginal job-seekers, yet it is already having problems absorbing potential Aboriginal workers. In 2001, the Aboriginal unemployment rate for Winnipeg was 14.3 percent, relative to 5.7 percent for the city overall; province-wide, these statistics were 15.1 percent and 6.1 percent, respectively (Statistics Canada 2001c).

The overrepresentation of Aboriginal people among the unemployed may be explained by low rates of secondary and post-secondary completion.

The 2001 Aboriginal Peoples Survey shows that 49.2 percent of Aboriginal adults in Manitoba did not finish high school, and that 30.1 percent of Aboriginal adults in Manitoba who have taken some post-secondary schooling did not finish the program in which they were enrolled (Statistics Canada 2001b). Poor access to communication technologies in Aboriginal communities may also play a role in their relatively high rates of unemployment: 6 percent of Aboriginal adults live in homes without telephones; 30 percent have not used a computer in the last twelve months; and 42 percent have not used the Internet in the last twelve months (Statistics Canada 2001f).

Structural Change in the Banking Industry

Structural changes since the late 1990s in the Canadian banking industry have had an impact on employment opportunities in Manitoba, where, as reported by the Canadian Bankers Association Web site, the total number of individuals employed in banking declined from 6,665 to 5,289 between 1997 and 2005. First, the introduction of federal legislation creating strict conditions for bank mergers has had a profound effect on employment patterns, since the inability to merge caused the banks to choose "internal restructuring and cost-cutting measures as an alternative to facing international competition" (Human Resources Development Canada 2001: 7). Second, financial institutions have come to rely on information technologies in an attempt to remain competitive.

Information technologies used by the banking industry belong to one of two categories: "front-office" services are used by banks when dealing directly with customers, while "back-office" services are those operations that are generally invisible to the customer (Berger 2003: 146, 151). Front-office banking technologies provide a cost-efficient alternative to traditional retail services. Technologies such as ATMs, Internet banking, electronic payments and the automation of telephone banking have revolutionized the industry by replacing front-office banking services. Meanwhile, back-office banking technologies, such as the electronic transfer of cheque information captured digitally (see Canadian Payments Association 2006 for further details on an initiative of this nature), enhance the collection, processing and distribution of financial information, allowing lending institutions to make substantial productivity gains.

OPPORTUNITIES FOR ABORIGINAL
EMPLOYMENT IN THE BANKING INDUSTRY

Representation of Aboriginal Employees by Occupational Category

Another important dimension of employment accessibility is the distribution of Aboriginal employees throughout the corporate hierarchy — it is not only the total proportion of employees that is Aboriginal, but also the advancement of Aboriginal employees through the company to senior positions that makes a financial institution a truly equitable employer. The representation of Aboriginal people in the different Employment Equity Occupational Groups (EEOGs) among the five chartered banks was determined from 2003 Individual Employer Employment Equity reports, which are available on the Human Resources Development Canada Web site. Information for credit unions and Aboriginal-owned financial institutions was acquired during interviews.

Chartered Banks

The proportion of Aboriginal persons working permanently, full-time in the banking sector across Manitoba ranges from 1.2 percent for CIBC to 5.6 percent for Royal Bank. Although the latter employer has a significantly greater number of total Manitoba employees than any of the other five major banks (1,240 as compared to less than 500 for each of the others), it still maintains the highest proportion of Aboriginal persons in its permanent full-time work force. Moreover, of ninety-nine permanent full-time employees hired by Royal Bank in 2003 — the highest number of new hires made by any of the banks — ten were Aboriginal. On the other hand, none of the forty-four permanent full-time Bank of Montreal hires were Aboriginal, nor were any of the twenty-eight new such CIBC employees. Of 197 permanent part-time hires made by Royal Bank, 7.1 percent were Aboriginal persons, again the highest number among the five banks. TD had the highest rate of Aboriginal permanent part-time hiring at 42.9 percent, though it should be noted that only seven new workers were taken on. CIBC hired the lowest proportion of Aboriginal part-time employees, at just one of forty-eight new hires.

Royal Bank advanced the highest proportion of Aboriginal employees to higher positions within the company for both permanent full-time and permanent part-time staff, and was the only employer to promote any permanent part-time Aboriginal employees. Aboriginal employees of this bank received 5.7 percent (nine of 157) of permanent full-time promotions and 8.7 percent (two of twenty-three) of permanent part-time promotions. Further, three of the nine promotions of permanent full-time Aboriginal employees were in the Middle and Other Managers EEOG. Each of Bank of Montreal, CIBC and Bank of Nova Scotia promoted only one Aboriginal employee, resulting in Aboriginal promotion rates of 2.3 percent, 4.0 percent and 2.1 percent, respectively.

Relative to their representation among permanent full-time employees in the banking sector, Aboriginal people are underrepresented in the highest and overrepresented in the lowest earning brackets. Nine Aboriginal persons earn $60,000 or more annually throughout the Manitoba banking sector, which amounts to just 2 percent of the industry's work force earning at least $60,000. A total of forty-seven Aboriginal persons in the banking sector earn less than $30,000, indicating that 7.1 percent of the work force at the lower end of the industry income spectrum is Aboriginal.

Aboriginal-Owned Financial Institutions

The first Aboriginal-owned financial institution, First Nations Bank, has one Manitoba branch, which is located in downtown Winnipeg. At the time of interview, two-thirds (four of six) of employees were of Aboriginal descent — this proportion had remained constant since the branch's opening two years prior. Two of these employees occupied entry-level positions, while the other two worked at the middle-management level. The second, MeDian Credit Union, is an Aboriginal-owned closed-bond credit union also located in downtown Winnipeg. The percentage of its employees who are Aboriginal has remained relatively constant, at 75 to 85 percent, over recent years. The credit union's Aboriginal workers were said to be distributed throughout the company. Finally, Peace Hills Trust is a trust company owned by the Samson Cree Nation of Hobbema, Alberta, which has one branch location in downtown Winnipeg (Peace Hills Trust Web site). According to the representative, approximately 85 percent of Peace Hills' employees are Aboriginal and are represented in all positions, from tellers to managers.

Credit Unions

Among the credit unions that participated in an interview, the Assiniboine Credit Union (ACU) has the highest proportion of Aboriginal people as a share of its total employees. As per 2005 data, 11.7 percent of the ACU work force is Aboriginal, a proportion that had increased from 9 percent in 2000 (Assiniboine Credit Union 2000) and had remained constant for the two years prior to the interview. These Aboriginal workers are distributed from entry-level positions through to the management level. Only three of the ten remaining credit unions also employ Aboriginal people in positions higher than the entry-level. All of the credit union representatives interviewed said there has been either no change or an increase in the share of Aboriginal employees over recent years, although this may be due to a reluctance to admit otherwise or to an increasing tendency for Aboriginal people to self-identify.

Conclusions

This analysis of opportunities for Aboriginal employment in the banking industry has shown work opportunities to be impeded by a number of fundamental barriers. Financial institutions are clustered in Winnipeg neighbourhoods and Manitoba census divisions with below average Aboriginal origin populations, meaning that banking jobs are concentrated in areas other than those where most Aboriginal people live. Aboriginal banking units have a fairly weak presence in Manitoba, further limiting employment opportunities for the residents of reserves and urban Aboriginal communities. It was also seen that, with the exception of Assiniboine Credit Union, the number of Aboriginal employees as a share of financial institutions' total work forces does not come close to reflecting their representation in the city and provincial populations at any occupational level, although Royal Bank is again deserving of mention for having accomplished much more than the other chartered banks toward achieving this goal. Finally, positions offering better pay and greater responsibility are particularly inaccessible, since the lowest rates of Aboriginal employment are found at the most senior levels.

INTERVIEW RESULTS

Twenty-three in-person and telephone interviews were carried out with representatives of high schools and post-secondary institutions, employment training organizations and labour force intermediaries; sixteen financial institutions also participated in an interview. Thirteen other interview requests received no response. Interviewees were asked about their organization's strategy for recruiting program participants/new employees; its partnerships with companies in the banking sector/the Aboriginal community; their perceptions of the effects of the increasing use of information technology on Aboriginal employment in the banking sector; and their opinions on other barriers to employment in the banking sector that Aboriginal people may face.

Education Institutions and Employment Training Organizations

Recruitment and Funding
Strategies for recruiting Aboriginal students vary in scope and intensity among high schools with vocational programs appropriate to future employment in banking, yet all secondary school educators whose facilities are located in areas with dense Aboriginal populations said they had made efforts to recruit Aboriginal participants for their programs. For example, while the Business/Computer Technology Program at R.B. Russell Vocational High School does not advertise independently, the school does place ads for its courses in Aboriginal newspapers. As well, feeder schools, which have many young Aboriginal students, are invited for tours, and open-house events promoting vocational education are held.

The recruitment strategies of post-secondary institutions are somewhat more intensive. The Aboriginal Business Education Program of the University of Manitoba uses its recruitment budget to attend career fairs as far away as Toronto and Thunder Bay; to visit high schools and adult learning centres; to place announcements on the Aboriginal Peoples' Television Network; to send videos and written promotional material by mail to high schools; and to offer tours and personal talks to high school students. Further, a $1,000 Citizenship Award is presented to the student who undertakes the greatest recruitment effort of his or her own. In rural areas, intensive Aboriginal recruitment strategies are not required due to the relatively higher Aboriginal population.

Providers of post-secondary education are in agreement that available funding is insufficient to attract and retain Aboriginal students to the necessary extent: their comments reflected a general desire for more funding meant specifically for Aboriginal students. Only two post-secondary institutions did not explicitly express dissatisfaction with the quantity of funding available to Aboriginal students, although it should be noted that one of these — the Aboriginal Business Education Program of the University of Manitoba — offers each student an admirable $5,000 to $6,000 annual scholarship funded by corporate donations. However, the director of this program also noted that band-funded students often enter the program only to have their funding not come through: it was also thought that the provision of more entrance awards could increase enrolment at the pre-program phase.

Among most Aboriginal employment training organizations interviewed, recruitment efforts are relatively indirect. For example, Partners for Careers and the Winnipeg Indian and Métis Friendship Centre post job orders at their local offices: the majority of individuals participating in PATH Resource Centre programs are self-referred. However, some Aboriginal employment training organizations undertake more direct recruitment initiatives that focus on youth or adult students. The Manitoba Metis Federation Provincial Recruitment Initiative, for instance, includes word-of-mouth recruiting, job fairs (for example, the Rotary Club Career Symposium) and promotional activities at schools and elsewhere. Another important example of less direct recruitment initiatives is the Manitoba Aboriginal Youth Career Awareness Committee, which campaigns both in Winnipeg and in rural and northern communities. This organization has involvement with about nine schools, using the recommendations of school counsellors and students' attendance and academic records to recruit program participants.

Strategic Partnerships with Industry

Representatives from both R.B. Russell Collegiate and the Aboriginal Business Education Program (ABEP) at the University of Manitoba said the Royal Bank has been a proactive partner in the creation of work placements for Aboriginal students. The director of the latter described the Royal Bank as a "well-oiled machine," since, as early as September, it plans the positions it will make available the following summer to the program's participants. Interns are often offered full-time positions to follow upon their graduation as early as the end of their third summer in the program. The ABEP director also noted that other financial institutions have expressed interest in establishing partnerships, but that such linkages have not been formed in order to protect the interests of current sponsors.

Aboriginal student work placement linkages at other high schools and post-secondary institutions are not as strong as at these two schools. Often, as in the case of the Business Administration Integrated Program at Red River College, the programs had recently been cut due to lack of enrolment. Assiniboine Community College noted that all business administration students must complete a four-month work placement in the summer, but that no special programs are in place for Aboriginal students. It was said that employment demand is so high in the rural areas the institution serves that no special program is necessary, and, moreover, that Aboriginal students have not been interested in receiving special treatment in the past.

The Urban Circle Training Centre incorporates a strong employment preparation component in all of its programs. The organization refers to its Mature Grade Twelve Diploma as its "Academic Education and Employment Program": in its literature, it declares that the program includes "job preparation skills, a six-week work placement and employment at the end of the program" (in Silver, Klyne and Simard 2003: 36). Assiniboine Credit Union and Peace Hills Trust accept many placement students from Urban Circle, as do Bank of Montreal and CIBC, all of which were said to be particularly attentive to their needs and to honour the organization's holistic approach to training.

Two other examples of relatively well-developed strategic partnerships were noted. The first is Taking Charge!, which has operated a business-banking retail program in past years. Program graduates have been placed as customer service representatives with a variety of banks and credit unions. Second, the department of Business Administration at the University College of the North includes a two-week work placement as part of its Computerized Business Applications, Community Economic Development and Business Assistant programs, through which banks in Thompson have accepted students in the past. Strategic partnerships with industry are relatively weak, in the development stage or nonexistent among the remaining education and employment training organizations serving the banking sector.

The Effects of Information Technology on Aboriginal Employment in Banking
None of the interviewees from either education institutions or organizations providing employment training services believe that information technology presents a barrier to Aboriginal employment in the banking industry. An educator at the high school level felt that the ability and desire to attend classes and acquire technical skills were more relevant. Three interviewees from post-secondary institutions noted that, although proficiency in information technologies seems to initially depend on whether or not students have arrived from a rural community, by the time of program completion there is no difference between Aboriginal and non-Aboriginal graduates. Interviewees representing two employment training organizations felt that poor mental health, poverty and a low level of education affect comfort with

new technologies — and thus employability — in an equal way for both Aboriginal and non-Aboriginal people. Another commented that a more important determinant of technological know-how is the period of time for which an individual has been out of school, with skills being higher the shorter this period is.

Participants did, however, identify poor access to new technologies at institutions providing employment training to Aboriginal people and, more generally, the relative scarcity and unreliability of information technology in the geographical areas where Aboriginal people tend to live as significant problems. The representative from the University College of the North said the increasing use of information technology was a challenge to the university itself, since it must ensure that the equipment and software used in business programs is up-to-date with local industry standards. Other interviewees in the education field observed that northern schools experience financial problems with the integration of technology into the classroom, and that Internet connections in that region are unreliable.

Perceived Barriers to Aboriginal Employment in Banking
Interviewees mentioned a wide range of social and economic issues that they believe present barriers to Aboriginal employment in the banking sector. Some individuals perceive Aboriginal people as suffering outright labour-market discrimination and exclusion from the person-to-person "network" that leads to word-of-mouth hiring. Some interviewees also mentioned that Aboriginal hiring tends to be concentrated in entry-level positions, which leads to discouragement and may inhibit future advancement.

Interviewees suggested that the misunderstandings created by differences between Aboriginal and mainstream culture result in learning difficulties for Aboriginal people during schooling and when seeking employment. Aboriginal education specialists suggested that the lack of Aboriginal content, the non-Aboriginal approach to education in the mainstream school system and the lack of funding for First Nations Schools create learning difficulties. Workplace problems said to be caused by the cultural divide include the perception by Aboriginal employees of unwelcoming physical and emotional environments; a lack of Aboriginal role models for new Aboriginal employees in the industry; an approach to problem-solving founded in the Aboriginal world-view, which, since it is based upon consensus, conflicts with the mainstream approach of argument and critical thinking; a lack of formal education (specifically, a lack of training in mathematics at the high school level); and the pervasive stereotype that employee retention rates are low among Aboriginal workers, which lowers the likelihood that they will be hired.

The lack of formal communication between Aboriginal communities and the banking industry was also named as a barrier to the employment of Aboriginal people. First, there are not enough financial institutions on reserves to provide significant employment opportunities to rural Aboriginal people. Second, the human resources departments of the major banks are, for the most part, located outside of Manitoba. As a result, banks remain unaware of a growing and increasingly skilled pool of prospective Aboriginal employees in this province.

Also relevant is the lack of formal communication between employers and employment training organizations. With the exception of Urban Circle, none of the interviewees said their organization was making a concerted effort to contact financial institutions in order to become aware of hiring standards for technological and other skills. As well, very few have developed work-experience components to their programs in cooperation with employers. By not using the input of prospective employers in the design of programs, these organizations cannot be sure they are adequately preparing their students for employment in the banking industry.

Not all interviewees, however, perceived Aboriginal people to be at a disadvantage in the banking industry labour market. The contact at Red River College observed that despite a relatively high rate of attrition among Aboriginal students, the success rate in the labour market for those who complete the course is extremely high. Moreover, although representatives from Assiniboine Community College and the Aboriginal Business Education Program at the University of Manitoba cited social issues as possible inhibitors to employment, both noted that these problems apply equally to non-Aboriginal students. Each of these individuals believes that financial institutions are eager to increase the proportion of Aboriginal graduates in their work forces. One must cautiously note, however, that the interviewees who did not perceive a disadvantage for Aboriginal relative to non-Aboriginal job-seekers represent institutions that have strong connections to the private sector, are located in major urban centres and whose graduates are highly coveted by employers by virtue of their post-secondary diploma or degree.

Companies in the Banking Sector

Recruitment Strategies and Strategic Partnerships
Efforts to recruit Aboriginal employees by the five chartered banks primarily involves attendance at career fairs, posting job openings at Aboriginal organizations and having membership to equity associations. It was noted by the CIBC representative that recruitment methods were more personal in rural areas, in the sense that branch managers communicate directly with Aboriginal organizations representing individuals seeking employment. Banks' working relationships with the Aboriginal community in Manitoba are not particularly well developed. Some companies, such as BMO, had a number of associations — it was said by a BMO representative that the com-

pany works with Urban Circle, an Aboriginal student group at Red River College and the Aboriginal Business Education Program at the University of Manitoba. The interviewee from CIBC, on the other hand, said that the bank has not had any formal partnerships with Aboriginal organizations located in Manitoba for the two years leading up to January 2005. [1]

All three of the Aboriginal-owned financial institutions interviewed actively recruit from Aboriginal organizations. Successful sources for new Aboriginal hires included the Centre for Aboriginal Human Resource Development, the Assembly of Manitoba Chiefs, the Manitoba Metis Federation and the Human Resources Development Canada Web site, in addition to Aboriginal training organizations within Winnipeg. None of these companies offered short-term work placements to Aboriginal learners at the time of interview.

Assiniboine Credit Union is the only credit union interviewed currently undertaking a well-organized effort to recruit Aboriginal people and to partner with Aboriginal organizations. Although the company is not federally legislated to meet diversity regulations, it chooses to do so out of commitment to employment equity as a business principle. Assiniboine aims to maintain a ratio of Aboriginal employees to its total work force equal to the rate at which Aboriginal people are represented in the surrounding community. Retention of employees who are members of the designated groups is another corporate goal. A turnover rate for Aboriginal people of less than one percent has been attained, which the interviewee noted to be ten times lower than the Aboriginal turnover rates of most other similar organizations.

The Assiniboine Aboriginal recruitment strategy is succinct, thorough and successful and should be used as a model by other financial institutions. This strategy has eight components: the establishment of relationships with Aboriginal networks and with employment and education agencies; the use of work experience and job shadowing programs, and summer employment opportunities for students; the definition of parameters around full-time and part-time employment; flexibility in compensation negotiations; the concerted effort to hire from colleges and universities and to provide on-the-job training towards positions in technical, professional and management roles; the provision of scholarships or bursaries for college or university students with the offer of potential employment upon graduation; the use of referrals from existing Aboriginal employers; and the inclusion of an Aboriginal person on the selection committee when hiring Aboriginal employees (Assiniboine Credit Union 2000). The company says it recruits directly from Aboriginal centres whose students are making life changes, such as Urban Circle, the Manitoba Aboriginal Youth Career Awareness Committee, Red River College, adult learning centres and Aboriginal job fairs, seeking out individuals whose education and employment backgrounds do not make them ideal job candidates.

Short-term work placements are an important component of Assiniboine's Aboriginal employment strategy. The partnership with Urban Circle, for which Assiniboine is a member of the Employer Advisory Committee, offers learners significant opportunity for career development through job-shadowing and the offer of employment upon graduation from the training program. These employees start at entry-level positions and subsequent efforts are made to advance them through the organization, with some being advanced to the management stream. Assiniboine has also participated in the Aboriginal and Black Youth Internship program in partnership with Manitoba Education and Training and the Province of Manitoba Career Start program (Assiniboine Credit Union 2000).

Aboriginal recruitment strategies and working partnerships with the Aboriginal community are almost nonexistent among the remaining Manitoba credit unions that participated in an interview. Two credit unions mentioned past partnerships with three different Aboriginal organizations, and one mentioned having attended a job fair at Assiniboine Community College where some inquiries — though no applications — were received from Aboriginal students. The representative from Vantis Credit Union commented that the company is putting together an initiative on Aboriginal employment, although it is still without a formal action plan.

The Effects of Information Technology on Aboriginal Employment in Banking
None of the company representatives who have had personal experience with Aboriginal applicants or employees perceived information technology to be a barrier to Aboriginal employment in the banking sector. Representatives of Aboriginal-owned financial institutions, which have particularly high rates of Aboriginal employees, were particularly strong on this point. One said that the Aboriginal community is becoming as astute with information technology as the non-Aboriginal community, since many individuals have taken computer software courses: another observed that information technology has been the backbone of the company's growth, and that their employees have had no difficulty with the increasing reliance on new technologies.

A number of interviewees mentioned that résumés are not examined for information technology skills because these can easily be taught on the job, although some noted that they would not want to hire an individual with zero computer experience. Rather than single out technology skills, most respondents made specific mention of customer service and sales experience and a positive attitude as the primary factors in hiring decisions.

Perceived Barriers to Aboriginal Employment in Banking
Financial institution representatives were generally in agreement regarding the barriers that may hinder Aboriginal people from gaining employment.

First, cultural differences were perceived to be an issue. Some individuals commented that Aboriginal people seem to prefer a work environment where they are surrounded by other Aboriginal people. For this reason, they may not be attracted to employment in a financial institution (although it was noted that this would work in the favour of the Aboriginal-owned companies) or, at a minimum, may be intimidated due to a false impression of a "stodgy" work environment. At least five employers observed that Aboriginal applicants are less forthcoming during interviews or tend to be less self-confident. All commented that such shyness conflicts with the sales- and service-oriented nature of entry-level banking positions.

Second, a few employers mentioned that a comparatively lower level of education among the Aboriginal population presents a barrier to their employment. It was recognized by one credit union representative that the Aboriginal population has a lower level of education, on average, due to relatively poor access to education, and not through any fault of their own. Finally, it was observed that post-secondary education is a requirement for high-level positions, and therefore may be a barrier to advancement through to senior levels of financial organizations.

Some employers acknowledged that their recruitment and retention efforts are insufficient. One chartered bank representative commented that, in order to attract Aboriginal applicants, her organization should be doing a better job of selling itself to the community as a prospective employer, and of promoting Aboriginal employees from within. The representative from Assiniboine Credit Union observed that many other financial institutions do not understand the principles of employment equity and are not sufficiently supportive of a diverse work force. For instance, Assiniboine provides diversity training to all of its employees: the company representative observed that such cross-cultural training is lacking in most other organizations' equity strategies.

Conclusions

This section has revealed that, with the exception of the Urban Circle Training Centre in Winnipeg, education institutions and employment training organizations offering programs for Aboriginal people seeking jobs in the banking sector generally do not have strong enough connections with industry to provide short-term work opportunities for students, nor is their approach sufficiently holistic to ensure students' comfort in the learning environment and success in the workplace thereafter. Similarly, except for Assiniboine Credit Union, the Aboriginal hiring and retention strategies of financial institutions were found to lack the sincerity, consideration of cultural differences and resourcefulness necessary to achieve an equitable rate of Aboriginal employment.

It has also been shown that access to employment in banking is not hindered in any important way by the increasing use of information technology by financial institutions. Although people who come from remote communities tend to enter education or employment training programs with a lower level of technology skills, they tend to graduate on par with their peers. Rather, a lack of experience in a sales- and service-oriented environment is generally considered to be the primary skill requirement that Aboriginal applicants are lacking. Negative stereotyping among employers about the poor work ethic of Aboriginal people, cultural differences and a relatively low level of education also present significant barriers to Aboriginal employment in the industry.

RECOMMENDATIONS

The following are sets of recommendations that education institutions/employment training organizations and companies in the banking sector should follow to foster improved rates of Aboriginal employment in the industry. These suggestions stress greater consideration of cultural differences, better communication and stronger connections between organizations working with Aboriginal learners and industry and an increased role for labour market intermediaries.

Recommendations for Education Institutions and Employment Training Organizations

- Increase the availability of financial support.
- Provide pre-program training in mathematics, science and the use of information technology.
- Improve recruitment strategies through personal engagement with the Aboriginal community.
- Create a culturally appropriate, non-intimidating learning environment.
- Emulate the welcoming, holistic approach of Urban Circle Training Centre.
- Communicate skills requirements to industry and increase awareness of a skilled Aboriginal labour pool.

Recommendations for Companies in the Banking Sector

- Work with labour force intermediaries to increase work placement and internship opportunities in the banking industry.
- Work with labour force intermediaries to develop the Aboriginal employment strategies of smaller financial institutions.
- Provide cultural sensitivity and diversity training to employees.
- Emulate the culturally appropriate, resourceful approach of Assiniboine Credit Union.
- Communicate skills requirements to education institutions and employ-

ment training organizations.
- Work with labour force intermediaries to create new banking positions in Aboriginal communities.

NOTE

1. Information on recruitment strategies and strategic partnerships was derived from both interviews and 2003 Individual Employer Employment Equity Reports for BMO and CIBC; information pertaining to RBC, TD and Scotiabank was derived from 2003 individual employer Employment Equity Reports only, since these banks did not respond to interview requests. The Employment Equity Narrative Reports of the five federally regulated chartered banks operating in Manitoba can be accessed on the Human Resources Development Canada Web site using the search tool for individual employer information at <http://www19.hrdc-drhc.gc.ca/~eeisadmin/cgi-bin/INTRO.cgi> accessed July 2007.

Chapter Fourteen

MANITOBA ALTERNATIVE FOOD PRODUCTION AND FARM MARKETING MODELS

Kreesta Doucette and Glen Koroluk

Research Advisory Committee: Vicky Burns, Janine Gibson, Blair Hamilton and Fred Tait

OVERVIEW OF AGRICULTURAL SECTOR IN MANITOBA

Manitoba's agricultural sector is currently experiencing a farm income crisis, a situation precipitated by the steady decline in grain prices since the 1980s, high interest rates during the early 1990s and the withdrawal of agricultural subsidies. While the gross value of agricultural production in Manitoba reached approximately $3.7 billion in 2001, an increase of 23 percent over 1997 levels, realized net farm income has been largely static (Manitoba Agriculture and Food 2003a). More revealing is that Manitoba's outstanding farm debt amounted to a record high of over $4 billion in 2001 (roughly $200,000 per farm), an increase of 43 percent over levels seen five years before (Manitoba Agriculture and Food 2002).

Many analysts attribute the farm income crisis to the industrialization-led consolidation of agribusiness. Ikerd (2002) defines agricultural industrialization as a three-stage process led by industrial specialization, which is followed by standardization and, finally, consolidation. By the final stage, the number of people (or corporations) holding decision-making power has been reduced. At this juncture vertical and horizontal integration are achieved, where "horizontal" refers to the merging of companies in the same line of business, and "vertical" to the merging of firms occupying different positions on the supply chain (such as a fertilizer company merging with a food processing company). Vertical and horizontal integration tend to reduce competition, as well as to increase the relative power of the new firm in the marketplace (Ikerd 2002). Indeed, Qualman (2001) demonstrates that ever-fewer corporations are controlling a large and growing share of the inputs and outputs that form the food industry chain.

Industry concentration has produced a modern farming and food-processing system characterized by Stonehouse (2001) as heavily dependent on sophisticated technologies, intensive use of resources, large-scale operation and extreme substitution of capital for labour. This system has provided opportunities for the growth of certain agricultural sub-sectors in Manitoba, such as the livestock, potato and genetically modified canola industries.

These changes are observable in Manitoba, where average farm size has increased almost 14 percent from 784 acres in 1996 to 891 acres in 2001 (Manitoba Agriculture and Food 2002). A similar expansion has occurred in segments of the livestock sector; notably, intensive hog operations have nearly doubled in average size over the same time period to 1250 hogs (Manitoba Agriculture and Food 2003b). As farm operations have grown larger, the land under production remains the same but fewer people are participating in farming: between 1997 and 2001 there was a loss of slightly more than 3,200 census farms in Manitoba, a decrease representing approximately 14 percent (Manitoba Agriculture and Food 2002). Manitoba Agriculture reports that the decline in farm numbers from 1996 to 2001 was the largest ever over a five-year period.

Shifting from Global to Local: Global Food Security and Sustainable Agriculture

This chapter investigates two producer-consumer food models which have been implemented in Manitoba farming communities as examples of alternatives to the industrialization and concentration of the agricultural sector: Community Shared Agriculture and The Winnipeg Humane Society Certified Labelling Program for dairy and meat products. Each of these intends to reduce the distance food travels "from gate to plate" and to decrease the use of agricultural practices deemed to be potentially damaging to ecosystems and consumers. Ultimately, these food models are intended to increase producers' share of revenues, or equally, to return a greater proportion of agricultural earnings to the farm "gate."

MANITOBA COMMUNITY
SHARED AGRICULTURE

In November of 1991, Manitoba farmers and interested individuals gathered for a series of five meetings to brainstorm ways of creating "an agri-food system that directly links the farmer with the consumer in an environmentally just way" (Dyck 1994: 234). The group developed the concept of "Shared Farming," a term coined by farmer/market-gardener Dan Wiens. Realizing that their concept was similar to international models such as *teikei* in Japan and Community Supported Agriculture (CSA) in the United States, the group attended a CSA conference in Michigan where they furthered their understanding of the system.

CSA is a partnership between a farmer and local consumers, wherein members of a CSA purchase a share of the farm's harvest prior to the growing season. This form of partnership guarantees a market to farmers, and ensures that the risks and benefits of agricultural activity are shared by the producer and consumers. CSA farms use organic, and sometimes biodynamic, principles. They may assume a number of organizational structures, which have included family operations, worker or consumer co-ops, non-profit organizations and multi-farm systems. Shareholder involvement ranges from subscription service CSAs, where consumers act only as "silent partners," to models where they actively participate in physical labour and decision-making.

The Shared Farming model was featured in newspapers and other publications across Manitoba. Dyck (1994: 238) states that, through media attention and "proselytizing efforts," over twenty Shared Farms were initiated across the Prairies in one year. As of 1995 there were approximately twelve CSAs operating in southern Manitoba (Ecological Farmer's Association 1995; Beeman and Rowley 1994; Salm 1997); by 1997, there were only seven remaining CSAs in the province (Salm 1997). In 2003, three of these continued as fully operating CSAs farms while a fourth was phasing out the CSA system. Only two farms had firm plans to offer shares in 2004; a third was seeking an individual to take over the operation of the farm for a one-year period. Together, the CSAs remaining in 2003 offered 363 shares, ranging in price from $260 to $325, and provided fresh produce to a reported 1044 people for approximately thirteen weeks of the year. These farms offered 11.5 seasonal employment positions.

Findings

Research on Manitoba CSA farms involved key document review, key informant interviews, in-person and telephone interviews and self-administered consumer surveys. An earlier study by Katkins in 1997 interviewed several of the same farms. In total, fourteen farmers on four (of four) current and five (of seven) former CSA farms were interviewed in January 2004. The four currently operating CSA farms are referred to as Farms #1 through #4 in the sections that follow. Farm #1 is family-run, ten acres in size and hires 2.5 additional farmers to farm cooperatively; Farm #2 is a registered, non-profit workers' co-op which employs five farmers and has four acres of land; and Farm #3 is family-run, two acres in size and relies on the labour of family members and volunteers. All three operations are organic, although Farm #3 does not have organic certification. Farm #4 was in its final year of CSA operation at the time of interview. Self-administered member surveys were conducted at each of Farms #1 and #3, with fifty (of a total of ninety-five) members responding for Farm #1 and eighteen (of a total of twenty) members responding for Farm #3. Results from a phone survey conducted by Hemery et al. (2003) provided data for sixty-three members of Farm #2.

Producer Motivations

While all current CSA farmers indicated that financial considerations factored into their decision to introduce the CSA model, social, environmental and ideological concerns were said to be primary motivations for their decisions. Farmers from Farm #1 clarify their motivations for initiating CSA farming as follows:

> [CSA] works well because I love the break from my office job… it's ideal. We love it. You couldn't ask for a better situation really, to do what you love during the summer… and have people involved and benefiting from it. We Shared Farm to build a form of agriculture that accounts for social, economic and environmental justice. We're idealists, but we make money as well. We love gardening and want to nudge agriculture back to a more human form doing what we love.

A farmer from Farm #3 states that:

> We farm because we believe it's important… Even though money is certainly important to us, it's not the main reason we do it. We could go and get part-time jobs and earn a whole lot more money per hour then we do doing this… never mind pension or health benefits. We do it to supplement our pension and… socially it connects us with other people we wouldn't otherwise connect with.

The main farmer from Farm #4 described her motivations as follows:

> We were already farming organically… I decided to stay home and still wanted to bring in income… I was interested in the educational aspect of city people reconnecting with the land and people were always finding their way out to our farm anyway so we just tried it. (Katkins 1997)

For all farmers cited above, the introduction of CSA was intended as a strategy for diversifying farming livelihood. Farm #2, which functions as a workers' co-op for new Canadians, focuses solely on farming. All farms also sell produce at farmers' markets.

Of the five former CSA farmers who participated in an interview, two began CSAs because they had excess produce they wished to sell, while a further two began CSA farming specifically to diversify their farm incomes. One former CSA farmer had initiated the operation primarily for philosophical reasons.

Consumer Motivations

Members of Farms #1 and #3 were asked to rank, from a set list, their top five reasons for having joined a CSA. "[To] get fresh produce" was the dominant reason for both, with 34 percent of respondents from Farm #1 and 63 percent from Farm #3 selecting this option. "Want to eat local produce" was the second most-chosen option, with 26 percent of Farm #1 consumers and 35 percent of those from Farm #3 including this reason in their ranking.

Consumers were also asked for their perceptions on the economic value of CSA shareholding. The weekly cost of shareholding is twenty-five dollars for Farm #1, twenty dollars for Farm #2 and $23.80 for Farm #3. Nearly all consumers from all three CSA farms indicated that they had received sufficient or excess produce (Farm #2 data: Hemery et al. 2003). A majority of respondents representing Farms #1 and #3 think the cost of their CSA share relative to that of produce purchased from the store to be either lower or the same. It should be noted that while 65.3 percent of respondents from Farm #1 said the price of their CSA share was lower than the cost of purchasing produce at the store, 38 percent of those from Farm #3 believed their share to be more expensive. Hemery et al. (2003) note that 87 percent of Farm #2 shareholders surveyed were satisfied or very satisfied with the price of their shares: 59 percent reported the overall value of their share as being good or excellent. Differing volumes of produce received at each farm and previous experience purchasing organic produce (often more expensive) may explain differences in satisfaction.

When asked, "What would improve your membership in the farm," 39 percent of respondents from Farm #1 and 50 percent of those from Farm #3 indicated their desire for increased produce choice. This sentiment was especially strong among Farm #3 respondents, the remaining 50 percent of whom named "More fruits/berries" as the way to improve their CSA membership.

Labour

Participant observation revealed that farmers who engage in CSA have diversified skill sets, since intermediaries are removed. A CSA farmer becomes manager, marketer, producer, processor, packager, retailer, distributor, delivery driver, public relations and volunteer coordinator, accountant and educator. In addition to diversification of labour, the CSA model increases the volume of labour for production. Current Manitoba CSA farmers indicated sources of increased labour requirements as follows: crop diversity, succession planting, diversified harvesting, seed saving, consumer expectations of bug- and dirt-free produce and associated labour, and research and techniques required for organic production.

Three of four current and all former Manitoba CSA farmers mentioned increasing age and decreasing physical ability as challenges to their operation of a CSA. Farms #1 and #4, as well as three former CSA farmers, indicated that decreased access to family labour was a further challenge. Of the five former CSA farmers interviewed, three noted the draining of available labour and low levels of consumer participation as reasons for having to discontinue CSA farming.

However a farmer from Farm#1 stated that:

> Any kind of market garden is a lot of work, I think CSAs are less work. You can regiment yourself better with CSA... it's a great thing for us because it is an assured market and the money [is] up-front. There is a lot of work that we put into any pound of produce, it's less in Shared Farming than it would be otherwise because it is all assured and it is paid for in advance. So in the end I think economically it makes a lot of sense, all the sense for us. We pick what we know we're going to need and we deliver it and that's the end.

All four currently operating CSAs use volunteers and employ labourers from outside the family. The two largest operating CSAs (Farms #1 and #2) have full-time apprentices and additional paid farmers; Farms #3 and #4 benefit from volunteers through the Willing Workers On Organic Farms program (WWOOF), as well as from other youth. Former CSA farmers reported using no labour external to self and family at the time of CSA operation.

Shareholder participation in CSA farming for educational and logistical purposes is central to the concept of CSA. However, to date, former and current CSAs in Manitoba attempting to include working shares — wherein members receive discounted or free memberships in exchange for farm labour — have met with little success.

Gender and Labour Patterns

Of the twelve current and former CSA farms interviewed, five were female-headed, two were male-headed, and four were co-headed by a female-male couple; the twelfth was run by a male head farmer, but involved board members of both genders. There was no strong indication among currently operating CSA farms of greater total participation in farm work by men or women: in two cases, more workers were male than female; in two others, contributions to farm work were either equal by gender or more time was put in by females. In terms of the actual tasks performed, women on the currently operating farms were responsible for bookkeeping, organic research, consumer relations and produce production. Meanwhile, men performed field work, including ploughing and share preparation, and tended livestock, with one being responsible for bookkeeping.

On Farms #1 and #3 some disagreements between men and women over time devoted to the CSA enterprise were observed. In these cases the men in the family were interested in increasing the scale of the CSA, requiring the family to spend more time participating in farm labour, while the women lobbied for decreasing its scale and increasing family time instead.

Economic Considerations

In comparison to a typical conventional family farm, the home-based and smaller-scale approach to CSA in Manitoba has decreased the costs of acquiring farming capital, since the relatively labour-intensive methods employed in small-scale organic production and other forms of sustainable agriculture have resulted in lower requirements for machinery and other mechanized physical capital. Further, farmers have been able to use their home facilities for processing and transportation, thereby reducing costs associated with post-harvest activities as well.

However, CSA farmers indicated that attaining the physical inputs necessary for agricultural activity is difficult due to the low profitability of CSA farming. An exception to this trend was Farm #2, whose non-profit status rendered it eligible for charitable grant funding, with which it procured greenhouse materials, a tractor and irrigation equipment. Farm #2 and Farm #4 also cited transportation costs as prohibitive relative to the financial returns of CSA farming. In order to overcome this barrier, the former plans to relocate at least part of its farming activity closer to the majority of shareholders.

In some cases, "organic farmers are motivated by emotion rather than economics.... Often, these people are subsidizing their farms through other income, although some may not realize just how much they are, in fact, subsidizing it" (Baker, cited in Comeau 1999). The head farmer from Farm #4 explains that her ideological motivations for CSA farming are strong, but that the drains the operation is causing to her asset base have resulted in her discontinuing her CSA operation:

> I remember from our accountant I had given him just the hours that I had kept track of and that was just when I was in the greenhouse... the hours that I was in the garden, well, I forgot about all that stuff. I didn't write down all my hours. So just with the spring hours he figured I made sixty-five cents an hour. So that means I must have went way below that because I didn't count my hours in July, August and September. Insane... You don't do it strictly for the money but you have to make something to survive. When you went over the

books [my husband's] wages off-farm were subsidizing us feeding those families in the city. You could see it directly.

Similarly, former CSA farmers cite drains to economic and human capital as their reasons for having to discontinue the model. Three of the five former CSA farmers interviewed found the financial returns to their labour too low to meet their needs. In fact, two of these were full-time farmers who had entered into CSA primarily for the purpose of improving their financial situation. One farmer stated, "the farm was my sole source of income, and between the customers' attitude[s] and my labour, I was going broke so I sold my property"; the other simply stated that it "wasn't worth our while."

Minimizing stress and keeping working hours to reasonable levels appear to carry much weight with farmers when defining their membership size. One CSA farmer, whose operation had a waiting list for membership, stated:

> We could actually do two hundred shares on this farm with the amount of land we have. We don't just do it just because we can. It's based on what kind of life we want to live. We base it on that.

Given the high priority placed on choice and quality of life, it appears that small-scale Manitoba CSA farmers would have to charge a higher share price to make a "fair" wage.

Currently operating CSA farms planning to continue CSA operations in the next growing year experienced financial outcomes in 2002 as follows: Farm #1 made $2,500 in profit; Farm #2 suffered a net loss of $21,000; and for Farm #3, pre-salary revenues were $3,800. It should be noted that both heads of household in Farm #1 have alternative sources of income and that both farmers from Farm #3 are retired: they therefore depend on the CSA for only a small percentage of their household income. The CSA model appears to meet the personal requirements of these remaining CSA farms on a sufficient scale to warrant its continued use as a livelihood activity.

Conclusions

In summary, our findings indicate that the CSA model can be used as a livelihood strategy for rural producer households to diversify household incomes through pre-paid consumer membership. The ability to choose one's livelihood appears to be a key element in the decisions of producer households to incorporate the CSA model into their farming activities. Other producer motivations include personal values, household sustainability, developing community bonds and the incorporation of intergenerational stewardship into financial planning. In addition, both producers and consumers are motivated to participate in the CSA system by a desire to participate in an alternative market structure, which promotes ethical choice, trustful exchange, environmentally sustainable practices and the development of social capital.

However, several challenges associated with CSA farming are apparent. Former CSA farmers identified low levels and seasonality of income, transportation of produce to shareholders and greater labour requirements than other forms of marketing as challenges that eventually caused them to abandon this agricultural model. Members also created some difficulties through unwillingness to contribute labour to the CSA, expectations of immaculate produce of greater variety and longer availability, and a lack of appreciation for the philosophical underpinnings of the CSA model. Above all, farmers' ability to participate in CSA is threatened by its seeming inability to ensure the financial sustainability of producer households.

HUMANE SOCIETY CERTIFIED
LABELLING PROGRAM

The Humane Society Certified (HSC) Labelling Program, established in 2002, provides certification and labelling for meat produced in accordance with the standards developed by animal welfare organizations. This program intends to respond to the inadequacies of existing legislation for animal welfare in meat production, described by Huddart (1999) as follows: "by focusing on conventional containment systems the recommended codes of practice for the care and handling of farm animals tend to support the status quo without generating incentives or recognition for enhancements to animal welfare." Currently there are no inspectors enforcing the recommended codes of practice, and existing animal welfare legislation is not called into play unless a breach of animal welfare is reported or observed.

Meat receiving certification from the Winnipeg Humane Society (WHS) has been produced at farms inspected by an independent certifier. The WHS standards with which these inspectors are trained to ensure compliance include:

- No hormones or unnecessary antibiotics in feed (that is, antibiotics can be administered when the animal is sick but not as growth promoters);
- No animal by-products in feed;
- Prohibition of the caging of animals for prolonged periods of time;
- Mandatory space allowances;
- Natural flooring and light; and
- Mandatory inspection by a WHS trained certifier. (Animalnet 2001)

The costs of certification are between $150 and $175 per year; however, farmers often receive a 10 percent price premium for certified meat through agreement with retailers and restaurants.

Findings

The following sections present the results of interviews with a local certifier, seven retailers, five restaurants, a meat broker and organizational program staff. Interviewees were identified by key document review, Internet searching and snowball sampling. Key informant and in-depth interviews were then conducted.

Sales

For the majority of the time that the program has been in operation it has not included a meat broker in its sales network. The current HSC meat broker indicated that the scale of demand is only sufficient to justify the marketing of specific or prime cuts. For example, one high-end grocery store/deli would be willing to order twenty carcasses' worth of pork loins per week; however, to do so would be unprofitable for the meat broker because there is currently insufficient demand for the rest of the carcass. This meat broker is currently selling turkey in Manitoba using the HSC label.

As of the fall of 2003, only two stores of the seven original retailers in Winnipeg continued to carry HSC meat, stocking mainly beef or turkey/chicken. Neither of these retailers was selling these products with the HSC sticker displayed. One store absorbs the HSC premium because it does not perceive consumers' willingness to pay to be high enough to achieve large sales volumes. The other store states that two to three percent of its meat sales are from HSC beef. While it has observed an increase in customer demand for naturally produced meat, it does not anticipate sales to exceed 1.5 times maximum levels unless a crisis occurs in the mainstream meat industry.

In addition, five restaurants/chefs currently purchase, or have purchased in the past, HSC meat. Among current purchasers, one restaurant procures 150 to 200 kilograms of turkey per week from a meat broker, but does not advertise the product as HSC-certified. Another occasionally purchases HSC beef, either through a meat broker or directly from a farmer. The final chef purchases HSC meat directly from the producer, but does not advertise the product as "humane." Rather than market this as HSC-certified, he feels it should be promoted as grass-fed so that restaurant patrons are not reminded of the slaughter. Among former purchasers, one restaurant was originally interested in purchasing HSC lamb and individual portion-sized chickens but has been unable to find a supplier. Another included a dish featuring HSC-certified meat on its menu, but had to drop the item because it was not profitable.

Overall, grocery stores, meat retailers and restaurants get the sense that consumers are more interested in purchasing a "natural" or organic meat product, raised without hormones and antibiotics, than one labelled as "humane." This identifies the need for broad-scale education campaigns on the value of humane meat labelling. Also, the lack of a meat broker for most of the program's operation forces producers to engage in the direct marketing of whole or half animals, a quantity that tends to be too great for most restaurants and individuals. As such, stakeholders identified the need for an intermediary, such as a large retail store, to meet buyers' needs for smaller-scale purchasing.

Barriers

The HSC Labelling Program has been attacked and discredited by a number of groups with interests in the conventional Manitoba meat industry. Both non-organic and organic producers appear to have been affronted by the label of a "humane" standard, rejecting the implication that their animals are reared in an inhumane manner. Large corporate meat producers also seem to have felt threatened by the HSC program: the reports of three sources suggest that retailers and restaurants were warned that they would not receive supplies of other meats from commercial packers if they carried HSC meat. Finally, HSC producers have faced opposition from the federal government, which has indicated that it will not allow the HSC label to make use of its slaughterhouses. In 2002, Howard Hilstrom, then a Canadian Alliance MP, called humane labelling confusing to consumers: "The biggest problem is that it tends to turn urban Canadians suspicious of how our livestock are raised in the countryside.... There's no truth to the fact that there's inhumane treatment of animals or that our food supply is unsafe" (CBC News Online 2002).

The U.S. Consumers' Union (2002) has developed a guide for evaluating the effectiveness of environmental labels. They suggest that an effective eco-label could be described as follows: meaningful and verifiable; consistent and clear; transparent; independent and protected from conflict of interest; and providing opportunities for public input. While the HSC program appears to meet the first three criteria, it may fall short of meeting the latter two. First, the Winnipeg Humane Society's membership and participation in the lobby group Hog Watch Manitoba may have jeopardized the perceived independence of the program. Second, public involvement in the design of the certification program should, according to the Consumers' Union, include consumers, environmentalists and social sector and industry representatives. However, industry representatives provided minimal support from the program's outset and continued to be hostile throughout its operation. The same can be said of government, as support from Manitoba Agriculture and Food, while never directly sought, was not forthcoming (personal communication, Burns 2004).

Conclusions

The HSC program did not reach the required threshold in the marketplace to make it economically viable and is currently in limited use. However, the

Manitoba experience does imply that humane labelling should be further explored as a model for meat production. In fact, established programs in other parts of the world are growing in consumer acceptance (for example: Freedom Farm in Great Britain; Free Farmed in the U.S.). The humane labelling system is further supported by a recent investigation carried out by the Leopold Center for Sustainable Agriculture (2003), whose findings suggest that a label indicating locally grown food with a connection to family farms surpasses even "grown locally, organically" in its marketing power. Since the current glut of meat intended for export has caused farmers to turn their attention to the local market, the use of eco-labelling can provide important opportunities to Manitoba meat producers to increase their sales through product differentiation.

OPPORTUNITIES FOR DEVELOPING
LOCAL FOOD SYSTEMS

This chapter recognizes that the development of a vibrant local food economy requires a diverse array of policy and financial instruments; it does not suggest that, under current conditions and at their current scale, the food models under investigation present "silver bullet solutions" to the farm income crisis in Manitoba. Along with other direct marketing programs such as U-picks, community gardens, road-side stands, food buying clubs and subscription services, these models present niche alternatives to the current food system which can be included in broader community economic development strategies working to create more self-reliant food economies.

Research has shown that in order for direct-to-consumer marketing models to have a positive effect on the local economy and to increase farm viability, they must pool their marketing resources (Kirschenmann 2003; Levins 2004; Mahoney 2004). Scott (2001) reported that in addition to direct marketing, producer cooperation and supply management schemes were found to increase farm product prices relative to expenses. By joining forces, farmers can increase their buying and marketing power, and non-financial resources such as knowledge and labour can be shared (Agriculture Rural Renewal Alliance 2000).

Just as important as farmer alliances is partnership between producers and consumers. Kirschenmann (2003) points out that rural-urban coalitions or food and agricultural councils are required because rural communities and farmers no longer have the political clout necessary to bring about a shift towards local food self-reliance, sustainable agriculture and food security. The Organic Food Council of Manitoba, one of twelve chapters of the Canadian Organic Growers, is a multi-party coalition which could provide organizational backing to this end at the provincial level. Comprised of gardeners, farmers, food distributors and retailers, its mission is to be a leading information and networking resource promoting the growing and distribution of organic food for its environmental, health and social benefits (OFCM 2004).

Resources, Education and Skills Development

Weurch et al. (2002: 35) identified "organic producers' lack of marketing knowledge and regulations needed to sell to retailers" as weaknesses in Manitoba's organic sector. They also found that "many producers are not trained in pricing, packaging, transporting, negotiating, selling and marketing of their products." In order to make the transition to sustainable and organic farming, adequate resources, skills development and training will therefore be required for farmers and rural communities. The Agriculture Renewal Alliance notes that farmers "must get off the technology treadmill; while not turning their backs on technology, farmers must focus on improving the pool of knowledge from which they can draw rather than uninformed acceptance of new and costly measures," because "knowledge, inasmuch as it is an investment in people rather than machines and technology, empowers farmers and allows them to achieve their full potential" (Agriculture Renewal Alliance 2000: 2).

The extension services offered by Manitoba Agriculture, Food and Rural Initiatives are very varied, and have significant geographical scope, ranging from financial planning and crisis management to business planning and on-farm diversification. However, the department's work is currently oriented toward Manitoba's agricultural policy, known as Destination 2010 and, to some extent, the Agricultural Policy Framework. This policy does not support local food systems and sustainability; rather, it advocates export-led expansion of the agricultural sector and the increasing size and degree of specialization of farms. Extension services must have a greater focus on the promotion of organic agriculture: Manitoba Agriculture, Food and Rural Initiatives, with over 650 full-time staff, lists only one employee as an organic agriculture specialist.

A 2002 national survey by Macey (2004) on the state of organic agriculture reveals that Manitoba has a long path ahead — a mere one percent of Manitoba farms (200 producers) have organic certification. MacRae (2003) suggests the program supports required to successfully move to organic farming include transition planning, conversion services, training programs and mentoring systems. The recent inclusion by Assiniboine Community College of organic agriculture in its curriculum has partly filled the gap in services. Also, the Organic Producers Association of Manitoba has launched a mentoring program to assist those wishing to make the transition to organic agriculture. It is unmistakeable that adequate financial investment will be required, especially in times of government spending cuts and program withdrawals. This could be accomplished by diverting the massive subsidy and incentive programs from specialized conventional farms, which encourage exports, to sustainable and organic agriculture for local consumption.

RECOMMENDATIONS

The following are specific recommendations that have emerged from this research and may assist the development of small-scale agriculture and alternative food systems.

1. Manitoba should endorse Canada's Action Plan for Food Security and also develop a provincial food policy, which would place greater emphasis on food self-reliance and sustainable food production systems.
2. Any future renewal of the Agriculture Policy Framework must place greater emphasis on sustainable and organic agricultural practices, local food systems and on-farm diversification, and must financially favour small- to medium-scale family farming enterprises.
3. Manitoba should adhere to its current *Sustainable Development Act* and Financial Management Guidelines, which call for the government to perform a sustainability impact assessment for major agricultural projects to which it provides assistance.
4. Program funding, subsidies, human resource allocations, training programs, education programs, outreach and research support provided by Manitoba Agriculture, Food and Rural Initiatives must shift towards local food systems, sustainable agriculture and organic production.

Chapter Fifteen

AGRICULTURAL LAND TRUSTS

Preserving Small Farm Heritage

Blair Hamilton

This chapter examines the suitability of an agricultural land trust as a community economic development (CED) intervention in the Rural Municipality (RM) of Franklin, located in south-central Manitoba. With a land area of 953 square kilometres, Franklin is divided into two distinct regions. The portion of land east of the highly visible escarpment is characterized by trees, rocks and sandy soil, and is used largely for beef or dairy cattle; to its west, the land is flat with few trees and has soil which can be described as "Red River gumbo," meaning that it is good for growing grain.

The 2001 Census Community Profiles (Statistics Canada 2001f) reported the RM of Franklin to have a population of 1,724 that is characterized by increasing age and low levels of education attainment, but also by a high level of employment. Specifically, Franklin reported a 0 percent unemployment rate in 2001, with many residents being employed in the agricultural field (by Industry of Employment classifications, 33 percent are considered to be employed as such). Despite this, residents have income levels at 71.6 percent of the Manitoba average, and also experience a gender gap in full-time earnings that is significantly greater than the Manitoba average.

The Manitoba agricultural sector has been moving toward increased farm size and higher capital investment. In fact, in 2001 Manitoba recorded the third-largest average farm size among all provinces (Statistics Canada 2001d). The average Manitoba farmer owns $162,811 worth of machinery, and about 44 percent of Manitoba farms have a total capitalization of $500,000 or more (Statistics Canada 2001d). In 2000, 46 percent of Manitoba farmers had off-farm employment (Manitoba Agricultural Review 2003): the average farm family received 73.5 percent of its income from off-farm sources (Agriculture and Agri-Food Canada 2001).

The realities of modern agriculture are manifest in the Census Division to which Franklin belongs (Census Division #2), which has a higher incidence of both high-grossing farms and low-grossing "hobby" farms (defined as farms earning less than $2,500 annually) (Statistics Canada 2001d). Analysis of assessment roll data for parcels of agricultural land of twenty acres or greater within the RM of Franklin in the period from 1982 to 2002 reveals the following:

- the total number of landowners is decreasing and the average size of holding is getting larger;
- the number of the very largest landowners (2,560 acres and greater) seems to have been static over the last twenty years;
- the number of very small rural acreages (159 acres or less) has gone up, suggesting an increase in the number of hobby farms;
- the number of holdings of 320 to 639 acres has seen a sharp decline; yet
- half of the agricultural landowners in Franklin own between 160 and 639 acres (Municipal Assessment Rolls, Rural Municipality of Franklin).

This suggests that the smaller family farm is under some pressure in Franklin, but that a critical mass of small acreages continues to exist.

Despite the many negative impacts globalization has had on rural communities, many people seem to cling to a free-market ideology. A model that places importance on the non-economic dimensions of farming, and takes an alternative approach to property rights, presents a challenge to this way of thinking.

THE LAND TRUST MODEL

Under the land trust model, donated and purchased land is assembled and made available for specified uses, which can vary according to the type of trust. These uses must be ones that are perceived to benefit the community, but that cannot generate sufficient revenues to compete for land in an unrestricted market. Land trusts are usually charitable organizations, which can issue tax receipts for donated land or money. Funds to purchase land are typically provided by individuals, foundations and government.

The proponents of the agricultural land trust model identify a few shared rationales. These include land affordability, access and sustainable use, as well as a belief in some broader community interest in how land is used. The land trust is seen as a way to balance the legitimate rights of the individual with the interests of the larger community, and to assemble land that is literally "held in trust" for community benefit in perpetuity. Having identified these common motivations, a review of the issues surrounding property rights, of the various types of land trust and of legal mechanisms for adjusting property rights is necessary for the development of a particular land trust model.

Types of Land Trusts

Different types of land trust exist to address the many possible combinations of property rights and interests. There are, however, some elements common to almost all land trusts, as recognized by the Institute for Community Economics (1982: 34) and Lawless (1994: Chapter 2):

- the land trust is incorporated as a non-profit corporation, separate from Government;
- the land trust is democratic in nature (one member, one vote);
- the land trust membership is open to all within a given community, balancing memberships between land users and the community at large; and
- the land trust exists to restrict land use in some defined way.

Land trusts often have two additional features:

- there is sometimes split ownership of the land and of improvements to the land — the trust owns the land and the lessee or the user owns the improvement; and
- the trust usually has first option to purchase any improvements, and the price is set by a formula that prevents windfall gains.

Lawless (1994: Chapter 2) offers what is probably the most useful categorization of land trust types:

Conservancy: These trusts aim to prohibit development in order to conserve habitat or sensitive ecological land. Sometimes trusts conserving local historical sites are included in this category.

Stewardship: These trusts are structured to provide for "principled management" of land. This would include trusts that stipulate organic agricultural production or sustainable forestry practices as a condition of using the land.

Economic: These trusts are structured to achieve certain social and economic goals, such as affordable housing, preserving family farms, or local economic development.

In this chapter, the agricultural land trust is seen primarily as an economic form of land trust, intended to address some of the adverse economic impacts of modern agriculture. An overview of the legal mechanisms used by land trusts will illustrate some of the different issues that may arise from the various types of trust.

Agricultural Land Trusts

The development of agricultural land trusts is a relatively new phenomenon: most of them are designed to address the loss of farmland to urban sprawl and ex-urban development. Another innovation, which is even less common, is the use of the agricultural land trust model to address land access issues created by agriculture itself. Consideration of an agricultural land trust assumes that the broader community has a legitimate interest in land as a resource and in how it is used. Lawless (1994: Chapter 2) indicates that an agricultural land trust should address four fundamental goals:

1. promote the economic stability of family farming;
2. increase the ability of new generations to enter farming;
3. preserve the quality of farmland by minimizing negative environmental impacts; and
4. minimize the negative impacts of some agriculture on rural communities.

It is presumed that smaller family farmers who are able to make a living from their farm and then pass that livelihood on to their children will be less likely to use farming techniques that have a negative impact on the land and environment. The model also assumes that smaller family farms will have greater motivation to mitigate negative impacts on their neighbours. Since the constitution of the family farm, and the weight given to each of the goals, will vary among communities, a proposed agricultural land trust must attempt to define these goals in a meaningful way to develop a common understanding of the project.

For a land trust to emerge there are three preconditions which must be met. These are:

1. The community must have a common identity and be bound by common issues or think of themselves as a community;
2. There must be a critical mass of interested people and potentially available land; and
3. The defined community must be small enough that the land trust will be viewed as a local, grassroots effort.

Once these preconditions are met, it will be possible to form a land trust. In order to subsequently launch and operate the land trust, four "necessary conditions" must also be met. These are:

1. Membership: The land trust must be able to define its membership;
2. Land Use: The land trust must include a definition of how land is ac-

cessed and what acceptable uses for it are;

3. Decision-Making Process: The land trust must be based on a consensual process for planning and making use decisions, including those regarding the granting of leases; and

4. Conflict Resolution Process: The land trust must have a consensual process for resolving conflicts over land use, production practices, interpretation of policy and other issues.

If each of these preconditions and necessary conditions is in place, a community can generally overcome organizational and logistical challenges to the successful initiation of a land trust.

THE GENESIS LAND CONSERVANCY

The Genesis Land Conservancy (Genesis) is an agricultural land trust based in Saskatchewan, dedicated specifically to assisting new farmers earn a livelihood and farm in a sustainable way.[1] It is a faith-based initiative, originally conceived and incubated by local religious orders as a way to pursue Christian principles of justice and stewardship. Genesis generally takes title to trust land and leases it to eligible farmers, rather than use easements.[2] In early 2004 Genesis had seven parcels of land totalling 2,800 acres: in 2007, the acreage has increased to over 3,000 acres. The land is located in mid-Saskatchewan, both east and west of Saskatoon, with the majority of parcels being located slightly north-east of this city.

Farmers wanting to lease Genesis land must be "beginning farmers," defined as having a net worth less than $250,000 and a net farm income of $20,000 or less. There is also a "softer," second criterion concerning commitment to sustainable farming practices. Genesis strongly encourages organic agriculture; at the time of interview, three of the seven parcels were fully organic and another was in the process of transition. Genesis trust land generally forms only a portion of the farming operation of the leasing farmer, who will normally have personal ownership of other land in the area. The Genesis land is therefore an incremental addition to the farmer's operation, and is intended to improve the operation's viability. At the time of interview, only one of the Genesis parcels included a residence, although two more parcels of land with residences were scheduled to be included in the near future.

The Genesis Land Conservancy is governed by a board with eight members: four represent the founding religious orders, two are elected from the general membership (including leasing farmers), and two are elected from major donors (those who have given a gift of a quarter-section of land or $50,000 at some point in the last five years). The Conservancy is "nested" within Earthcare Connections, a non-profit organization which operates other programs supporting sustainable agricultural and sound environmental practice. While Genesis receives no direct government funding of any significance, it does have the ability to issue charitable tax receipts, which can be viewed as an indirect source of government support. Virtually all of the land has been acquired as voluntary contributions.

The strength of the Genesis land assembly strategy is threefold. First, it offers a number of mechanisms by which land can be donated, including direct gift, bequest made in a will, preferred sale, joint ownership and retained life interest.

The second strength of the Genesis land assembly strategy lies in its focus on communication with prospective contributors of new land; thus the organization successfully puts a human face on the land trust arrangement by showcasing individual donors and explaining their motives for participation in the land trust agreement.

The third strength of the Genesis model lies in its long-term approach to planning. The organization's estate planning and retained life interest approach reflects the acknowledgement that it may have to wait for years to realize the incorporation of some enlisted land into the trust. Also, the past histories of land parcels are emphasized and linked to future use as part of the Genesis communication strategy. In these ways, the overall strategy reinforces the conceptualization of the land trust as a permanent community institution.

Several features of the Genesis model, however, raise questions and concerns. The first potentially problematic issue is that, when compared to other land trusts, the tenants/lessees of trust land appear to be under-represented in the Genesis governance model. A second matter of concern is the model's wide geographic scope: Genesis land is spread over a large area, making it less likely to be viewed as a local initiative. A third concerning feature of the Genesis model is the lack of easements among the properties it holds. If Genesis were to develop its land acquisition strategy to include the use of easements, the land area impacted would increase, thereby enhancing its capacity to have a positive impact on farmers in the region.

It would be presumptuous to characterize these observations as shortcomings; rather, these issues should be monitored over time to make a proper assessment of their impacts. The Genesis Land Conservancy can generally be considered a strong agricultural land trust model with much direct relevance to the development of land trusts in the Red River Valley.

SOUTHERN ALBERTA LAND TRUST SOCIETY

The Southern Alberta Land Trust Society (SALTS) is an agricultural land trust based in south-western Alberta, which came about as the result of intense development pressures created by the expansion of the city of Calgary.[3] The purpose of the organization is to preserve the land base and agricultural livelihood involved in cattle ranching. The SALTS uses the term "conservation" extensively when describing its activities and purpose. The organization uses conservation easements to preserve existing cattle ranches and prevent future owners from changing the use of ranch lands. The trust appears to include seven easements, totalling 3,800 acres.

The SALTS does not aim to provide access to new farmers, but rather to facilitate the intergenerational transfer of existing ranches without jeopardizing their working cattle-ranch status. The use of easements is therefore particularly appropriate to the SALTS model. As part of its easement-focused strategy, the SALTS undertakes broad education initiatives on the danger of fragmenting or losing ranch land, and provides extensive tax, estate and succession planning resources to current ranch owners.

The organization's self-described "rancher-driven" approach is reflected in its governance structure, since stewards (ranchers) hold 50 percent of the eight existing director positions. Other directors are drawn from the community at large, and have experience or expertise in the areas of conservation or environment, or in the non-profit sector.

The SALTS appears to be supported by a diverse range of funding and in-kind contributors. It is not clear if it receives any direct funding from government, although Alberta Agriculture, Food and Rural Development, the British Columbia Ministry of Agriculture, Fisheries and Food and the Saskatchewan Department of Agriculture and Food are listed as partners. The organization has also established an endowment fund, the proceeds of which will underwrite its operational costs over the longer term.

The SALTS has two major strengths as an agricultural land trust model. The first is the diversity of its funding contributors and fund-raising strategy, seeing that it has been able to build an impressive level of support among government, foundations, the corporate sector and individuals. The second is the articulation of its reasons for preserving ranch land. The SALTS explicitly recognizes that the linkages between land, the natural environment, human use, economic activity and food production cannot be reduced to an economic calculation. The communication of this notion is central to enlisting support for the development of a land trust.

The principal shortcomings of the SALTS model are its exclusive focus on cattle ranching, and its failure to address how new farmers might gain access to land. From a local perspective, however, these are not seen as shortcomings, but as evidence that the SALTS has been locally designed to meet specific local needs. Even with these apparent limitations, the SALTS would appear to be a significant potential resource for any future land trust contemplating the use of easements in southern Manitoba.

COMMUNITY RESPONSE

Three community meetings were held during March of 2004 for the purposes of this research. These meetings began with a presentation that discussed general trends in agricultural economics, as well as agriculture and land ownership in Franklin; gave an introduction to the land trust concept; and provided two examples of land trust models operating in Canada. During the second half of the meeting, community members were asked to comment on the presentation and to give feedback on the local applicability of the land trust model.

Participants agreed that land ownership is becoming more concentrated, that the capital requirements for farming are increasing and that farms have been increasing in size. As one participant observed: "Thirty years ago, you could make a living off of fifty cows; today you need two hundred." Half-section farms are no longer seen as viable, and most felt it was imperative for farm survival that they grow. There was some concern that continued growth in the size of farm operations may result in absentee landownership and a growing group of commuting agricultural labourers, neither of whom would be active in community institutions in the same way as residents. One participant said that while the land trust may provide an alternative, a model that helps ten to twenty people will not have an impact sufficient to reverse these trends.

Although they were concerned about developments in agriculture, they saw these changes as eventualities and seemed somewhat resigned to their inevitable impacts. People were concerned about rural depopulation and the impact it has on the community's ability to retain businesses, services and infrastructure. As a consequence of this phenomenon, rural residents are forced to travel farther for, and to face less choice of, suppliers, retailers, trades people, health care and education.

Participants were asked if small-scale farming should even be preserved. It was made very clear in their responses that in choosing to farm on a small scale, one must be prepared to have either outside employment or a very modest standard of living. This is not to say that the quality of life is not good on small-scale farms; it simply implies that a minimum standard of living must be upheld. Some people felt it is possible to scratch a living out of a mixed farm of 640 acres, although this would result in simple living. Even if one is prepared to work outside the farm or take in less income, other pressures may arise from small size. For example, suppliers of feed, machinery and inputs have less time for small producers, who face higher per-unit prices, and the need to comply with food safety and environmental regulations is more burdensome on the smaller operator.

Participants were asked to identify positive features of the land trust concept. Their comments included: its permanent nature as a community institution; its being removed from the political cycle; that it uses longer leases, making it more practical to improve land and to plan; its incorporation of the principle of sustainability; that the model lends itself to cooperative and neighbourly collaboration; that the model leaves open the possibility of government assistance; and that professionals, non-farmers and other external people sit on the board, providing a more objective opinion. Trusts that help new or young farmers are seen as particularly attractive, as are those that have a local design, and thereby meet local needs.

Meeting participants were also asked to rate the desirability of a list of features which could be incorporated into a land trust. Most were ambivalent as to whether the leasing family should live on the leased land or not. It was generally felt that the most important goal of the land trust is that it be of assistance to new farmers. Local heritage preservation was seen as highly important by about half of respondents. It was clear that the issue of whether lease land is chemical-free has the potential to be divisive. Some respondents were quite sceptical, feeling that organic standards are too strict and could dramatically reduce the number of people willing to lease land. In contrast, there was general support for the idea of requiring lease families to use non-intensive, traditional production techniques. There was also general support for using the land trust to conserve the natural environment and wildlife habitat, although this was not seen to be necessary as an overriding principle. Rather, preservation was seen as secondary to the economic goal of promoting small-scale sustainable farms.

Meeting participants were also asked to identify the features of the land trust model that most concerned them. Responses included: that successful land lease applicants may face jealousy or resentment from unsuccessful applicants, leading to damaged social relations; that the trust's board might place unreasonable restrictions on land use; that the model is likely to require off-farm employment; and that it addresses only land issues, and not equipment or stock needs. Furthermore, conservation easements were not generally seen as a popular feature.

SUITABILITY FOR LOCAL USE

The overarching objective of this study was to determine whether a land trust is suitable for the Rural Municipality of Franklin. The researchers used a two-step approach to assess the suitability of the model. First, the appropriateness of the goals of an agricultural land trust to Franklin was determined, as well as how these goals might be interpreted in the local context. The second step was to ascertain if the necessary preconditions exist, or can be made to exist. The results of this analysis are presented below. A general match of goals and the meeting of preconditions were considered sufficient to say that a land trust might be suitable for Franklin. The specific strategy for planning and implementing the land trust would have to be determined by the citizens who undertake the initiative.

Goals for an Agricultural Land Trust

The first goal of an agricultural land trust is to promote the economic stability of family farming. Indeed, farm and land ownership in Franklin continue to be rooted in the family, and family farming is a still a reasonable economic proposition for some families in the area; however, their number is shrinking. Moreover, Franklin has experienced a loss of young adults, particularly those who are educated, which may be related to the lack of economic stability in farming. There is also evidence of a growing class of agricultural labourers who do not necessarily have access to land and who earn relatively low wages. These factors indicate that an agricultural land trust designed to lower the cost of accessing farmland could be beneficial for family farming.

Local response to the changing face of agriculture in Franklin indicates that the impacts of globalization and structural adjustment in the farming sector are of concern to the area's residents. However, locals also seem to assume that these forces are beyond their control, and invariably measured the potential benefits of land trusts using conventional agriculture as the yardstick. When this discussion turned to the ability of agricultural land trusts to provide a full-time living, a livelihood approach that centred on several different income sources (including farming) was perceived as a necessary but undesirable option for small farmers. Overall, there was little evidence of desire to explore an alternative economy.

Area residents felt land trusts may help some farming families economically, but that they were not a general solution for the problems facing agriculture and rural populations.

The second goal for an agricultural land trust is to assist new generations, since younger farmers face numerous barriers when entering into farming. In this sense, the land trust was seen as only a partial solution, which is useful in its ability to make a tangible difference in the cost of accessing incremental land (presuming the farmer also owns other land). It does not address issues related to machinery, equipment, stock or working capital, nor does it target the difficulties created by other agents along the value chain who assume that they will be dealing with large-scale operations, that is, whether buying inputs or selling outputs, farmers face price, delivery and minimum order requirements in which a certain scale of operation is implicit. Nonetheless, Franklin residents see the land trust concept as, at a minimum, a step in the right direction, and the most favourably viewed characteristic of the land trust model was its ability to assist new farmers. Any agricultural land trust proposed for Franklin would likely need to make this a central feature.

The third goal for an agricultural land trust is preserving the quality of farmland by minimizing negative environmental impacts. Some qualified support for sustainable agriculture did seem to exist among community respondents. This was expressed as a favourable rating for trust farms that use "traditional non-intensive techniques," but that stop short of recommending organic agriculture. The concept of chemical-free trust land was seen as too restrictive, since it was perceived as undermining the ability of the farmer to make income from the land. Therefore, a proposed land trust for Franklin might take a "best practices" approach that encourages sustainable agriculture and seeks to minimize environmental harm.

The fourth and final goal for an agricultural land trust is to minimize the negative impacts of larger-scale agriculture on rural communities. The most apparent example of this damage is the above-mentioned nuisance effect of intensive livestock operations, and particularly that of hog barns. Although the creation of a land trust that excludes intensive livestock operations would not directly resolve the ongoing controversy in that sector, it might, at best, incrementally add to the pool of non-intensive livestock operators in the area.

Another potential negative impact on rural communities occurs when ex-urban developments and hobby farmers buy small acreages, fragmenting the agricultural land base. This can lead to higher land prices, loss of productive acreage and conflict over nuisances. An agricultural land trust could be an effective tool for preventing or mitigating the loss of productive farmland to residential or commercial development.

Preconditions for an Agricultural Land Trust
The first necessary precondition for the development of an agricultural land trust is the existence of a common identity or sense of community, derived from a set of common issues. While it is true that people in Franklin share similar issues and the same municipal government, it is equally true that the situation and needs of farmers vary greatly throughout the municipality: it appears that echoes of the topographic division etched by the escarpment (described above) ripple through levels of income and net worth, differences in linguistic and cultural heritage, types of agricultural activity performed and places where people shop. This is not to say that the residents of Franklin could not collaborate on a land trust project or other community initiative; rather, it implies that the design of an agricultural land trust should reflect the differences in the needs of local farmers.

The second necessary precondition for establishing a land trust is the existence of a critical mass of land and people. This precondition is met to the extent that there is no shortage of farmers or former farmers in the area, and to the extent that there is plenty of agricultural land, much of it in small holdings, owned by people with an historical link to the community.

The more critical question is whether a critical mass of supporters and potential land donors exists. Regarding the first, there seems to be a great deal of potential support among individual community residents for the core objectives of a land trust. The key to the long-term survival of any proposed land trust is support during the development process from one or more community organizations. The Triple R Community Futures Development Corporation (CFDC) and the local Franklin CDC could potentially play this role; other prospective allies which have a regional presence include the Nature Conservancy of Canada and the Crow Wing Trail Association, although their role would depend on the specific goals of the trust. Nonetheless, the emergence of a small group of activist community leaders is necessary to build and promote a vision for turning this potential into active support.

The third precondition for establishing a land trust is that the community be small enough for the initiative to be conceived of as a local, grassroots effort. This precondition, however, runs counter to the need to cast a wider geographic net in order to assemble the critical mass of people, land and technical expertise necessary to run a viable land trust. In the case of Franklin, there is no doubt that a land trust initiative would be small enough to be seen as local, although the bisected nature of its land would present a challenge. Use of a regional land trust structure with locally defined projects would allow different approaches to be taken in different parts of the municipality. It would also imply collaborating with a wider regional community to operate an effective land trust organization.

CONCLUDING COMMENTS

There is no doubt that ongoing changes to the face of Canadian agriculture are affecting Franklin: there is sufficient evidence to suggest that the small family farm is disappearing as a consequence of high capitalization requirements and concentration of land ownership. At the same time, it is apparent that a window of opportunity remains to preserve smaller farms, at least in the eastern portion of the municipality. Based on comparative earnings, many families in Franklin also have an implicit need for supplemental sources of income.

Objectively speaking, therefore, conditions appear to be appropriate for use of the agricultural land trust model as a suitable CED strategy for Franklin. Equally important are research findings that some residents would like to see smaller family farms preserved and are sympathetic to the goals of agricultural land trusts. Residents sensed that the changes to agriculture and the loss of the small family farm were inevitable, and that agricultural market forces would dictate outcomes. Yet the distinguishing feature of CED models is their recognition that market forces alone are not sufficient to address human needs. In this respect, Franklin participants seem receptive to the CED message implicit in the agricultural land trust model. It is also apparent, however, that they have not yet internalized this way of thinking.

Examination of the interplay of the necessary preconditions for agricultural land trust development (community identity, a critical mass of people and land, and maintenance of a local character), leads to the conclusion the citizens of Franklin would have to collaborate with residents of other municipalities to create a land trust. It appears that a regional land trust organization with the flexibility to sustain various local projects would offer a viable approach to achieving the right balance between local control and a critical mass of resources.

The implementation of an agricultural land trust in Franklin, or variations on the theme in other areas, will also have to grapple with the issue of vision and leadership. The land trust concept is built on the belief that alternative approaches to land management, and to the economy in general, are both possible and desirable. Bringing this to fruition will require a leadership that can articulate the non-economic value of family farming as a way of life and part of a community's heritage. It will require a vision that inspires local residents to look to other jurisdictions and say, "We have something worth preserving. We can do that here."

NOTES

1. Information on Genesis Land Conservancy was derived from the organization's Web site <http://www.earthcare.sk.ca/genesis/trusts.html> (accessed July 2007), supplemented by a telephone interview with staff.
2. An easement is the right to use property for a specific purpose.
3. Profile of SALTS is taken from its Web site <www.salts-landtrust.org> (accessed July 2007).

Chapter Sixteen

ECONOMICS FOR CED PRACTITIONERS

John Loxley and Laura Lamb

Despite the growing popularity of community economic development (CED) as a policy framework, it remains under-theorized in economic, political and sociological terms. On the economic side, there are two main reasons for this. First, because CED is itself a vague concept, open to many different definitions and approaches, developing a coherent theory to explain it is difficult. Second, orthodox economic theory has no interest in CED, however defined. Rather, mainstream models are preoccupied with profit maximization, short-run efficiency and individual self-interest, within a framework that accepts perfect competition as the ideal industrial structure. Huge sectors of the economy in which the market plays only a peripheral role and in which women's labour figures prominently, what Bakker and Elson (1998) have called the "care economy," are excluded from analysis, even though the market economy could not function without them.

The logic of this underlying competitive model is based on increasing scale, concentration and centralization. In reality, industrial organizations deviate from this structure and so are considered to be less than optimally efficient; this becomes the focal point of interest. Class, gender and regional inequalities are the inevitable outcomes of the orthodox theoretical model, but are treated only as irrational occurrences which would disappear if the market were given free reign. State intervention is called upon to ameliorate these inequalities, both to minimize resulting social friction and to assist the process of private accumulation. In this sense, state subsidization of the private sector is intrinsic to the system; the private sector is dependent on both overt public support, as in the granting of concessions to attract business to a particular geographic location, and that which is hidden, in the form of tax expenditures or state support for health, education and infrastructure (O'Connor 1973).

Orthodox economic theory makes no attempt to consider alternative, more cooperative forms of industrial organization, nor does it assess the macro-scale, economy-wide implications of their growth or widespread adoption. CED would fall into the group of analytical paradigms calling for a different approach to economic theorizing, insofar as it is driven by motivations other than private accumulation and narrow individual self-interest. This chapter will attempt to throw light on those aspects of the economics of CED thought to be important to CED practitioners, by examining different philosophical approaches to CED, as well as different economic strategies for its implementation.

CED AS A CHALLENGE TO
ECONOMIC ORTHODOXY

One of the difficulties in CED theorizing is the eclectic nature of its definition. To some, CED covers any economic development initiative, be it private, public or community-driven, taking place within some definition of "community" that is usually geographic. In this view, there is no necessary inconsistency between orthodox economics and CED. More demanding definitions of CED, which are coming to dominate the literature, seem to call for more radical departures from the orthodox (see, for instance, Canadian CED Network 2004; Loxley 1986b). These more rigorous approaches define CED as a social decision-making process, departing from orthodox theory in a number of ways: they replace the individual "consumer" with the collective community; they see the meeting of collective "needs" as taking precedence over the satisfaction of individual consumer "demands"; they do not artificially split decisions about production from those about consumption; they take a long view of economic activities as opposed to that of short-term profit maximization; and they see economic decisions as being inextricably linked to social, environmental, political and cultural considerations.

Within this more demanding view of CED, two schools of thought exist. The first, associated with a more radical, communal tradition, sees CED as a form of social organization that presents an alternative to capitalism. The second is more limited in its vision, seeing CED as a desirable and workable approach to dealing with particular problems facing communities, such as "unemployment, poverty, job loss, environmental degradation and loss of community control" (Canadian CED Network 2004). These problems are seen as a direct outcome of the differential and uneven effects of capitalism on certain communities, and CED is seen as a way to help fix them within the confines of the capitalist system as a whole.

The most complete set of CED principles in practice in Manitoba is the one that underlies the Neechi Foods CED model. Neechi Foods Co-op Ltd. is an Aboriginal, worker-owned, cooperative retail store in Winnipeg whose CED approach is one of building a strong, inward-looking, self-reliant economy based on goods and services consumed by people who live or work in a community. The Neechi model favours cooperative ownership, small-scale production and popular control over economic decision-making; it is a holistic approach, in which the safety, health and self-respect of residents are of paramount importance (Loxley 2002). In theoretical terms it is a convergence strategy of economic development (Thomas 1974).

This CED strategy can be contrasted with alternative approaches which implicitly assume that communities are too small to offer economic opportunities based purely on the local market, and hence should build their economic bases on the export of goods or services. These approaches incorporate the logics of large-scale production and orthodox economics into their assumption scts.

EXPORT BASE APPROACH

The export base approach is a commonly used strategy, wherein production within a community is geared to satisfying extra-community market demand. Although it is a theory of regional economic growth and development, it is pertinent to CED because a community's economy can be analyzed in the same way as that of a small region. The export base model is grounded in the assumption that all economic activity within a community is a function of export activities; export expansion is considered the primary source of economic growth, either from an improved cost position of existing exports relative to competing areas or as a result of the development of new exports (North 1955). The export base approach is outward looking, and thus contrasts greatly with the Neechi model: by focusing on developing an economic base through production of goods for the export market, little consideration is given to the needs of the community.

The export base becomes instrumental in shaping the distinctive quality of the community's economy. The economic base model conceptualizes the economy as being divided into two sectors: the export or "basic" sector, which consists of all economic activity whose final market lies outside the community; and the non-export or "non-basic" sector, which consists of all economic activity whose final market is local. Employment and income in the basic sector are a function of external demand for a community's exports (Davis 1993; Hewings 1977). Total economic activity is modelled as a function of export activity in economic base analysis, a tool of regional economics used to examine the economic impact of export activity in a region or community. If export activity increases, then total economic activity will increase by the amount of the change in export activity times a multiplier (which always has a positive effect, as it is equal to the ratio of non-basic to basic activity plus one).

Export base theory is a derivative of the staple theory of growth, which was developed to explain the economic development of Canada as a process of diversification around an export base (Watkins 1963). The argument is that Canada's economy took the shape it did because of the characteristics of various staples it exported — including beaver, cod, timber, wheat and oil. In this line of thinking, therefore, the term staple refers to the main commodity produced by a region, and is generally thought of as describing the products of extractive industries. The central concept of staple theory is the impact of export activity on the local economy and society. ◢

Staple theory analyzes the impact of export expansion on an economy through the classification of its income flows. The inducement of domestic investment resulting from increased export activity can be broken down into three linkage effects: backward linkages, forward linkages and final demand linkages (Hirschman 1965; Watkins 1963). A backward linkage is a measure of the extent of expenditure on inputs produced in the community, including capital goods. Backward linkages are created when a sector's input requirements are comprised of resources and technologies produced or owned by the community. A forward linkage is a measure of the extent to which a sector's output is sold as inputs to other sectors in the community. Forward linkages are formed when the product of one industry requires further processing by, and thus investment in, another industry in the community. A final demand linkage is a measure of the extent to which domestic industries are producing consumer or investment goods for use in the community. The greater the proportion of domestic production sold inside the region, rather than as exports, the greater the final demand linkage effect will be. Linkages are also determined by supply-side expansion of the export sector; in other words, the growth of a community's export sector resulting from the increased efficiency of markets for the inputs used in export production. The degree of supply-side export expansion therefore depends on the relationship between staple production and the supply of entrepreneurship and complementary inputs, including technology. If the staple or staples generate strong linkage effects which are adequately employed to the community's advantage, then eventually the economy will grow and diversify to the point where the term "staple economy" will no longer apply (Watkins 1963).

Export base theory is limited in that it is only appropriate for small, isolated economies whose growth and development are dependent on export-oriented industries (Davis 1993). The theory fails to acknowledge sources of economic stimuli other than exports, such as the remaining components of gross regional product (consumption, government expenditures, and business investment and residential construction). Exports are neither the only, nor the most important, source of economic stimuli. In fact, it has been found that economic activities are rarely a function only of export activities (Loxley 1986b). The role and source of capital is a critical component of export-led development. Since new and rebuilding communities typically depend on imported capital to develop their export staple industries, external investors have decision-making power over investment projects. These individuals are typically reluctant to invest in new, unproven activities where risks are greater;

thus new investment goes to expanding the base rather than diversifying the local economy (North 1955). Resource firms do not tend to diversify: since many of the exports are products with little or no further processing from raw material (Watkins 1963), linkages are rarely established at the point of production of the export commodity. Environmental concerns may also arise from outside ownership of capital, for which reason Schumacher (1973: 34) argues that community ownership is preferable: "men (*sic*) organised in small units will take better care of *their* bit of land or other natural resources than anonymous companies or megalomaniac governments which pretend to themselves that the whole universe is their legitimate quarry." Further, profits from the imported capital typically flow out of the community, reducing linkage effects even more.

The term "leakage" is used as a measure of the income flows leaving a region through sources such as migratory labour, interest paid on capital borrowed from outside the region and immigrants' remittances abroad, to name but a few. As a consequence of these leakages and, as described above, of the failure to establish linkages at the point of production, the development of a resource base into a staple export does not necessarily lead to CED. Loxley (1986b) describes staple economies as divergent, a concept first introduced by C.Y. Thomas (1974) that implies that what is locally produced is not locally consumed, and what is locally consumed is not locally produced.

CONVERGENCE OR COMMUNITY-BASED ECONOMIC DEVELOPMENT

A convergence or community-based approach attempts to match community needs to locally available resources (Wismer and Pell 1981). This inward-focused method suggests the convergence of local use and demand through the creation of a series of industries producing "basic goods," which, in this case, are said to be goods that feature prominently in the production of a wide range of consumption and investment goods (Loxley 1986b). The nature of the community resource base and the structure of community demand and needs determine what will be produced. Community participation and ownership are necessary components of convergence and community-based approaches because they play a part in reversing income flows, reducing income inequalities and ensuring that production meets community demand and needs (Loxley 1986b). Although somewhat compatible with a subsistence strategy, the very nature of which is the convergence of local resources with need, a convergence strategy goes well beyond it to integrate production for monetary exchange and to suggest how this might be organized (Loxley 1986b).

The economic theory underlying this approach perceives underdevelopment as a consequence of increasing divergence and unresponsiveness of domestic production to the needs of the local community (Thomas 1974). Divergence, in part, describes a lack of self-sufficiency: foreign ownership and control of domestic resources is a key reason for it. The economic development process transpires through economic activity with an inward focus; that is, the convergence of a community's resource base with its demands and needs. Production decisions are based on the demands and needs of the community rather than demands from outside it (which arise in the form of exports).

The import domestic expenditure coefficient is a quantitative measure of divergence which relates the value of imports for domestic use to domestic expenditure (Thomas 1974), or equally, reveals the share of a community's spending that goes toward imported goods and services. This measurement provides relevant information on the extent of the gap between, and the differences in the structures of, a community's production and demand. The import domestic expenditure coefficient is a number between zero and one: a community whose coefficient is close to one is described as a divergent economy, meaning that nearly all domestic spending is on goods and services imported into the community; whereas a community whose coefficient is close to zero is described as a convergent economy. Disadvantaged communities typically have import domestic expenditure coefficients closer to one. The import domestic expenditure coefficient is useful for planning development strategies: initiatives based on the principles of the Neechi model, for instance, aim to reduce the import domestic expenditure coefficient through small business initiatives to provide goods and services consumed by those who live and work in the community.

The formation of linkages between the different production sectors is the mechanism through which community economic growth and development occurs. Staple theory (Watkins 1963), convergence theory (Thomas 1974), big push theory[1] (Lynn 2003), as well as theoretical work by Loxley (1986b), all emphasize the importance of linkages for economic development. Practical examples of linkage formation are provided by Neechi Foods: backward linkages are formed when the co-op purchases moccasins and other home-made crafts made by neighbourhood Aboriginal women for sale in its store; forward linkages occur when it sells food items to a community bakery or restaurant; and final demand linkages are created by its offering of a better selection of food at better prices to community residents. The maximization of linkages and the minimization of leakages strengthen the growth and development processes. Optimization of these processes is achieved to the extent that output, including social services such as housing and child-care, are locally owned with profits staying in the community, and also to the extent that output is sold to other businesses and individuals within the community.

Smallness of scale is imperative to convergence and community-based approaches to community development (Schumacher 1973; Thomas 1974; Wismer and Pell 1981; Loxley 1986b). Small-scale production is perceived as desirable because it allows for a more spatially balanced economy, a less impersonal work environment, the possibility of community participation and control, the opportunity to tailor technology to local skill and employment levels and less deleterious effects on the environment (Loxley 1986b; Schumacher 1973: 33).

The emphasis on small-scale production for community development may be in conflict with microeconomic theory, which generally supports the view that economies of scale are crucial in determining the appropriate nature and level of production. Those who support a convergence approach to community development argue that minimum efficiency scale, the production level at which unit costs are at a minimum, is not as important for deciding levels of production as the critical minimum level of production, the output level at which the rate of fall in unit costs, as output increases, is at its greatest (Thomas 1974). They argue that most benefits which are perceived to occur from that large scale of production where average costs are at a minimum actually accrue at, or below, the critical minimum level of output, which may be well below the production level at which unit costs are minimized. This supports the idea of efficient small-scale production by showing that the benefits which are thought to be realized through economies of scale, such as the advantages of labour and managerial specialization and efficient capital equipment, actually arise at lower output levels than mainstream neoclassical theory suggests. The economic and social benefits stemming from the formation of inter-industry linkages are viewed as more important than economics of scale in community development (Loxley 1986b).

Nonetheless, the convergence approach acknowledges that small-scale projects will normally carry higher unit costs than those that are large in scale, and that firms may require subsidies to compensate for the foregone benefits of large-scale production. Some ways in which firms can endeavour to curtail unit costs are inter-community cooperation, the minimization of capital costs through multi-usage of facilities and, perhaps, a shorter work week. The higher costs of small-scale production may also be offset by external economies; in other words, any individual community enterprise may see its costs reduced and revenues improved by the existence of other enterprises in the community, since these allow for the sharing of some production expenses, stimulation of the market and general encouragement of a suitable economic environment. External economies can be developed through linkages as well as through activities such as marketing organizations, credit facilities, labour force training programs, housing projects, recreation centres and social institutions (Blakely 1984). Finally, exports can play a pivotal role by enlarging the market for a community's output just enough so that unit costs can fall to their critical minimum level. Trade outside the community therefore serves a different function than in export base theories, because it serves only to extend domestic demand and domestic need (Thomas 1974).

The convergence approach is confronted by challenges to its focus on community ownership. It is reasonable to expect fundamental opposition from those who control the economy and those who hold power to approaches turning these over to the community. The main challenge is that this approach requires basic and long-term state support, which may be withheld if it challenges the private sector or empowers the community to voice its demands and discontents (Shragge 1993). Challenges to the convergence strategy also arise from its political assumptions. These are very ambitious, including the political system's ability to regulate or prohibit trade flows, impose taxes, take property into public sector hands, redistribute income and plan production (Loxley 1986b). Such a political system stands in contrast to that which is dominant in present-day society, wherein unfettered free markets and a minimized role for the state are held as the correct formula for development. In Canadian society, at best only approximations of a pure convergence approach can be followed (Loxley 1986b).

OTHER CED STRATEGIES

Between the extremes of convergence strategy and export base approach, three other strategies of CED can be identified (Loxley 1986b). The first, which is really a strategy of defeatism or despair, is that of a social assistance or migration strategy, wherein people either survive locally on transfer payments or leave the community for other centres because the state and community have effectively given up on economic development. This approach has characterized state policy towards some, often relatively isolated, communities, and underlies so-called "market solutions" to Aboriginal economic problems (see Riggs and Velk 1993). The problem with this approach is that the lack of local economic development opportunities is often assumed *a priori*, rather than concluded after a detailed examination of possibilities. A second problem is that economic conditions for migrants are often little better in the towns to which they arrive than they were in the remote communities from which they came. Market solutions are often, therefore, no solution at all.

Second, in many communities the provision of government services — from local government to infrastructure building and maintenance, including education and health care facilities, policing and garbage disposal — is the main, or at least an important, aspect of economic strategy. It is common for these activities to account for most jobs and a high proportion of community income in Aboriginal communities.

Finally, some communities pursue what economists would describe as an import substitution strategy, meaning that they undertake to provide services and produce goods locally which were previously being imported. The local provision of government services, implying that local people take over jobs previously occupied by people from outside the community, is particularly attractive to communities because these jobs are relatively secure and available over the long term, and also because it implies a greater degree of local control. The replacement of non-government services and imported products by local initiatives and production may face problems of scale. However, these consequences are overcome by the benefits of import substitution; for example, the market demand of these services and products is known with some degree of certainty. Although import substitution has a role in convergence strategies, there is some contradiction between these two approaches since the latter do not accept the existing distribution of income, and hence current market demand, as given. A further fundamental difference is that convergence strategies do not accept that output should be driven only by the market, placing a much greater emphasis on meeting needs as opposed to demand.

THE ROLE OF SUBSIDIES IN CED

Underlying most approaches to CED is a philosophy of self-reliance and community independence. In reality, however, CED ventures have to compete with other, often monopoly producers; CED initiatives often have to accept the prices these more powerful competitors fix, which are based on much larger scales of production and wages close to or below subsistence levels (a prime example being the well-known retailer Wal-Mart). In contrast, in CED projects, the scale of production is usually very small, overhead costs are relatively high, wage levels must be socially acceptable, and workers are often in need of training and facing social problems not necessarily experienced by the general labour force. For all these reasons, and until prices generally in the economy are arrived at by considerations other than those of short-run, market-driven profit maximization, CED projects will find it difficult to prosper without some degree of subsidization.

Subsidies for CED projects can take many forms, from someone picking up the bottom-line losses of a project to the provision of a wage or training subsidy, a protected market for products at a higher than market price, physical assets at less than cost, cheap capital, a protective tariff or tax on competitors' products, or help towards meeting overhead costs. All of these can be found, in one way or another, around the world.

In places where CED is very well-established along convergence lines, with many enterprises and agencies providing a range of goods and services, some products may be subsidized by others. In this case, "cross-subsidization" is said to be taking place. Some examples of cross-subsidization in CED may include a community-owned credit union's provision of credit on favourable terms to other community-based projects, or a locally owned restaurant being supplied with locally produced food at prices not determined by the market. Another form of cross-subsidization occurs when locally produced products are being sold at prices higher than those seen elsewhere, in which case it is the consumers who are subsidizing CED activities. The extensive cross-subsidization of CED projects in a community through higher final sales prices than those in neighbouring communities is justified by the jobs the project creates, which would not otherwise exist (see *We're the Boss*, National Film Board 1990, a film about the experiences of Evangeline, in Prince Edward Island, with this problem). In this respect, support for CED projects is not unlike support for fair trade products or for cooperatives generally; consumers may, quite simply, have to pay more to support broader social goals.

Usually one resorts to the principles of cost-benefit analysis to provide an economic rationale for subsidization. Projects that are not commercially viable may yet be socially viable if the market does not accurately capture the true costs and benefits to society of the project in question. Market prices do not, in fact, normally capture the true *opportunity cost* of employing resources, or, in other words, the foregone opportunities that arise when resources are not put toward the use that optimizes social benefits. Thus, for a community experiencing widespread unemployment, the true social cost of employing labour is not the wage that would have to be paid to hire workers, but rather the loss of output to society of using funds to offer work to the unemployed instead of for other, potentially more productive purposes. Often, that loss is zero or negligible, in which case a subsidy could be justified because it would put wages well below market levels, improving the apparent profitability of the project. The rationale for this subsidy is, therefore, one of job creation, wherein the state or some other entity would have to pay the project the difference between market and social wage costs. The correct way to proceed, in general, is to calculate true social costs and benefits, analyze effects on project accounting, and then limit subsidies to the amount that brings the project out of deficit spending.

In reality, however, these calculations are difficult to make, and government policy-makers may find them hard to follow. In such cases, another, closely related approach may be pursued. This other approach to the determination of government subsidy consists of measuring a project's fiscal impact, and gearing the amount of the subsidy to improving the fiscal position of government(s). Such improvement may come from a number of sources. First, if the project increases employment, it may reduce either Employment Insurance (EI) claims (expenditures made by the federal government) or social assistance payments (usually paid by provincial or municipal governments). Second, once employed, workers will contribute to government revenues through EI payments, as well as income, sales and other taxes. Third, projects may reduce social problems either directly or indirectly — logically, when unemployment is reduced government spending to address social problems should go down. In theory, it is possible to add up all these positive fiscal impacts and to use the result to justify government subsidization of CED projects.

Though there are similarities in the two approaches, they can, and normally will, give different results for the amount of subsidy considered to be justified. Politicians can usually relate more easily to the fiscal impact approach, finding it more accessible than justifications for subsidies based on cost-benefit analyses. One potential problem of this preferred method, however, is that net fiscal benefits are spread among the different levels of government, so that the level of government that gains the most may not be the one that has made the greatest amount of subsidy available. Despite this drawback, it is worthwhile to undertake fiscal impact studies to justify state support for CED undertakings.

Subsidies may be a feature of all alternative CED strategies (except, by definition, a pure subsistence strategy). However, export base strategies are not likely to work where production costs are too high to compete in the external market. Import substitution approaches may need some additional form of protection so that import substitutes can compete against cheaper goods and services produced outside the community. Finally, the basis of a convergent CED strategy can be formed where state and third sector funding is available for activities such as provision of housing, education and training: this takes on a huge importance in this approach because it immediately addresses peoples' basic needs as well as providing sources of income, employment and linkages.

Voluntary labour inputs from members of the community are another source of project "subsidization," which is often important but under-recognized. It is also often gendered, with women playing disproportionate roles. It needs to be recognized, therefore, that pursuing a convergence strategy might place new demands on community members, especially on women. Nonetheless, successful pursuit of the strategy might reduce other burdens on women by improving child care facilities, creating job opportunities, improving incomes and reducing the social problems that affect them.

SUMMARY AND CONCLUSION

This chapter has examined solely the economics of CED; this aspect of the process, however, cannot be separated from the broader discussion on different philosophical approaches to the concept. This is because, within the overarching dialogue on CED, there are competing views of what CED actually is and how one should go about implementing it. While there are no single "right" and "wrong" ways of proceeding, the vision chosen and the strategy pursued will necessarily have economic implications. It is hoped that the outlines of the various approaches to the economic development component of CED provided above will help practitioners to make careful programming decisions which take long-term economy-wide effects into account.

This chapter has discussed the economics of CED in the context of that line of theorizing which considers CED as a means of dealing with the problems posed to communities by capitalism, rather than in the context of thought which sees CED as a replacement method of social and economic organization. Common to all approaches attempting to pursue CED within capitalism will be the need to find sources of support for projects, given competition for funding from much larger and more mainstream capitalist projects. As CED theory is further developed and options for its implementation expand, concerns over finding support may diminish, since state subsidization may be replaced by broader consumer support in the forms of cross-subsidization or social pricing. Until this level of support among the public is achieved, it is important that those working in the field continue to raise awareness of the broad, equitable benefits that CED can offer to disadvantaged communities.

NOTE

1. Big push theory, premised on the belief that industrialization leads to economic development, proposes a series of complementary projects, even if none is big in itself, to create the necessary linkages and external economies for successful development.

Chapter Seventeen

THE MANITOBA COMMUNITY ECONOMIC DEVELOPMENT LENS
Local Participation and Democratic State Restructuring

Byron M. Sheldrick with
Kevin Warkentin

BACKGROUND

In Manitoba there is a deeply rooted appreciation for community economic development (CED), which has arisen from a unique set of factors. The inner city in Winnipeg is beset by problems of chronic poverty; yet, there is a vibrant left-wing political tradition committed to concepts of economic and social justice, as well as a large urban Aboriginal population with an activist leadership that is inspired by ideals of self-governance and self-determination. Together, these factors contributed to the emergence of a "CED vision." This vision became more coherent as a result of the neo-liberal political agenda pursued throughout the 1990s by the Conservative government of Gary Filmon, since it did not lend a great deal of support to local, community-driven initiatives. The Filmon Tories largely abandoned the inner city, leaving questions of economic and community development to the community itself.

The result, particularly in Winnipeg, was the development of a diversity of community development organizations that, for the most part, occurred independently of the state. These organizations were often small and poorly resourced, and depended on project funding cobbled together from a variety of sources. In many instances they remained dependent on some degree of state funding and subsidization. That funding, however, was often precarious and vulnerable to government cutbacks and priority changes.

With the election of the New Democratic Party (NDP) under Gary Doer in 1999, there was some expectation that CED and support for civil society organizations working in the inner city would become a higher priority — Manitoba NDP governments have historically identified with the left side of the political spectrum, and have been broadly committed to social and economic justice. These hopes seemed justified when the Doer government undertook to include CED issues in its policy agenda. The centrepiece of this commitment was the implementation of the Community Economic Development Lens, which was to be a policy tool for integrating a CED perspective into government policies across programs and departments. From the perspective of communities, it was hoped that this new orientation would permit a more coherent and supportive approach to CED, ending the fragmented and tenuous strategy that had been taken by the Filmon Tories.

The expectations around the CED lens remain, however, largely unrealized: its integration into the policy framework of the state has been at worst a failure, and at best incomplete. This is due, in part, to the inadequacy of the mechanism chosen for the implementation of the lens. The lens was put into operation through the creation of a central agency — the Community and Economic Development Committee of Cabinet (CEDC) — which was to coordinate economic policy across departments. One of the strengths of the central agency approach is its ability to create frameworks overarching a number of line departments. In the case of the CED lens, however, the CEDC had competing objectives, such that CED was mostly a secondary concern. Moreover, committee members working on the CED lens had little capacity to direct the activities of departments and no program authority. In other words, programs and policies remained the responsibility of individual line departments. For those departments not sympathetic to CED, therefore, it was relatively easy simply to ignore the lens.

One of the critical tasks faced by the proponents of the CED lens was, to a certain extent, changing the fundamentals of bureaucratic culture: the implementation of the lens required policy-makers across departments to conceptualize their roles and to understand the policy framework under which they operated in a different way. This was necessary because previous governments had successfully transformed bureaucratic culture, reorienting processes along neo-liberal lines. "New Public Management," as this process widely came to be known, had revolutionized public services throughout the western world, resulting in the restructuring and downsizing of state bureaucracies. Its implementation had resulted in a wholesale change in the "culture" of bureaucracies, with greater emphasis on marketization, privatization and entrepreneurialism (Osborne and Gaebler: 1993). To the extent that CED represented an alternative conception of economic development, its promotion would require radical changes to the way bureaucrats and policy-makers approached the question.

This chapter is divided into four parts. The first provides a brief discussion of what is meant by CED, and of its radical potential as an alternative strategy for economic development. The second part discusses the origins of the CED lens in Manitoba, and the difficulties the state has faced in its development. Interviews were conducted by Kevin Warkentin with individuals working in the Community and Economic Development Committee of Cabinet Secretariat, and with departmental representatives on the CED working group. Interviews were also conducted with CED activists about their perceptions of the CED lens. The third part examines the reasons for which the transformation of bureaucratic culture along CED lines is so difficult, and shows that policy culture in Manitoba remains non-conducive to CED. Finally, the conclusion offers some ideas as to how democratic change could be pursued more effectively.

COMMUNITY ECONOMIC DEVELOPMENT

CED can be understood in a number of ways. For the purposes of this chapter, CED is understood as a community-driven process that combines social, economic and environmental goals to build healthy and economically viable communities. CED aims to revitalize and renew community economies by developing community resources. Local control and ownership of such resources is considered vital to enhancing the self-reliance of communities; it also ensures that economic development efforts will be responsive to local priorities as defined by the community itself.

CED challenges traditional approaches to policy development and implementation at both the collective and individual level. For example, economic development policy has generally been understood in market terms. Levers of economic development therefore tend to involve a range of incentives to private business, such as tax incentives and a variety of other direct enticements. In this context, the role of the state is limited to creating a "business-friendly" climate in which companies will want to locate. As such, the state's frame of reference is largely at the macro level: it is concerned with economic development at the level of the nation, province or city, depending on the level of government in question.

Within the traditional economic development framework, the state does not concern itself with the products/outputs of economic development. In other words, profits generated from economic activity remain in the hands of private business, and what is done with those profits is not the concern of the state. Therefore, the state has an extremely limited capacity to direct the reinvestment of those profits into the community for local benefit. From the state's perspective, the establishment of a new manufacturing plant in an inner-city neighbourhood, for example, might constitute an example of successful economic development; however, from a CED practitioner's point of view this would only be successful if the plant were to employ community members and reinvest profits into the community. Moreover, the CED perspective would see the community itself, and not just the company, involved in setting those priorities. In traditional economic development models, the questions of who to employ and what to do with earnings remain within the exclusive purview of the private company.

CED, then, offers a radical alternative to conventional approaches to economic development. CED can also be conceptualized as an alternative model of state-community relations. In particular, the democratic possibilities embedded within CED notions of local autonomy and decision-making provide the basis for creating state-community partnerships that are more participatory and developmental in nature. In this way, CED offers the potential to go beyond traditional models of policy-making and service delivery, which are all too frequently oriented from the top down and are bureaucratically driven. It has the potential to develop partnerships that are less one-sided, and that are capable of genuinely enabling community organizations to set the terms and priorities of service delivery.

THE CED LENS IN MANITOBA

After the election of the NDP under Gary Doer in 1999, a series of discussions developed between CED groups and the government: these talks centred on the disjuncture between the objectives of the former and the policy framework of the latter. CED groups felt the state agencies they dealt with did not understand CED, and were not sympathetic to or supportive of the ways in which they were organized and operated. Overall, the government's policy framework and approach to service delivery was considered antithetical to the achievement of the CED goals of enfranchising and empowering communities. In modern bureaucracies, policy development and implementation conceive of accountability and expertise in ways that privilege the authority of state experts, and that are generally not supportive of the mechanisms of community participation and self-determination. The government's top-down approach to economic development provided little or no opportunity for local participation. This was compounded by the belief that civil servants had poor comprehension of CED principles. Activists felt that, unless government policy-makers had a better understanding of CED principles, they would continue to receive limited support.

These discussions led to the development of a CED initiative that generated a number of changes to the structure of the state. Most notable was the creation of the Community and Economic Development Committee of Cabinet (CEDC) in March of 2000, along with a secretariat to provide administrative support. The cabinet committee was chaired by the Premier and included six ministers representing the following departments: Industry, Trade and Mines; Advanced Education and Training; Aboriginal and Northern Affairs; Culture, Heritage and Tourism; Agriculture and Food; and Intergovernmental Affairs. A parallel committee of deputy ministers was chaired by a senior public servant and influential member of the NDP. This committee included representatives from the above departments as well as a representative from Family Services and Housing.

For CED activists, the creation of the CEDC and the adoption of the lens seemed to be very positive developments. For the first time it appeared that CED was being taken seriously at very senior levels of government: there appeared to be some political will to restructure policy processes in a way that would be more sensitive to and supportive of CED values.

The initial optimism of community CED activists that the creation of the CEDC would increase the visibility of inner-city economic issues was soon replaced by a certain degree of frustration. This was because the new cabinet committee confronted a number of obstacles to integrating community-based principles into broader notions of economic development. The CEDC is responsible for economic development issues generally, and CED, while important, is only one priority among many. In this regard it is important to note that the name of the cabinet committee is conjunctive: it is the Community *and* Economic Development Committee, not the Community Economic Development Committee. Consequently, it has been involved in a number of traditional economic development ventures, such as the creation of a "single gateway" for new businesses interested in moving to Manitoba, and the encouragement of outside investment in the province. The CEDC also oversees and smoothes the way for new development projects. These have included very traditional initiatives, including, for example, the development of meat packing and potato processing plants, the construction of a new arena and a new downtown campus for Red River College (Rabson 2003).

There has, however, been some movement towards the integration of CED principles into a broader policy framework at the level of the CEDC Secretariat, which provides staff resources and assistance for the cabinet committee. The secretariat is divided into nine project areas, although only one project officer is charged with the Community Economic Development file — this individual was drawn from the community and had an extensive background working in CED organizations. The remaining officers deal with more traditional economic concerns.

This has resulted in the establishment of an interdepartmental working group, chaired by the CEDC project officer responsible for CED. The working group is made up of sixteen members, including three staff members and a "CED champion" nominated from within the ranks of each department. These representatives are from Aboriginal and Northern Affairs; Culture, Heritage and Tourism; Advanced Education/Education, Training and Youth; Family Services and Housing; Healthy Child Committee of Cabinet; Industry, Trade and Mines; and Intergovernmental Affairs, which has three representatives on the working group. The notion of a CED lens as a policy tool developed out of the work of this committee. The lens was to provide a framework, or a set of indicators, that departments could utilize to evaluate policy initiatives in order to ensure that they are consistent with CED principles. The lens would also allow departments to identify policy areas where CED opportunities exist and could be developed. As part of its work, the NDP has taken responsibility for the development of this policy framework.

While the idea of using the CED lens as a policy tool is promising, its operationalization has proven more difficult: the integration of a more participatory and locally driven approach to economic development into existing policy frameworks has been frustrated by the realities of bureaucratic organization. The CED lens is meant as an internal tool for self-analysis that will permit policy-makers to identify possibilities for CED applications — it has not been utilized as a vehicle by which community groups are brought into that process. Although the need for the CED lens may have emerged from a dialogue with community groups, discussions since then have primarily been internal. The background documents prepared by the committee have not been shared with CED groups and practitioners, nor are they publicly available. (The materials are kept on a government intranet, accessible only by public servants.) Moreover, although the interdepartmental working group invites individuals from the community to make presentations to it, these occasions are rare, and are conceptualized as "information gathering" by the committee, rather than as opportunities to involve community groups in the committee's discussions and planning. Finally, while most members of the working group are very supportive of and enthusiastic about the lens, they are still in the process of self-education as to what constitutes CED. There is a consensus that this needs to take place before education can begin at a broader level.

While some departments have utilized the CED lens as a basis for conducting an inventory of programs, those departments most embedded in traditional modes of economic development — Industry, Trade and Mines, and Energy, Science and Technology — have not. The departments that have done so are those in which a well-developed policy community exists: these departments have a history of consultation and involvement by members of that community in policy processes. This would certainly describe the Labour and Immigration Department: both business and labour groups have traditionally been very involved in labour policy development, as have a number of organizations representing immigrant communities in Manitoba for policy concerning immigration. The same can be said of the Aboriginal and Northern Affairs Department, in which the logic and language of self-governance is very current and predominates the bureaucratic discourse. Since there is congruence between the language of CED and the aims and aspirations of self-governance, the development and integration of CED principles into the operation of the department has been more easily achieved.

However, at the time of writing, very few departments had conducted inventories using the CED lens. This reflects the fact that many participants in the working group do not understand or appreciate the relevance of its work to the daily activities of the departments involved — in fact, interviews conducted with members of the working group reflect that they do not perceive the principles of CED to be particularly applicable to their day-by-day operations. To a certain extent, the lens operated within a "double bind." Departments without a strong economic focus found it difficult to conceptualize its relevance to their operations; and working group members from departments most associated with traditional models of economic development were sceptical of its approach. The project was seen as an interesting exercise, but as one with limited applicability; the promotion of CED in general was understood as a significant gesture to the broader social justice ambitions of the government, but one which was ancillary to its primary economic agenda.

The fact that the lens was not viewed to be compatible with traditional models of economic development can be readily seen in the approach some departments have taken toward it. A representative of Industry, Trade and Mines, for example, identified the department's vision as "bringing economic prosperity and identifying Manitoba as a competitive marketplace for industry." To this end, the department's objective was to stimulate and facilitate economic growth, particularly by promoting Manitoba as a location for investment and by improving access to capital for potential investors. As a result, the working group member from this department felt that CED "did not really fit in with a large proportion of what the department does."

The case of Manitoba Agriculture and Food is also instructive. The representative to the working group conceptualized his department's work as consistent with CED. However, this understanding was linked to conceptions of "value added diversification" within the context of agri-business. Effectively, this means the expansion of economic activity beyond primary agricultural activities — planting and harvesting — to include manufacturing and tertiary activities such as food processing and retailing. Clearly, this approach understands CED not as a community-driven and participatory process, but rather as one of helping rural communities adjust to the harsh realities of the global market. Although there is a sense that this should take place within a context of sustainability and support for the family farm, this is still a far cry from CED as it is understood within the framework of the lens.

TRANSFORMING BUREAUCRATIC CULTURE

It is useful to examine the factors that contributed to the success of New Public Management at shifting the culture of the public service in order to assess the capacity of the current NDP government to reorient public services in a fashion consistent with CED values and principles.

Some members of the interdepartmental working group hoped to restructure the policy culture of the state, and to create changes that will outlast the current administration. However, fiscal pressures in Manitoba run counter to the implementation of CED in a serious way, and as a result render the development of a CED culture within the bureaucracy extremely difficult. Although it is certainly true that building economically sustainable communities would save the Manitoba government a great deal of money in the long run by greatly reducing the amount currently spent on social assistance, health care, child welfare, and policing and corrections, these savings would likely not be realized in the foreseeable future, and possibly not for several generations. Moreover, given the small nature of current CED initiatives, to increase their size and scope to the point where they would begin to have a significant impact on the opportunities of disenfranchised communities would involve large increases in expenditures. Yet the Manitoba government is still feeling the fiscal legacy of New Public Management. Balanced budget legislation precludes running a deficit, and the government is committed to not raising taxes; in fact, the Doer government believes electoral victory to depend on being consistent in its adherence to these two principles. Consequently, there is no great desire to embark on a policy direction that would involve significant increases in expenditures in the short term with cost savings not being realized for some time.

The lack of fiscal incentive to adopt CED principles might be overcome if there were sufficient support from the Premier's office; yet this seems to be lacking. Though some support for the initiative is evidenced by the fact that the CEDC is chaired by the Premier, and the secretariat is headed by a particularly influential government figure whose appointment was seen as reflecting the Premier's commitment to the project, the CED aspect of the secretariat's work remains a limited portion of its mandate.

This points to a broader problem — namely, that the government's conception of CED differs significantly from that of local community activists and CED practitioners. CED can be reinterpreted fairly easily so as to be consistent with very conventional notions of economic development; and the democratic and participatory elements of CED can easily be jettisoned. The commitment of the government to CED, therefore, may be more limited than it appears. For the most part, the work of both the CEDC and the secretariat can be understood within a relatively traditional economic framework. Their primary concerns are with business development, training and creating an economic climate that is favourable to private business — objectives that can easily be incorporated and articulated through a language of CED that has little to do with the objectives of the lens. This same ambivalence can be seen among some of the participants in the project.

CED as a more progressive and radical alternative is, at best, an add-on. In some respects it is a concession to inner-city activists who have been pushing the government to devote more resources to problems in inner-city neighbourhoods. The absence of a true commitment to CED can be seen in a number of recent examples of development projects that have proceeded without a significant CED component, despite their obvious potential to do so. For example, the construction of the new Red River College Campus in Winnipeg's Exchange District proceeded without any requirements to employ local residents even though the campus is adjacent to one of the poorest neighbourhoods in Winnipeg.

In other instances, "partnerships" between the provincial government and not-for-profit organizations continue to be structured by "service agreements": these agreements often impose terms on the community group with very little possibility for negotiation. Community groups are frequently so under-funded that, in the scramble for resources, it is relatively easy for government agencies to engage in a top-down process. From the government's perspective, this approach has the merit of providing fairly clear mechanisms of accountability with strict reporting schedules and performance obligations, without any of the potential complications that might arise from a more democratic or participatory process. It also retains control in the hands of state policy experts, and does not share authority and responsibility with local communities. Under this scenario, community groups have very little choice but to accede to the dictates of government.

CONCLUSIONS

One should not be overly critical of the Doer NDP government, since the situation of many community groups has certainly improved relative to their circumstances under the Filmon Conservatives. Nonetheless, the existing policy framework around CED remains inadequate. CED, if it is to provide a basis for restructuring the relationship between community groups and the Manitoba government, needs to be given a higher priority status as a state objective. This will require several changes to government structures. First, CED needs to be integrated more effectively into the government's overall agenda, an achievement that will require a commitment from the Premier and his office. More concretely, CED needs to be made a priority at the level of the CEDC and at that of its secretariat. The CEDC, while an important economic committee, does not have the same degree of authority over government policy as does the Treasury Board, and there is no requirement that all new policies be vetted as to their CED potential prior to going to Cabinet for approval. In this sense, it has yet to become a true central agency of control. As a result, the exhortations of the interdepartmental working group are its only mechanism for ensuring that government policies conform to CED principles.

Second, several changes to the interdepartmental working group will be required. At the moment, each department approaches the question of CED from its own particular perspective, resulting in widely varying understandings of the concept. The interdepartmental working group is attempting to formulate a common perspective, but this will depend on the cooperation and agreement of representatives from a wide range of departments. Therefore, the group needs to develop its own policy and program capacity: it must have the ability to develop training programs, to create best practices manuals, tailored to the needs of particular departments, and to sponsor pilot projects. At the same time, a performance evaluation component permitting the group to undertake external evaluations of the integrity of the CED efforts of line departments would be extremely useful. As well, because it is simply too easy for departments and agencies to utilize the language of community without actually integrating genuine CED principles into their operations, the working group may have to be transformed into an agency in its own right. This would allow it to develop a coherent CED approach.

Nevertheless, it would be a mistake to believe that simply adjusting the operational form of the CEDC secretariat and working group can provide an adequate solution — there is a more fundamental contradiction at the heart of the CED lens project. That is, the objective of the lens is to adjust bureaucratic behaviour and attitudes so as to render them more amenable to community-based initiatives; yet this project has been conceived as an effort that is largely internal to the state, without sufficient participation from community groups. The lens is an attempt to facilitate the state in developing a top-down process of promoting more democratic participation in economic decision-making, rather than working with the community to develop its own democratic capacity.

To this extent, an appropriate strategy may be to hand the CED lens over to the community: greater involvement of community participants through community-based assessments of departmental policies and of joint civil servant and community planning forums, as well as hiring project officers directly into departments with the explicit role of facilitating and developing new forms of state-community participation could be extremely useful in expanding the application of true CED principles. Such approaches have been attempted with some success in other jurisdictions, particularly in New Zealand (Larner and Butler 2005): these approaches would likely have been more fruitful than was the traditional model of policy development undertaken.

To date, the success of the interdepartmental working group at raising the profile of CED within the provincial government has not been great. Though the CEDC has only been in existence for six years, one might nevertheless have expected greater output from the interdepartmental working group. Certain community activists are disappointed that more has not been accomplished, and that the CED lens does not seem to have much purchase in the operations of most departments. In part, this reflects the nature of bureaucracy: it is frequently slow to act, and many quarters of the state will be unreceptive to any initiative intending to increase the capacity of community groups to influence and direct policy. However, the failure of the CED lens initiative to produce substantive change to public service delivery also reflects a lack of support from the centre. Fundamentally, the Doer NDP government's approach to governing in Manitoba is based on the model of the "third way," pioneered by Tony Blair's New Labour government (Bradford 2002; Sheldrick 2002), which depends on a fairly careful engagement in brokerage politics. In the Manitoba context, the government has adopted a strategy of appeasing business: the business community is given the concessions it wants — primarily, lower taxes — and, with its leftover capacity, the government makes marginal investments that are intended to be seen as advancing the cause of social justice. It is in this context that the inadequacies of the CED lens can be explained: it is perceived by the government as a nice idea — one, however, that will not be permitted to interfere with the traditional economic development strategies it considers key to its electoral success.

Chapter Eighteen

REFLECTIONS ON ACCOMPLISHMENTS AND CHALLENGES

John Loxley and Jim Silver

This book has consistently emphasized the importance of community. In the introductory chapter, and in one way or another in each of the chapters that followed, we have argued that development, as we conceive of it — as part of community economic development — starts with, and is rooted in, decisions made by the community and the active involvement of the community. The authors of many of the chapters in this book have used methodologies — like participatory action research and life stories — that reflect a belief in the importance of community involvement in the research process. As well, the design of the research project as a whole reflects our belief in the importance of the real and genuine involvement of the community in CED, and of ongoing research about CED. In this concluding chapter, we first describe the way in which we organized the research undertaken by the Manitoba Research Alliance (MRA), which we believe reflects our belief in the value of community involvement: we then consider some of the areas in which the MRA intends to do further research.

In 2002, three universities in Manitoba cooperated with the Canadian Centre for Policy Alternatives–Manitoba (CCPA–MB), a number of community-based organizations and the provincial and federal governments, to form the Manitoba Research Alliance on Community Economic Development in the New Economy. The Manitoba Research Alliance was successful in its application for an $895,000 SSHRC grant to conduct research into CED and the new economy, one outcome of which is this volume. This was a unique project, led by a non-academic, community-based research organization, the CCPA-MB, and supported by such CED agencies as the North End Community Renewal Corporation, the Ma Mawi Wi Chi Itata Centre, the West Broadway Development Corporation, SEED Winnipeg and many others. This alliance was based on cooperation between academics and non-academics interested in CED.

Our purpose in this large research undertaking has been to examine the impact of the so-called "new economy" on those who have historically been excluded by the profit-oriented capitalist economy, and to determine the ways, if any, in which CED might be beneficial in improving their circumstances.

Our research has had an inner-city, rural and northern focus: we have also attempted to pay particular attention to the circumstances of Aboriginal people and of women. We have wanted to ensure the active involvement in the research process of those who are the objects of our research.

The Manitoba Research Alliance on CED and the New Economy remains a unique organization in the province. It brings together a wide variety of community-based organizations active in CED, a progressive research and policy formulation think-tank (the CCPA–MB), representatives of the two senior levels of government, and members of the academic community affiliated with three universities who are interested in CED. Together, they have designed a research program of common interest, ensuring, in the process, that academic research has a direct tie into community needs and aspirations, as well as into the formulation and implementation of government policy and programs, and that community needs and aspirations are reflected in the research that is done, as well as the way in which that research is done.

Because the Alliance explicitly bases its research agenda on matters of importance to CBOs, community-based organizations (CBOs) have remained involved in the Alliance. Several individual research projects have drawn directly on CBOs, their staff or community activists known to them, to help undertake the research agenda that they themselves have helped shape. In some cases, these participants receive funding from the MRA to define and to conduct that research which they believe will bring broader benefits to them. Without the Alliance, much of this research would not have been conducted, or it would have entailed hiring expensive outside consultants. But even where no funding was received, and the direct benefits may be, at best, slight, community organizations are still participants in designing and managing a research agenda which is of interest to them in broad and general terms and which, hopefully, will bring many indirect benefits, such as, for example, a better understanding of obstacles to employment in certain important local industries, the problems faced by women in participating in CED and the difficulties encountered by government in building into all its activities a concern for furthering CED.

Involving Aboriginal people as researchers is one of the biggest accomplishments of the Alliance. A total of thirty-eight community researchers have participated in the MRA's research work.[1] Given the continuing dependent, colonial relationship that Aboriginal people endure with the larger society, there is an understandable wariness on the part of Aboriginal people about non-Aboriginal researchers, their motives, methods and intent. But when the research agenda is driven by the perceived needs of Aboriginal people, and conducted by Aboriginal researchers, these problems are reduced. There is a general feeling that Aboriginal people speak more freely with Aboriginal researchers, who can more easily create "a relationship of mutuality, respect and shared purpose" (Deane, Morrissette, Bousquet and Bruyere 2002: 8). This brings to the research a depth, insights and sincerity that might otherwise be lacking. It also creates an Aboriginal awareness about the results of the research that is otherwise difficult to achieve. Thus, when a major publication of the Alliance, *In their Own Voices: Building Urban Aboriginal Communities* (Silver 2006b), was released, the audience was packed with Aboriginal people, present because of the research but also because of the researchers. The pride of the researchers in being part of this project was apparent for all to see.

Being directly and actively involved in research undertaken by the MRA not only has contributed significantly to the skills of Aboriginal researchers drawn from the community, but has also added noticeably to their self-confidence and self-esteem. Several Aboriginal people involved as researchers with MRA projects will undoubtedly be among the future leaders of Winnipeg's urban Aboriginal community.

THREE FOUNDATIONS OF THE
MANITOBA RESEARCH ALLIANCE

Community-based organizations play an important role in managing the Alliance on an ongoing basis: they are involved in defining the overall research objectives and strategy, allocating funding to particular research projects, monitoring approved projects and ensuring proper evaluation and dissemination of results. They bring to the research process their expertise and community perspective while, at the same time, gaining insights into how research priorities are arrived at in a situation of constrained funding, how cash flows are managed and how problems of research quality and timeliness of reports are addressed. They also participate fully in discussions about the dissemination of research results, and can have a big impact on the design of dissemination programs, an example being the recruitment of a well-known Aboriginal film-maker, Coleen Rajotte, to help project the results of our research. (Her video, *In Their Own Voices: Urban Aboriginal Community Development*, is available from the Canadian Centre for Policy Alternatives–Manitoba). Community-based organizations are, therefore, active in all facets of the work of the Alliance, keeping it firmly rooted in the reality of the community in which CED is practised: they constitute one of the three foundations of this unique research undertaking.

Having a non-profit research and policy think tank as the lead organization is also very unusual but decidedly beneficial to the work of the Alliance. The CCPA–MB, the second foundation of this research undertaking, has extensive contacts in the progressive community and is an active voice for social and economic reform. With a reputation for quality research, it is an important counterpoint to the Fraser Institute, the Fraser's local associate, the Frontier Institute, and its "academic" soul-mate, the C.D. Howe Institute, all of which have far more resources, far closer and more lucrative relationships with the corporate sector and far more influence with the media than do those voices which, like the CCPA–MB, are associated with the poor and excluded of modern society. Putting forward an alternative perspective on public policy is crucial because otherwise, the corporate point of view would be the only one heard. The CCPA–MB has a wide network of well-published and highly regarded researchers upon which it can draw, and an established and effective distribution system through which to disseminate its research results. And, unlike other think tanks, the CCPA–MB puts social justice, equity and the rights of ordinary women and men front and centre in its research agenda. As a result, it makes an ideal partner for activists and academics concerned about the problems of poverty and social exclusion faced by many people living in Manitoba.

Conversely, the Alliance is important to the CCPA–MB for a number of reasons. First, it helps consolidate the CCPA–MB's organic links to the local community, in the process enhancing its reputation for socially relevant policy research. Second, it broadens the CCPA–MB's research and publications agenda, giving it greater public prominence. Third, it provides the CCPA–MB with a small but important contribution to its funding base to help pay for publications and administrative overhead. At the same time, it adds a whole new layer of responsibility onto the shoulders of the director and board of the CCPA–MB to ensure that large research projects are managed properly. In this respect the Alliance was fortunate to be able to engage the services of an outstanding project manager, who bore much of that responsibility. We believe that the MRA, because it was successfully led by a non university, community-based, public policy research institute, has set an important precedent in the conduct of large research projects that seek to actively and meaningfully engage the community.

Academic researchers are the third foundation of the Alliance and are drawn from three universities: the University of Manitoba, the University of Winnipeg and Brandon University. They span a number of disciplines — political science, sociology, economics, urban studies, women's studies, rural development, anthropology, native studies, social work, management — that share a common interest in the research themes of the Alliance. For many, this was the first time working together with academics from neighbouring universities, so that collaborative ties have been created; for others those ties have been consolidated. A Web site was established to share information on the project, its management details as well as research undertakings, participants and outcomes.[2] A peer-review process was also set up under which all research findings were reviewed before publication.

The Alliance has offered unique research opportunities for students at all levels. It has employed thirty-seven undergraduate students and fourteen graduate students as well as a post-doctoral fellow. Several students had full responsibility for research projects, from conception to final publication. Students were also given the responsibility, and the funding, to organize two well-attended and very successful colloquia at which they presented research proposals and results. For most of the students this was their first opportunity to present research methods and findings to peers; for many it was a formative experience. The Alliance has arranged seven student internship placements with CED and community organizations, and created a whole new awareness around CED issues in the student community. This in itself is likely to have a lasting impact. Several researchers completed graduate theses in the area, while others, having participated in the work of the Alliance as undergraduates, have gone on to study CED and related issues at the graduate level. Several student participants are now working full-time in CED jobs, including the CED network, United Way of Winnipeg and several community-based organizations.

THE NEED FOR SUSTAINED
RESEARCH OF THIS KIND

The participation of the Alliance has been important in deepening cooperative relations between community-based organizations, the CCPA–MB and universities in Manitoba, in expanding the capacity of CED practitioners in Manitoba, in bringing together academic researchers and in broadening the opportunities for community members and students interested in CED. It has also generated a great deal of research into CED and the new economy, some of which is included in this volume and much of which has direct relevance to government policy. Little of this would have been possible without the SSHRC grant that funded it.

Herein lies the dilemma. Without such funding there is little prospect that the Alliance, in its current form, can survive. As a research alliance, its funding sources are limited. On the basis of the SSHRC funding, the Alliance was able to leverage a further $293,000 from research partners, of which $20,000 was in kind. About a third of this was money obtained from the provincial government to undertake research on opportunities for low- income people to secure employment in the knowledge economy (see Chapter 9 in this volume by Loewen and Silver), the rest was obtained from organizations working with individual projects. Little of this would have materialized without the underpinning of the large SSHRC research grant. It is for this reason that the Alliance applied for further SSHRC funding in 2007 and was successful in being awarded a $1 million five-year Community University Research Alliance (CURA) grant. The grant application lays out where the Alliance believes future research efforts on CED should be focused.

FUTURE RESEARCH ON COMMUNITY DEVELOPMENT/COMMUNITY ECONOMIC DEVELOPMENT

Alliance members believe that the growing incidence of poverty that is increasingly spatially concentrated, multi-generational, racialized and feminized, in both inner cities and in non-urban Aboriginal communities, constitutes the biggest challenge facing public-policy-makers today. The problems associated with poverty are equally complex and pernicious in both geographic locations — inner cities and non-urban Aboriginal communities — and, of course, are interrelated through processes of migration in both directions between urban centres and rural and northern Aboriginal communities. Urban poverty, however, goes well beyond the Aboriginal community, in which it has its own historical specificity: it embraces people of all ethnic backgrounds, including, to a growing extent, recently arrived African refugees. Traditional one-dimensional strategies have little effect on the complex and multifaceted problems associated with the incidence of poverty, but effective community development and community economic development strategies have helped deal with these problems, leaving a legacy of creative and effective community-based organizations. It is our view that these CBOs have to be strengthened, creative solutions found elsewhere need to be transferred to Manitoba, and our understanding of how people can transform marginalized communities has to be expanded and deepened. Our hope is that the research agenda that we initiated with the MRA will generate a deeper understanding of the evolving problems in Manitoba's inner cities and Aboriginal communities. Our intention is to build on our recent research and experience to identify genuinely transformative solutions that communities can use.

This research agenda is important and would need to be carried out with or without SSHRC funding, but the awarding of the grant greatly simplifies the research task. Finding funding for socially useful research is an issue of importance not only to the Manitoba Research Alliance, but also to progressive and collaborative research undertakings of a wide variety of kinds. Good quality research matters, especially when undertaken in close collaboration with the communities that are the objects of the research. But when these communities are among those most disadvantaged by the current socio-economic arrangements of society, and when the researchers are committed less to finding ways of improving corporate profits than of contributing to social justice, funding such efforts can be difficult. The new SSHRC grant will enable us to solve this problem and to carry on with what we believe is an important research agenda. Without it, the task would be much more difficult.

NOTES

1. See <http://www.manitobaresearchallianceced.ca/documents/MRAFinalReport1.pdf>.
2. See <http://www.manitobaresearchallianceced.ca> accessed July 2007.

ACRONYMS

ABEP	Aboriginal Business Education Program
ACU	Assiniboine Credit Union
AECF	Annie E. Casey Foundation
AET	Advanced Education and Training
AHI	Affordable Housing Initiative
ALO	Aboriginal liaison officers
AMICA	Indigenous Women's Movement (Nicaragua)
ARDA	Agricultural Rehabilitation and Development Administration
ATM	automatic teller machine
BHE	Bachelor of Human Ecology
BMO	Bank of Montreal
CBC	Canadian Broadcasting Corporation
CBO	community-based organization
CCEDNET	Canadian CED Network
CCPA	Canadian Centre for Policy Alternatives
CCPA–MB	Canadian Centre for Policy Alternatives–Manitoba
CD	community development
CDC	community development corporations
CED	community economic development
CEDA	Community Education Development Agency
CEDC	Community and Economic Development Committee of Cabinet
CEDF	Communities Economic Development Fund
CEDTAP	CED Technical Assistance Program
CEP	Communications, Energy and Paperworkers Union of Canada
CFDC	Community Futures Development Corporation
CIBC	Canadian Imperial Bank of Commerce
CMHC	Canada Mortgage and Housing Corporation
COS	Community Ownership Solutions
CSA	Community Supported Agriculture
CUPW	Canadian Union of Postal Workers
CURA	Community University Research Alliance
EEOGs	Employment Equity Occupational Groups
EI	Employment Insurance
ETS	Education Training Services
FRED	Fund for Rural Economic Development
HRDC	Human Resources Development Canada)
HSC	Humane Society Certified

ICT	information and computer technology
IDA	Individual Development Account
IRPA	*Immigrant and Refugee Protection Act*
IT	information technology
LITE	Local Investment Toward Employment)
LGD	Local Government District
LMDA	Labour Market Development Agreement
LMI	labour market intermediaries
LMP	labour market partnerships
MCCA	Manitoba Customer Contact Association
MFI	Manitoba Fashion Institute
MIT	Massachussets Institute of Technology
MP	Member of Parliament
MRA	Manitoba Research Alliance
MTS	Manitoba Telecom Services
NAFTA	North American Free Trade Agreement
NDP	New Democratic Party
NFA	Northern Flood Agreement
NGO	non-governmental organization
OECD	Organisation of Economic Co-operation and Development
OFCM	Organic Food Council of Manitoba
OFE	Opportunities for Employment
P3	public-private partnership
PATH	Pathways to Alternative Tomorrows with Hope
PLAR	Prior Learning Assessment and Recognition
RBC	Royal Bank of Canada
RCAP	Royal Commission on Aboriginal Peoples
RM	Rural Municipality
S-SEED	Small-Scale Entrepreneurial Economic Development
SSHRC	Social Science and Humanities Research Council.
SSHRC/INE	Social Science and Humanities Research Council, Initiative on the New Economy.
SALTS	Southern Alberta Land Trust Society
SEED	Supporting Employment and Economic Development
SJI	Seattle Jobs Initiative
SMO	sewing machine operator
TD	Toronto Dominion (bank)
URL	universal resource locator
WED	Western Economic Diversification
WHS	Winnipeg Humane Society
WWOOF	Willing Workers On Organic Farms

REFERENCES

Aboriginal and Northern Affairs, Manitoba. 2006. *Community Economic Development Fund Summary.* Available at <www.gov.mb.ca/ana/interest/cedf_summary.html>.

Adams, R.J. 2006. *Labour Left Out: Canada's Failure to Protect and Promote Collective Bargaining as a Human Right.* Ottawa: Canadian Centre for Policy Alternatives.

Agriculture and Agri-Food Canada. 2001. *Profile of the 1998 Taxfiler Farm Family Data.* Canada: Agriculture and Agrifood.

Agriculture Renewal Alliance. 2000. "Recapturing Wealth on the Canadian Prairies." Annual Conference.

———— 2001. "Alliances for Recapturing Wealth on the Canadian Prairies." Conference Executive Summary. Available at <www.umanitoba.ca/afs/plant_science/agrenewal/2001.htm#ExeSum> accessed July 2007.

Alderson, L., and M. Conn. 1988. *More Than Dollars: A Study of Women's Community Economic Development in British Columbia.* Vancouver: Women Futures Community Economic Development Society.

Anderson, E. 1999. *Code of the Street: Decency, Violence and the Moral Life of the Inner City.* New York: W.W. Norton.

Animalnet. 2001, "Winnipeg Humane Society Unveils Animal Friendly Product Label " Available at <http://archives.foodsafetynetwork.ca/animalnet/2001/4-2001/an-04-30-01-01.txt> accessed July 9, 2007.

Annie E. Casey Foundation. 2001. *Taking the Initiative on Jobs and Race: Innovations on Workforce Development for Minority Job Seekers and Employers.* Baltimore, MD: The Annie E. Casey Foundation. Available at <http://www.aecf.org> Accessed 7 July 2005.

Assiniboine Credit Union. 2000. "Aboriginal Employment Strategy." Received electronically on December 3, 2004, from Director of Human Resources, Assiniboine Credit Union.

B.C. Working Group on CED. 1995. *Sharing Stories: Community Economic Development in B.C.* Vancouver: B.C. Ministry of Small Business, Tourism and Culture.

Bain, Peter, and Phillip Taylor. 1998. "'Bright Satanic Offices': Intensification, Control and Team Taylorism." In C. Warhurst and P. Thompson (eds.), *Workplaces of the Future.* London: Macmillan.

Bakker, I., and D. Elson. 1998. "Towards Engendering Budgets." *Alternative Federal Budget Papers.* Ottawa: Canadian Centre for Policy Alternatives.

Baldry, C., P. Bain and P. Taylor. 1998. "Bright Satanic Offices:Intensification, Control and Team Taylorism." In P. Thompson and C. Warhurst (eds.) *Workplaces of the Future.* Houndmills, Basingstoke, Hampshire: Palgrave.

Beeman, C., and T. Rowley. 1994. *Our Field: A Manual for Community Shared Agriculture.* Wroxeter, Ontario: Community Supported Agriculture Resource Centre.

Berger, A.N. 2003. "The Economic Effects of Technological Progress: Evidence from the Banking Industry." *Journal of Money, Credit, and Banking* 35 (2): 141–76.

Betcherman, G., K. McMullen and K. Davidman. 1998. *Training for the New Economy: A Synthesis Report.* Ottawa: Canadian Policy Research Networks.

Black, E., and T. Scarth. 2003. *Rising Job Tide Not Lifting Low-Wage Boats: Review of Economic and Social Trends in Manitoba.* Winnipeg: CCPA–Manitoba

Blakely, E.J. 1994. *Planning Local Economic Development: Theory and Practice*. Second edition. London: Sage Publications.

Blau, F., M. Ferber and A. Winkler. 1998. *The Economics of Women, Men and Work*. Upper Saddle River, NJ: Prentice-Hall.

Bradford, N. 2002. "Renewing Social Democracy? Beyond the Third Way." *Studies in Political Economy* 67: 145–59.

Brandt, B. 1995. *Whole Life Economics: Revaluing Daily Life*. Gabriola Island, BC: New Society Publishers.

Brown, A. 1997. *Work First: How to Implement an Employment-Focused Approach to Welfare Reform*. New York: Manpower Demonstration Research Corporation.

Bryant, C.R. 1994. "The Corporate and Voluntary Sectors as Partners in CED." In B. Galaway and J. Hudson (eds.), *Community Economic Development: Perspectives on Research and Policy*. Toronto: Thompson Educational Publishing.

Buckley, H. 1992. *From Wooden Ploughs to Welfare: Why Indian Policy Failed in the Prairie Provinces*. Montreal and Kingston: McGill-Queen's University Press.

Callahan, M. 1997. "Feminist Community Organizing in Canada: Postcards from the Edge." In B. Wharf and M. Clague (eds.), *Community Organizing: Canadian Experience*. Toronto: Oxford University Press.

Canada Mortgage and Housing Corporation. 1991. *Core Housing Need in Canada*. Ottawa: CMHC.

Canadian CED Network. 2004. "Home page." Available at <http://www.ccednet-rc-dec.ca/en/pages/home.asp> accessed May 2004.

Canadian Payments Association. 2006. "Cheque Imaging in Canada: A Change Whose Time has Come" (updated to February 2006). Ottawa: Canadian Payments Association. Available at <http://www.cdnpay.ca/publications/pdfs_publications/imaging.pdf> accessed September 6, 2006.

Carter, T., C. Polevychok and K. Sargent. 2005. *Canada's 25 Major Metropolitan Centres: A Comparison*. Research Highlight No. 6, January. Winnipeg: Institute of Urban Studies, University of Winnipeg.

Cates, F. 2003. *Community Based Housing Development in Winnipeg*. Paper prepared for "Building on the Momentum: CD/CED Gathering," Winnipeg, November 26, 2003.

CBC News Online. 2002. "Manitoba Humane Society endorses 'humane meat'." Available at <http://www.cbc.ca/story/2002/03/27/humanemeat_020327.html> accessed May 27, 2004.

Chorney, P. 2003. "Neighbourhood Development Activity in Winnipeg." Paper prepared for "Building on the Momentum: CD/CED Gathering," Winnipeg. November 26, 2003.

City of Winnipeg. 2004. "Census 2001: City of Winnipeg Neighbourhood Profiles." Available at <http://www.winnipeg.ca/census2001/> accessed January 15, 2005.

Clark, P., and S.L. Dawson, with A.J. Kays, F. Molina, and R. Surpin. 1995. *Jobs and the Urban Poor: Privately Initiated Sectoral Strategies*. Washington, DC: Aspen Institute.

Comeau, S. 1999 "Finding Funds for Farmers." *McGill Reporter*, April 22. Available at <http://reporter-archive.mcgill.ca/Rep/r3115/baker.html> accessed July 2007.

Community Resilience Team. 1999. *The Community Resilience Manual: A Resource for Rural Recovery & Renewal*. British Columbia: Centre for Community Enterprise.

Conn, M. n.d. "Women, Co-ops and CED." *Making Waves* 12 (1).

COS (Community Ownership Solutions). n.d. "Who We Are." Available at <www. communityownershipsolutions.com/about/index.html> accessed January 12, 2007.

Cretchley, G., and J. Castle. 2001. "OBE, RPL and Adult Education: Good Bedfellows in Higher Education in South Africa?" *International Journal of LifeLong Education* 20 (6): 487–501.

Damaris, R. 2001. "Revisiting Feminist Research Methodologies." Working Paper. Ottawa: Status of Women Canada.

David, A. n/d. "Assessment Process: Overview." Available at <http://www.victorialaw. com/process/pgeneral.php> (accessed July 16, 2005).

Davidson, K. 2002. "News of the World: PPPs are a Disaster." Sydney: Evatt Foundation. Available at <http://evatt.labor.net.au/news/92.html> (accessed May 10, 2005).

Davis, C.H. 1993. *Regional Economic Impact Analysis and Project Evaluation.* Vancouver: UBC Press.

Deane, L., L. Morrissette, J. Bousquet and S. Bruyere. 2002. "Explorations in Urban Aboriginal Neighbourhood Development." Unpublished paper, Faculty of Social Work, Winnipeg Education Centre, University of Manitoba.

Decter, M.B., and J.A. Kowall. 1990. *Manitoba's Interlake Region: The Fund for Rural Economic Development Agreement, 1967–1977.* Ottawa: Economic Council of Canada.

Department of Justice Canada. "Citizenship Act (R.S. 1985, c. C-29)." Available at <http://laws.justice.gc.ca/en/C-29/index.html> accessed July 31st, 2005.

Destination Winnipeg. 2005. *Winnipeg Contact Centre Industry Profile.* Winnipeg: Destination Winnipeg.

Dickens, W.T. 1999. "Rebuilding Urban Labor Markets: What Community Development Can Accomplish." In R. Ferguson and W. Dickens (eds.), *Urban Problems and Community Development.* Washington, DC: Brookings Institution Press.

Dreier, P. 1996. "Community Empowerment Strategies: The Limits and Potential of Community Organizing in Urban Neighbourhoods." *Cityscape: A Journal of Policy Development and Research* 2 (2).

Drolet, M. 2001. "The Persistent Gap: New Evidence on the Canadian Gender Wage Gap." Statistics Canada, Analytical Studies Branch, Research Paper Series.

Dyck, B. 1994. "From Airy-Fairy Ideas to Concrete Realities: The Case of Shared Farming." *Leadership Quarterly* 5 (3/4): 227–46.

Ecological Farmers' Association. 1995. *Community Shared Agriculture.* Wroxeter, ON: Ecological Farmers' Association.

Economic Council of Canada. 1990. *Manitoba's Interlake Region: The Fund for Rural Economic Development, 1967–1977.* Ottawa: Economic Council of Canada.

Fals-Borda, O. 1992. "Evolution and Convergence in Participatory Action Research." In J. Frideres (ed.). *A World of Communities: Participatory Research Perspectives.* North York: Captus.

Fernandez, L.P. 2005. "Government Policy Towards Community Economic Development in Manitoba." M.A. Thesis, University of Manitoba. Available at <http://www.manitobaresearchallianceced.ca/Documents/24-CEDPolicyDevelopment.pdf> accessed August 28, 2006.

Fischer, D.J. 2005. "The Road to Good Employment Retention: Three Successful Programs from the Jobs Initiative." Baltimore, MD: Annie E. Casey Foundation. Available at <http://www.aecf.org/upload/PublicationFiles/FES3622H335. pdf> accessed July 7, 2005.

Fisher, R., and E. Shragge. 2002. "Organizing Locally and Globally: Bridging the Divides." *Canadian Dimension* 36 (3).

Fixico, D.L. 2000. *The Urban Indian Experience in America*. Albuquerque: University of New Mexico Press.

Fleischer, W. 2001. *Extending Ladders: Findings from the Annie E. Casey Foundation's Jobs Initiative*. Baltimore, MD: Annie E. Casey Foundation. Available at <http://www. aspenwsi.org/publications/Extending_Ladders.pdf> accessed July 2007.

_____. (n.d.) "Education Policy and the Annie E. Casey Jobs Initiative." Annie E. Casey Jobs Initiative Policy Brief #3. Available at <http://www.aecf.org/up-load/PublicationFiles/edpolicy.pdf> accessed July 2007.

Fleischer, W., and J. Dressner. 2002. *Providing the Missing Link: A Model for a Neighbourhood-Focused Employment Program*. Baltimore: Annie E. Casey Foundation. Available at <http://www.aecf.org/upload/PublicationFiles/missing%20link%20employm ent.pdf> accessed July 2007.

Fontan, J.M., P. Hamel, R. Morin and E. Shragge. 1999. "Community Economic Development and Metropolitan Goverance: A Comparison of Montreal and Toronto." *Canadian Journal of Regional Science* 22 (1–2).

Fontan, J., and E. Shragge. 1994. "Employability Approaches in CED Practice: Case Studies and Issues." In B. Galaway and J. Hudson (eds.), *Community Economic Development: Perspectives on Research and Policy*. Toronto: Thompson Educational Publishing.

Francis, D. 1992. *The Imaginary Indian: The Image of the Indian in Canadian Culture*. Vancouver: Arsenal Pulp Press.

Freire, P. 1973. *Education for Critical Consciousness*. New York: Seabury Press.

Ghorayshi, P. 1990. "Manitoba's Clothing Industry in the 1980s: Change and Continuity." In J. Silver and J. Hull (eds.), *The Political Economy of Manitoba*. Regina: Canadian Plains Research Centre, University of Regina Press.

Giloth, R.P. 2004a. *Workforce Development Politics: Civic Capacity and Performance*. Philadelphia: Temple University Press.

_____. 2004b. *Workforce Intermediaries for the Twenty-First Century*. Philadelphia: Temple University Press.

Gingras, Y., and R. Roy. 2000. "Is There a Skill Gap in Canada?" *Canadian Public Policy/Analyse de Politiques*, Vol. 26, Supplement.

Gittell, M., I. Ortega-Bustamante and T. Steffy. 2000. "Social Capital and Social Change." *Urban Affairs Review* 32 (2).

Good, Tom, and Joan McFarland. 2003. "Technology, Geography and Regulation: The Case of Call Centres in New Brunswick." In Leah Vosko and Jim Stanford (eds.), *Challenging the Market: The Struggle to Regulate Work and Income*. Montreal: McGill-Queen's University Press.

Government of Manitoba. 2006. "Prior Learning Assessment and Recognition (PLAR) Policies and Procedures Guide for Adult Learning Centers." Available at <http://www.edu.gov.mb.ca/ael/all/publications/plar/plar_policies_final. pdf> accessed March 7, 2006.

Gracey, M. 1999. *A Case Study: The Northern Star Collection. A Community Economic*

Development Project of the North End Women's Centre. Winnipeg: The North End Women's Centre.

Gramsci, Antonio. 1978. *Selections From Political Writings 1921–1926*. Trans. Quentin Hoare. New York: International Publishing.

Green, G.P., and A. Haines. 2002. *Asset Building & Community Development*. Thousand Oaks: Sage Publications.

Grieshaber-Otto, J., and M. Sanger. 2002. *Perilous Lessons: The Impact of the WTO Services Agreement (GATS) on Canada's Public Education System*. Ottawa: Canadian Centre for Policy Alternatives.

Guard, Julie. 2003. *Manitoba's Call Centre Explosion: A Preliminary Overview*. Toronto: United Steelworkers Canada. <http://www.uswa.ca/program/adminlinks/docs//call_guard.pdf> accessed August 2007.

Guard, J., J. Garcia Orgales and M. Steedman. 2006. "Organizing Call Centres: The Steelworkers' Experience." In P. Kumar and C. Schenk (eds.), *Paths to Union Renewal: Canadian Experiences*. Toronto: Broadview Press.

Halter, M. 1995. "Introduction — Boston's Immigrants Revisited: The Economic Culture of Ethnic Enterprise." In M. Halter (ed.), *New Migrants in the Marketplace: Boston's Ethnic Entrepreneurs*. Boston: University of Massachusetts Press.

Hanselman, C. 2003. *Shared Responsibility: Final Report and Recommendations of the Urban Aboriginal Initiative*. Calgary: Canada West Foundation.

Harrison, B., and M. Weiss. 1998. *Workforce Development Networks: Community-Based Organizations and Regional Alliances*. Thousand Oaks, CA: Sage Publications.

Hart-Landsberg, M., and P. Burkett. 2001. "Economic Crisis and Restructuring in South Korea: Beyond the Free Market-Statist Debate." *Critical Asian Studies* 33 (3): 403–30.

Head, K., and J. Ries. 1998. "Immigration and Trade Creation: Econometric Evidence From Canada." *The Canadian Journal of Economics* 31 (1): 47–62.

Hemery, T., M. Kicenko, N. Luz, N. Mardis and T. Markovic. 2003. *Earthshare Ideas on Sustainability: From Seed to Social Venture*. Winnipeg: I.H. Asper School of Business, University of Manitoba.

Henderson, H. 1996. *Creating Alternative Futures: The End of Economics*. West Hartford: Kumarian Press.

Hewings, G.J.D. 1977. *Regional Industrial Analysis and Development*. London: Methuen.

Hirschman, A.O. 1965. *The Strategy of Economic Development*. New Haven and London: Yale University Press.

HRDC (Human Resources Development Canada). 2001. *2000 Employment Equity Annual Report*. Ottawa: Human Resources and Skills Development Canada.

_____. 2005. "Aboriginal Human Resource Development Strategy, Standard Contribution Agreement, Final Version." Available at <http://www17.hrdc-drhc.gc.ca/AHRDSInternet/general/Publication/PublicationDocs/ahrda_english.pdf> accessed September 2005.

Huddart, S. 1999. "Coming Soon-Humane Farming Standards." Available at <http://cfhs.ca/info/coming_soon_humane_farming_standards/> accessed July 2007.

Ikerd, J. 2002. "Revitalising Rural Communities." Presentation to Third Annual Conference of Recapturing the Wealth in the Prairies, October 29–30, 2002, organized by the Agriculture Renewal Alliance: Brandon.

Informetrica Limited. 2000. "Recent Immigrants in Metropolitan Areas: Winnipeg,

A Comparative Profile Based on the 1996 Census." Available at <http://www.cic.gc.ca/english/resources/research/census2001/winnipeg/intro.asp> accessed July 9, 2005.

Institute for Community Economics. 1982. *The Community Land Trust Handbook*. Pennsylvania: Rochdale Press.

Institute of Urban Studies. 2003. "First Nations/Métis/Inuit Mobility Study: Interim Report One: Results from Initial Survey Final Draft." Winnipeg: University of Winnipeg. Available at <http://ius.uwinnipeg.ca/pdf/Interim%20Report%20One-%20Weeb.pdf> accessed July 26, 2005.

Jackson, A. 2004. *Home Truths: Why the Housing System Matters to all Canadians*. Ottawa: Canadian Centre for Policy Alternatives.

Jahid, D. 2005. "Migration in a Dream Land: A Review of the Literature Available and Related to the Problems and Constraints of Immigration and Settlement Services in Manitoba Canada." *Samajkantha: Voice of Society* 57. Available at <http://www.samajkantha.com/Migration%20in%20a%20dreamland.html> accessed July 9, 2005.

Jenkins, D. 1999. *Beyond Welfare-to-Work: Bridging the Low-Wage, Livable-Wage Employment Gap*. Chicago: Great Cities Institute.

Just Income Coalition. 2004. "Minimum Wage in Manitoba." Brief submitted to the Manitoba NDP Caucus, April 26. Winnipeg: Just Income Coalition.

Kaktins, S-L. 1997. "Community Shared/Supported Agriculture: Overcoming the Barriers." Master of Environmental Studies. Halifax: School for Resource and Environmental Studies, Dalhousie University.

Khatun, Amena. 1998. "Occupational Health of Women Garment Workers in Dhaka City." Unpublished M.Sc. Thesis, Gender and Development, Asian Institute of Technology. Bangkok, Thailand.

_____. 2005. "Worker Views on Changes in the Winnipeg Garment Industry: In-depth Interviews with Ten Immigrant Garment Workers." In R. Wiest (ed.), *The Winnipeg Garment Industry: Industry Development and Employment*. A report for the Manitoba Research Alliance on Community Economic Development in the New Economy, Project #4. Winnipeg: Manitoba Research Alliance. Available at <http://www.manitobaresearchallianceced.ca/Documents/4-GarmentIndustry-revNov22.pdf> accessed July 2007.

Kirschenmann, Fred. 2003. "Presentation to What Does It Mean to be Successful in Rural Manitoba." Fourth Annual Event for Recapturing Wealth on the Canadian Prairies. Agriculture Renewal Alliance. October 29. Dauphin, Manitoba. Available at <www.umanitoba.ca/afs/plant_science/agrenewal/2003.htm#Dr.FredKirschenmann> accessed July 2007.

KiSquared. 2004. "Winnipeg Customer Contact Centre Industry Research Study: Final Report." Winnipeg: Kisquared.

Knack, M.C., and A. Littlefield. 1996. "Native American Labor: Retrieving History, Rethinking Theory." In A. Littlefield and M.C. Knack (eds.), *Native Americans and Wage Labor: Ethnohistorical Perspectives*. Norman, OK: University of Oklahoma Press.

Korten, David C. 1999. *The Post-Corporate World: Life After Capitalism*. San Francisco: Kumarian.

Kuyek, J.N. 1990. *Fighting for Hope*. Montreal: Black Rose Books.

Labrecque, M.F. 1991. "Les Femmes et le I: de qui parle-ton at juste?" *Recherches*

Feministe 4 (2).

Lamb, Laura. 2007. "Towards an Economic Theory of Community Economic Development." In John Loxley (ed). *Transforming or Reforming Capitalism: Towards a Theory of Community Economic Development.* Halifax and Winnipeg: Fernwood Publishing and CCPA-MB.

Larner, W., and M. Butler. 2005. "Governmentalities of Local Partnerships: The Rise of a Partnering State in New Zealand." *Studies in Political Economy* 75: 85–108.

Lawless, G. 1994. "The Community Land Trust Model Applied to Farmland: A Case Study of the Wisconsin Farmland Conservancy." Unpublished Masters Thesis, University of Wisconsin-Madison, Madison, Wisconson.

Leopold Centre for Sustainable Agriculture. 2003. "Ecolabel Value Assessment Report." Available at <http://www.leopold.iastate.edu//pubs/staff/ecolabels/ecolabels.pdf> accessed May 24, 2004.

Levins, R.A. 2004. "Farm Income Rethinking." Presentation to the Fourth Managing Excellence in Agriculture Conference, February. Niagara Falls, ON.

Lewis, M. 1994. *The Development Wheel: A Workbook to Guide Community Analysis and Development Planning.* Second Edition. West Coast Series on CED. Vernon, BC: Westcoast Development Group.

Lewis, M., and R.A. Lockhart. 1999. *CED in the High Arctic: Progress and Prospects — A Documentary Review.* British Columbia: Centre for Community Enterprise.

Lezubski, D., J. Silver and E. Black. 2000. "High and Rising: The Growth of Poverty in Winnipeg." In J. Silver (ed.), *Solutions that Work: Fighting Poverty in Winnipeg.* Halifax: Fernwood Publishing and Winnipeg: CCPA, Manitoba.

Light, I., et al. 1995. "Ethnic Economy or Ethnic Enclave Economy?" In M. Halter (ed). *New Migrants in the Marketplace: Boston's Ethnic Entrepreneurs.* Amherst: University of Massachusetts Press.

Lloyd, A.J. 1967. *Community Development in Canada, Vol. Document 1.* Ottawa: Canadian Research Centre for Anthropology, Saint Paul University.

Loewen, G. 2003a. "Employment Development Activity in Winnipeg." Summary of Community Development and Community Economic Development in Winnipeg. Prepared for Building on the Momentum—CD/CED Gathering, Winnipeg November 26, 2003.

_____. 2003b. "Social Enterprise Development in Winnipeg." Prepared for Building on the Momentum—CD/CED Gathering, Winnipeg November 26, 2003.

Loewen, G., J. Silver, M. August, P. Bruning, M. MacKenzie and S. Meyerson. 2005. *Moving Low-Income People In Winnipeg's Inner City Into Good Jobs.* Winnipeg: Canadian Centre for Policy Alternatives–Manitoba.

Looker, D., and V. Thiessen. 2003. *The Digital Divide in Canadian Schools: Factors Affecting Student Access to and Use of Information Technology.* Ottawa: Statistics Canada.

Loxley, J. 1981. "The 'Great Northern Plan'." *Studies in Political Economy* 6: 151–82.

_____. 1985. *The Economics of CED: A Report Prepared for the Native Economic Development Program.* Winnipeg: University of Manitoba.

_____. 1986a. *Chapter 3: Strategies for the Economic Development of Native Communities.* Winnipeg: Native Economic Development Program.

_____. 1986b. *The Economics of Community Development: A Report Prepared for the Native Economic Development Program.* Winnipeg, MB: H.K.L. and Associates.

_____. 1990. "Economic Planning Under Social Democracy." In J. Silver and J. Hull (eds.), *The Political Economy of Manitoba.* Winnipeg: Canadian Plains Research

Centre, University of Regina.

_____. 2000. "Aboriginal Economic Development in Winnipeg." In J. Silver (ed.), *Solutions that Work Fighting Poverty in Winnipeg*. Winnipeg: Canadian Centre for Policy Alternatives–Manitoba and Fernwood Publishing.

_____. 2002. "Sustainable Urban Economic Development: An Aboriginal Perspective." *Journal of Aboriginal Economic Development* 3 (1): 29–32.

_____. 2003a. *Aboriginal People in the Winnipeg Economy: A 2003 Update*. Unpublished paper. Winnipeg: University of Manitoba, Department of Economics, mimeo, in author's possession.

_____. 2003b. "Financing Community Economic Development in Winnipeg." *Économie et Solidarité* 34 (1): 82–104

Loxley, J., and F. Wien. 2003. "Urban Aboriginal Economic Development." In D. Newhouse and E. Peters (eds.), *Not Strangers in These Parts, Urban Aboriginal Peoples*. Policy Research Initiative, Government of Canada.

Lynn, S.R. 2003. *Economic Development: Theory and Practice for a Divided World*. New Jersey: Prentice Hall.

Macey, A. 2002. "The State of Organic Farming in Canada 2002." *Eco-Farm and Garden* 7 (1): 44–47.

MacKinnon, S. 2006. "The Social Economy in Manitoba: Designing Public Policy for Social Inclusion." *Horizons* 8, 2. Available at <http://policyresearch.gc.ca/page.asp?pagenm=v8n2_art_06> accessed July 27, 2006.

MacRae, R. 2003. "Evidence and Policy Support for Organics." Presentation to Making Manitoba Food Secure Conference, March. University of Winnipeg.

Mahoney, E. 2004. "Farm Diversification." Presentation to the Fourth Managing Excellence in Agriculture Conference, February. Niagara Falls, ON.

Mandell, A., and E. Michelson. 1990. "Portfolio Development and Adult Learning." *Council for Adult and Experiential Learning (CAEL)*. Chicago, IL.

Manitoba Aboriginal and Northern Affairs. 2006. "Aboriginal People in Manitoba 2000, Education and Training (Chapter 4): Labour Market Training." Available at <http://www.gov.mb.ca/ana/apm2000/4/d.html> accessed August 28, 2006.

Manitoba Agriculture and Food. 2002. "Manitoba Agricultural Profile 2001." Winnipeg: Manitoba Agriculture and Food, Program and Policy Analysis Branch, May 17.

Manitoba Agriculture and Food, Market Analysis and Statistics Section. 2003a. *Manitoba Livestock Industry Profiles*. June. Winnipeg: Manitoba Agriculture and Food.

_____. 2003b. *Manitoba Agricultural Review 2002*. Winnipeg: Manitoba Agriculture and Food.

Manitoba Agriculture, Food, and Rural Initiatives, 2003. *Manitoba Agricultural Review*. November. Available at <http://www.gov.mb.ca/agriculture/statistics/aac01s01.html> Accessed May 24, 2004.

Manitoba Bureau of Statistics. 1997. "Manitoba's Aboriginal Populations Projected 1991–2016." Prepared for the Native Affairs Secretariat and Manitoba Northern Affairs. Winnipeg: Native Affairs Secretariat.

Manitoba Hydro Web Site. "History and Timelines." Available at <www.hydro.mb.ca/corporate/history/hep_1960.html> accessed July 2007.

Manitoba Research Alliance on Community Economic Development in the New

Economy. "Guiding Principles of Community Economic Development." Available at <http://www.manitobaresearchallianceced.ca/cedall.html> accessed August 28, 2006.

Margolis, J., and A. Fisher. 2002. *Unlocking the Clubhouse: Women in Computing*. Cambridge: MIT Press

Martin, Pat (MP for Winnipeg Centre). 2005. "Garment Industry Debate: 38th Parliament, 1st Session, Number 035." Available at <www2.parl.gc.ca./house-publications/publication.aspx?DocId=1516241&Language=E&Mode=1&Parl=38&Ses=1> accessed July 9, 2005.

Mason, J. 2002. *Qualitative Researching Second Edition*. London: Sage Publications.

Mayo, M. 2000. *Cultures, Communities, Identities: Cultural Strategies for Participation and Empowerment*. New York: Palgrave.

MCCA (Manitoba Customer Contact Association). 2006a. *Aboriginal HR Liaison, Aboriginal Representative Workforce Strategy*. Winnipeg: Manitoba Customer Contact Association. Available at <http://www.mcca.mb.ca/4.training.7.htm> accessed August 28, 2006.

_____. 2006b. *Industry Approved Entry Level Curriculum*. Winnipeg: Manitoba Customer Contact Association. Available at <http://www.mcca.mb.ca/4.training.4.htm> accessed August 28, 2006.

_____. 2006c. *Video Library Catalogue*. Winnipeg: Manitoba Customer Contact Association. Available at <http://www.mcca.mb.ca/4.training.2.htm> accessed August 28, 2006.

McEwen, E.R. 1968. *Community Development Services for Canadian Indian and Metis Communities*. Toronto: Indian-Eskimo Association of Canada.

McFarland, J. 2002. "Call Centres in New Brunswick: Maquiladoras of the North?" *Canadian Woman Studies*. Special issue: *Women, Globalization and International Trade* 21/22 (4/1): 65–70

McMullin, J., M. Cooke, and R. Downie. 2004. *Labour Force Ageing and Skill Shortages in Canada and Ontario*. Ottawa: Canadian Policy Research Networks Inc.

McPherson, C.B. 1965. *The Real World of Democracy*. Toronto: CBC Massey Lectures.

Mendelson, M. 2004. *Aboriginal People in Canada's Labour Market: Work and Unemployment, Today and Tomorrow*. Ottawa. Caledon Institute.

Merriam, S.B. 2001. "Andragogy and Self-Directed Learning: Pillars of Adult Learning Theory." *New Directions for Adult and Continuing Education* 89: 3–14.

Milloy, J.S. 1999. *A National Crime: The Canadian Government and the Residential School System, 1879–1986*. Winnipeg: University of Manitoba Press.

Morgan, M. 1996. "Working for Social Change: Learning From and Building Upon Women's Knowledge to Develop Economic Literacy." In P. Ghorayshi and C. Belanger (eds.), *Women, Work and Gender Relations in Developing Countries: A Global Perspective*. Westport, CT: Greenwood Press.

Moser, C. 1989. "Gender Planning in the Third World: Meeting Practical and Strategic Gender Needs." *World Development* 17 (11): 1799–825.

Mossman, Kathryn. 2005. "Training of Labour in the Winnipeg Garment Industry." In Raymond Wiest (ed), *The Winnipeg Garment Industry: Industry Development and Employment: A Report for the Manitoba Research Alliance on Community Economic Development in the New Economy*. Winnipeg.

_____. 2006. "Experiences of Immigrant Women in the Winnipeg Garment Industry: Gender, Ethnicity and Class in the Global Economy." Unpublished MA Thesis,

Department of Anthropology. Winnipeg: University of Manitoba.

Ms. Foundation for Women. 2001. *The New Girls' Movement: Implications for Youth Programs.* New York: Ms. Foundation for Women.

Nagler, M. 1970. *Indians in the City.* Ottawa: St. Paul University Press.

Naples, N.A. 2002. "The Challenges and Possibilities of Transnational Feminist Praxis." In N.A. Naples and M. Desai (eds.), *Women's Activism and Globalization: Linking Local Struggles and Transnational Politics.* New York and London: Routledge.

National Council of Welfare. 2005. "Poverty Lines 2004." *Welfare Incomes 2004.* Ottawa: National Council of Welfare. Also available at <http://www.ncwcnbes. net/en/publications/pub-123.html> accessed August 28, 2006.

National Film Board of Canada. 1990. *We're the Boss.* Directed by Brian Pollard. Ottawa: National Film Board of Canada.

Neechi Foods Co-op Ltd. 1993. *It's Up to All of Us.* Winnipeg: Neechi Foods.

Neighbourhoods Alive! 2002a. "CED Principles 2002." Independent Report. Winnipeg: Neighbourhoods Alive! Manitoba, MB.

_____. 2002b. "11 CED Principles: Using CED Principles to Build Strong Neighbourhoods." *Neighbourhoods Alive! Forum,* February 22. Winnipeg, MB.

Nelson, J. A. 2000. "Feminist Economics at the Millennium: A Personal Perspective." *Signs: Journal of Women in Culture and Society* 25 (4): 1178.

Ninacs, B., and L. Favreau. 1993. *CED in Quebec: Features in the Early 1990s.* British Columbia: Centre for Community Enterprise.

Norris, D.T., and S. Conceicao. 2004. "Narrowing the Digital Divide in Low-Income, Urban Communities." *New Directions for Adult and Continuing Education* 101: 69–81.

North, D.C. 1955. "Location Theory and Regional Economic Growth." *Journal of Political Economy* 63 (3): 332–45.

O'Connor, J. 1973. *The Fiscal Crisis of the State.* New York: St Martin's.

O'Donnell, S., and S. Karanja. 2000. "Transformative Community Practice: Building a Model for Developing Extremely Low-Income African-American Communities." *Journal of Community Practice* 7 (3): 67–84.

OECD (Organisation of Economic Co-operation and Development). 2000. *Learning to Bridge the Digital Divide.* Paris: OECD.

OFCM (Organic Food Council of Manitoba). 2004. "Down to Earth." Winnipeg: Organic Food Council of Manitoba.

Okazawa-Rey, M., and M. Wong. 1997. "Organizing in Communities of Color: Addressing Interethnic Conflicts." *Social Justice* 24 (1).

Osborne, D., and T. Gaebler. 1993. *Reinventing Government: How the Entrepreneurial Spirit is Transforming the Public Sector.* New York: Plume.

Pateman, C. 1970. *Participation and Democratic Theory.* Cambridge: Cambridge University Press.

Peace Hills Trust. "Locations." Available at <www.peacehills.com/default. aspx?PageID=1006> accessed July 4, 2007.

Perry, S. n.d. "Some Terminology and Definitions in the Field of Community Economic Development." *Making Waves* 10 (1).

Prentice, S., and M. McCracken. 2004. "A Time for Action: An Economic and Social Analysis of Childcare in Winnipeg." Winnipeg: *Childcare Coalition of Manitoba.* Available at <www.childcaremanitoba.ca/projects/docs/CCCM_WP_report5_04.pdf> accessed July 2007.

Province of Manitoba. 1973a. *Guidelines for the Seventies, Volume 1: Introduction and Economic Analysis*. Winnipeg: Queen's Printer.

_____. 1973b. *Guidelines for the Seventies, Volume 3: Regional Perspectives*. Winnipeg: Queen's Printer.

Qualman, D. 2001. *The Farm Crisis and Corporate Power*. Ottawa: Canadian Centre for Policy Alternatives.

Rabson, M. 2003. "Province Scores French Fry Operation, 'SWAT team' lures $120 m. potato plant." *Winnipeg Free Press*, March 17: B1.

Rankin, K. 2002. "Social Capital, Microfinance, and the Politics of Development." *Feminist Economics* 8 (1): 1–24.

RCAP (Royal Commission on Aboriginal Peoples). 1993. *Sharing the Harvest: The Road to Self-Reliance: Report of the National Round Table on Aboriginal Economic Development and Resources*. René Dussault and Georges Erasmus, Co-Chairs. Ottawa: Minister of Supply and Services, Government of Canada.

Richard, P. 2004. *Transformed by Community Economic Development: Southwest Montreal Now Has a Future as Well as a Past*. British Columbia: Centre for Community Enterprise.

Riggin, L., P. Grasso and M. Westcott. 1992. "A Framework for Evaluating Housing and Community Development Partnership Projects." *Public Administration Review* 52 (1): 40–46.

Riggs, A.R. and T. Velk. 1993. "Native People of North America and the Dependency Issue." *McGill Working Papers in Economics* 4.

Robertson, H., D. McGrane and E. Shaker. 2003. *For Cash and Future Considerations: Ontario Universities and Public-Private Partnerships*. Ottawa: Canadian Centre for Policy Alternatives.

Ross, A. (ed.). 1997. *No Sweat: Fashion, Free Trade and the Rights of Garment Workers*. London: New Left Books.

Rothney, R. 2003. *Winnipeg Co-operative Business Development Pilot Project Overview and Assessment*. Winnipeg: Assiniboine Credit Union.

Rubin, H. 1994. "There Aren't Going to Be Any Bakeries Here if There Is No Money to Afford Jellyrolls: The Organic Theory of Community Based Development." *Social Problems* 41 (3): 401–24.

Rural Municipality of Franklin. 2001. *Municipal Assessment Roll 2001*. Franklin, MB.

Sabagh, G., M. Bozorgmehr, and C. Cer-Martirosian. 1995. "Ethnic Economy or Ethnic Enclave Economy?" In M. Halter (ed.), *New Migrants in the Marketplace: Boston's Ethnic Entrepreneurs*. Boston and Amherst: University of Massachusetts Press.

Salm, A. 1997. Direct Connections: Farmer-Consumer Communication in a Local Food System. Unpublished MSc. Thesis. Wageningen Agricultural University, Netherlands.

Sanger, M. 2001. *Reckless Abandon: Canada, the GATS, and the Future of Health Care*. Ottawa: Canadian Centre for Policy Alternatives.

Schetagne, S. 2001. *Building Bridges Across Generations in the Workplace: A Response to Aging of the Workforce*. Vancouver: Canadian Council on Social Development, Columbia Foundation.

Schumacher, E.F. 1973. *Small is Beautiful: Economics As If People Mattered*. New York: Harper Colophon.

Scott, J. 2001. *Farm Viability and Economic Capacity in Nova Scotia: The Nova Scotia Genuine*

Progress Index — Soils and Agriculture Accounts. Glen Haven, NS: GPI Atlantic.

Sen, A. 1999. *Development as Freedom.* New York: Anchor Books.

Sheldrick, B.M. 2002. "New Labour and the Third Way: Democracy, Accountability and Social Democratic Politics." *Studies in Political Economy* 67: 133–44.

Shor, I., and P. Freire. 1987. *A Pedagogy for Liberation: Dialogues on Transforming Education.* South Hadley, MA: Bergin and Garvey.

Shragge, E. 1993. *Community Economic Development: In Search of Empowerment.* Montreal: Black Rose Books.

_____. (ed.). 1997. *Community Economic Development: In Search of Empowerment.* Revised edition. Montreal: Black Rose Books.

_____. 2002. "What is Left of the Community?" *Canadian Dimension* 36 (2): 41–42.

Silver, J. (ed.). 2000. *Solutions That Work: Fighting Poverty in Winnipeg.* Winnipeg: CCPA Manitoba and Fernwood Publishing.

_____. 2006a. *Gentrification in West Broadway: Contested Space in a Winnipeg Inner City Neighbourhood.* Winnipeg: Canadian Centre for Policy Alternatives-Manitoba.

_____. 2006b. *In Their Own Voices: Urban Aboriginal Community Development.* Halifax: Fernwood Publishing.

Silver, J., D. Klyne and F. Simard. 2003. *Aboriginal Learners in Selected Adult Learning Centres in Manitoba.* Winnipeg: Canadian Centre for Policy Alternatives-Manitoba.

Silver, J., K. Mallett, J. Greene and F. Simard. 2002. *Aboriginal Students in Winnipeg Inner-City High Schools.* Winnipeg: Canadian Centre for Policy Alternatives-Manitoba.

Skelton, I. 2000. "Cooperative and Nonprofit Housing in Winnipeg: Toward a Re-engagement of the Provision of Infrastructure." *Canadian Journal of Urban Research* 9 (1): 177–96.

Sommers, S. 2000. *Advanced Technology Bridge Training: Implementation Guide.* Chicago: Great Cities Institute.

Sparr, P. 1994. *Mortgaging Women's Lives: Feminist Critique of Structural Adjustment.* London: Zed Press.

Stall, S., and R. Stoecker. 1997. "Community Organizing or Organizing Community: Gender and the Crafts of Empowerment." *Working Paper Series for COMM-ORG: The On-Line Conference on Community Organizing and Development.* June. Available at <http://comm-org.wisc.edu/papers96/gender2.html> accessed July 2007.

Statistics Canada. 1995b. *As Time Goes By: Time Use of Canadians.* Ottawa: Minister of Industry.

_____. 1999. "Long Working Hours and Health." *The Daily*, Tuesday November 16.

_____. 2001a "Agricultural Census: Initial Release." catalogue #95F0301XIE, Ottawa.

_____. 2001b. "2001 Aboriginal Peoples Survey." Available at <http://www12.statcan.ca/english/profil01aps/home.cfm> accessed September 6, 2006.

_____. 2001c. "Aboriginal Peoples of Canada." Available at <www12.statcan.ca/english/profil01/AP01/Index.cfm?Lang=E> accessed August 10, 2004.

_____. 2001d. "2001 Census of Canada." Available at <http://www12.statcan.ca/english/census01/home/index.cfm> accessed September 6, 2006.

_____. 2001e. "2001 Census: City of Winnipeg." Available at <http://winnipeg.ca/census/2001>.

_____. 2001f. "Community Profiles." Population Statistics for Franklin, Manitoba.

Available at <http://www12.statcan.ca/english/profil01/PlaceSearchForm1. cfm> accessed May 26, 2004.

Stephens, S. 2005. "Labour Recruitment Strategies of the Winnipeg Garment Industry." In R. Wiest (ed.), *The Winnipeg Garment Industry: Industry Development and Employment*. Report for the Manitoba Research Alliance on Community Economic Development in the New Economy, Project #4. Available at <http://www. manitobaresearchallianceced.ca/Documents/4-GarmentIndustry-revNov22. pdf> accessed July 2007.

Stephens, S., and K. Mossman. 2005. "Biases and Beliefs: Impacts of Perspectives on the Garment Industry." In R. Wiest (ed.), *The Winnipeg Garment Industry: Industry Development and Employment*. Report for the Manitoba Research Alliance on Community Economic Development in the New Economy, Project #4. Available at <http://www.manitobaresearchallianceced.ca/Documents/4-GarmentIndustry-revNov22.pdf> accessed July 2007.

Stoecker, R. 2001. "Community Development and Community Organizing: Apples and Oranges? Chicken and Egg?" Available at <www.yepp.community.org/ downloads/empowerment/Community%20Development%20Stoecker.pdf> accessed December 10, 2003.

Stone, C., J. Henig, B. Jones and C. Pierannunzi. 2001. *Building Civic Capacity: The Politics of Reforming Urban Schools*. Lawrence: University Press of Kansas.

Stonehouse, P. 2001. "Intensive Livestock Operations and Sustainability Issues." Report for the Department of Agriculture Economics and Business, University of Guelph. Presentation to Sustainable Livestock Farms: Healthy Communities Conference. London, ON, March 24.

Supreme Court of Canada. 1973. *Calder vs. Attorney-General of British Columbia*. Ottawa: Supreme Court of Canada.

Taylor, P., and P. Bain. 1999. "'An Assembly Line in the Head': Work and Employee Relations in the Call Centre." *Industrial Relations Journal* 30 (2): 101–17.

Teeple, G. 2000. *Globalization and the Decline of Social Reform: Into the Twenty-First Century*. Toronto: Garamond Press.

Thomas, C.Y. 1974. *Dependence and Transformation: The Economics of the Transition to Socialism*. New York: Monthly Review Press.

Tilley, C. 1996. *The Good, the Bad and the Ugly: Good and Bad Jobs in the United States at the Millenium*. New York: Russell Sage Foundation.

Todaro, M.P. 2000. *Economic Development, Seventh Edition*. Don Mills, ON: Addison-Wesley.

Torjman, S. 1999a. *A Labour Force Development Strategy for Ottawa-Carleton*. Ottawa: Caledon Institute for Social Policy.

_____. 1999b. *Reintegrating the Unemployed Through Customized Training*. Ottawa: Caledon Institute of Social Policy.

_____. 2000. *Survival-of-the-Fittest Employment Policy*. Ottawa: Caledon Institute of Social Policy.

U.S. Consumers' Union. 2002. "The Consumers Union Guide to Environmental Labels." Available at <http://www.eco-labels.org/> accessed July 2007.

United Nations Development Program. 1995. "Human Development Report 1995: Gender and Human Development." United Nations Human Development reports Web site. Available at <www.undp.org/dpa/publications/hdro/98-htm> accessed July 30, 2004.

Veltmeyer, H., and A. O'Malley. 2001. *Transcending Neoliberalism: Community-based Development in Latin America*. Bloomfield, CT: Kumarian Press.

Vidal, A.C. 1997. "Can Community Development Re-Invent Itself?" *Journal of the American Planning Association* 63 (4): 429–37.

Voyageur, C., and B. Calliou. 2003. "Aboriginal Economic Development and the Struggle for Self-Government." In L. Samuelson and W. Antony (eds.), *Power and Resistance: Critical Thinking About Canadian Social Issues*. Third edition. Halifax: Fernwood Publishing.

Watkins, M. 1963. "A Staple Theory of Economic Growth." *Canadian Journal of Economics and Political Science* 29 (2): 141–58.

Wiest, R. (ed.). 2005. *The Winnipeg Garment Industry: Industry Development and Employment*. A report for the Manitoba Research Alliance on Community Economic Development in the New Economy, Project #4. Available at <http://www.manitobaresearchallianceced.ca/Documents/4-GarmentIndustry-revNov22.pdf> (accessed September 13, 2006).

Wiest, Raymond, Amena Khatun and Helal Mohiuddin. 2003. "Workplace, Residence and Relationships among Garment Workers in the Globalizing Export Economy of Bangladesh." In Matiur Rahman (ed.), *Globalization, Environmental Crisis and Social Change in Bangladesh*. Dhaka: University Press Limited.

Wilson, W.J. 1996. *When Work Disappears: The World of the New Urban Poor*. New York: Alfred A. Knopf.

Winnipeg Foundation. 2006. "Website." Available at <http://www.wpgfdn.org> accessed August 19, 2006.

Winnipeg Partnership Agreement. 2005. *Annual Report, 2005*. Available at <www.winnipegpartnership.mb.ca/pdf/annual_rpt_2005.pdf>.

Winnipeg Technical College. 2006. "Business Administrative Assistant: Course Content." Available at <http://www.wtc.mb.ca/index.cfm?pageID=93> accessed March 7, 2006.

Wismer, Susan, and David Pell. 1981. *Community Profit: Community-Based Economic Development in Canada*. Toronto: IS Five Press.

Wong, A.T. 1996. *Prior Learning Assessment: A Guide for University Faculty and Administrators*. Saskatoon: University Extension Press, University of Saskatchewan.

Woodiwiss, A. 2002. "Human Rights and the Challenge of Cosmopolitanism." *Theory, Culture and Society* 19 (1–2).

Wuerch, D., H. Urbina and K. Diachun. 2002. *Manitoba Organic Report*. Winnipeg: Agriculture and Agri-Food Canada.

Yanz, L., B. Jeffcott, D. Ladd and J. Atlin. 1999. *Policy Options to Improve Standards for Garment Workers in Canada and Internationally*. Ottawa: Status of Women Canada.

Zimmerman, B., and R. Dart 1998. *Charities Doing Commercial Ventures: Societal and Organizational Implications*. Canada: Trillium Foundation and Canadian Policy Research Networks Incorporated.

INDEX